NORMATIVE JURISPRUDENCE

Normative Jurisprudence aims to reinvigorate normative legal scholarship that both criticizes positive law and suggests reforms on the basis of stated moral values and legalistic ideals. It looks sequentially and in detail at the three major traditions in jurisprudence – natural law, legal positivism, and critical legal studies – that have in the past provided philosophical foundations for such normative scholarship. Over the past fifty years or so, all of these traditions have taken a number of different turns, although for different reasons, toward empirical analysis, conceptual analysis, or Foucauldian critique and away from straightforward normative criticism. As a result, normative legal scholarship – scholarship that is aimed at criticism and reform – is now lacking a foundation in jurisprudential thought. This book criticizes these developments and suggests a return – albeit with different and, in many ways, larger challenges – to the traditional understanding of the purpose of legal scholarship.

Robin West is Associate Dean for Research and Frederick Haas Professor of Law and Philosophy at the Georgetown University Law Center. She is the author of several books and more than a hundred articles on feminist legal theory, law and literature, law and humanities, jurisprudence, Constitutional law and theory, and, most recently, of *Marriage, Sexuality, and Gender* (2007) and *Re-Imagining Justice* (2003). She is the recipient of a J. B. White Lifetime Achievement Award from the Association for the Study of Law, Culture and Humanities, and she has held the John Carroll Research Chair at Georgetown.

CAMBRIDGE INTRODUCTIONS TO PHILOSOPHY AND LAW

Series Editors

Brian H. Bix
University of Minnesota

William A. Edmundson
Georgia State University

This introductory series of books provides concise studies of the philosophical founda-tions of law, of perennial topics in the philosophy of law, and of important and opposing schools of thought. The series is aimed principally at students in philosophy, law, and political science.

Matthew Kramer, *Objectivity and the Rule of Law*

William A. Edmundson, *An Introduction to Rights*

Normative Jurisprudence

AN INTRODUCTION

ROBIN WEST

Georgetown University Law Center

CAMBRIDGE
UNIVERSITY PRESS

CAMBRIDGE UNIVERSITY PRESS
Cambridge, New York, Melbourne, Madrid, Cape Town,
Singapore, São Paulo, Delhi, Tokyo, Mexico City

Cambridge University Press
32 Avenue of the Americas, New York, NY 10013-2473, USA

www.cambridge.org
Information on this title: www.cambridge.org/9780521738293

First published 2011

Printed in the United States of America

A catalog record for this publication is available from the British Library.

Library of Congress Cataloging in Publication data

West, Robin, 1954–
Normative jurisprudence : an introduction / Robin West.
    p.   cm. – (Cambridge introductions to philosophy and law)
Includes bibliographical references and index.
ISBN 978-0-521-46000-2 (hardback) – ISBN 978-0-521-73829-3 (paperback)
1. Jurisprudence.   I. Title.   II. Series.
K230.W475A36   2011
340–dc22   2011009193

ISBN 978-0-521-46000-2 Hardback
ISBN 978-0-521-73829-3 Paperback

To my children, Nick, Ben, and Molly; my husband, Robert Green; and my friend and colleague, Deborah Epstein

Contents

Introduction

Toward Normative Jurisprudence

Lawyers, judges, legal scholars, and law students – collectively, the legal profession – all, at various times, criticize, pan, praise, or laud laws. Thus, lawyers are inclined to say, in any number of formal and informal contexts, "this law is a good law (or a bad law)," or "this regulation is a godsend (or a calamity)"; "that piece of legislation is a breach of trust (or an act of good faith)"; "that legal regime, even, is a boom (or a bust) for mankind." How do we do that? What is it that lawyers know, if anything, about law, society, or political morality that informs their nonadversarial critical work? Somehow, the scholar, judge, American Law Institute committee member, legislator, or student reaches a judgment that a strict liability rule with respect to automobile accidents or defective products is *better* than a negligence regime, that the holder of a promissory note *should* take that note free of defenses on the basis of fraud in the underlying transaction, that a sexually harassed worker *should* have a cause of action under Title VII of the Civil Rights Act, and that the First Amendment *should* protect purveyors of hate speech no less than advocates of evolution or creation science against state censure. Knowledge of the law that exists cannot alone generate the basis of our conclusions regarding the law that ought to be – although it is surely true, as countless scholars have pointed out for the past one hundred years, that our judgments regarding the law that ought to be influence our understanding of the law that is.

So what fills the gap from the legal is to the legal ought for the legal critic? Do lawyers have a sense, in any way different from that of nonlawyers, of the good that law, or a law, does, can do, or fails to do, or of the justice that a law ought to promote? Do lawyers have a better or a different moral sense than nonlawyers, perhaps of the attractions of the Rule of Law and the dangers of legalist dystopias? Do lawyers understand something about what justice requires of law? If lawyers don't have some distinctive moral knowledge, then against what base are they judging it, when they praise, laud, pan, or denounce law? If they do have some distinctive moral knowledge, then what is it? What is the human good, or goods, that lawyers, distinctively, take to be law's goal, or a law's goal, or the Rule of Law's goal? What is the justice we rightly demand of law?

These questions – the demands of justice, the ideals we have or should have for law, or the nature of the "good" that a good law exhibits and that a bad law lacks – should be defining questions of jurisprudence. If there is a field of study that could profitably ask questions about our normative framework for evaluating, criticizing, praising or panning law, it should be jurisprudence – both analytic jurisprudence, which might ask what we mean by the justice, or the good, against which we evaluate law, and critical jurisprudence, which might ask how we should, and how we can, sufficiently distance ourselves from the profession in which we participate, so as to better criticize our deepest and most defining legal commitments. They are not, however. With only a few exceptions, the major practitioners of our dominant contemporary jurisprudential movements do not ask what justice requires of law, what makes a good law good or what makes a bad law bad, or what the good is that law can, or should, accomplish, against which we might judge particular laws or legal regimes. We do not ask how we know that a good law is good or a bad law bad, or what lawyers generally seem to assume to be the case about a good law or a bad law, or whether those assumptions are warranted or unwarranted. Even more clearly, we do not often ask what it is about social life that seemingly requires address by or recompense from the law, or how a good law might respond to a social ill in a desirable fashion, or how a bad law, or no law, might do so poorly. We do not often ask whether we have insufficient law to address ills of private or social life, or how we would know that, if it is true. We do not often ask, anymore, whether the legal regime in which we live and which we have constructed with law is promoting good lives for us and our neighbors. We do not ask whether our legal commitments, as well as our moral commitments about law – commitments to its generality, its rationality, its justice – are complicit in the moral calamities our nation, and our nations, face: a dangerously changing climate, implacable struggles over religious beliefs, a seemingly unbridgeable gap between rich and poor, both globally and nationally. We ask neither ethical questions about a legal regime's or a law's moral goodness nor meta-ethical questions about our own or our fellow lawyers' unexamined practices regarding the legal criticism in which we all nevertheless engage. Jurisprudence has largely turned its back on these normative questions about law's value.

This is a significant omission. These normative questions – the meaning of justice, the quality of the legal good that a good law possesses and a bad law lacks, the quality of life our legal regimes promote or frustrate, the complicity of our law and our legal consciousness in contemporary injustices – all ought to be jurisprudential questions. They ought to be pressing, urgent jurisprudential questions, I believe, but more minimally, they ought to be at least on par with what are today regarded as the central questions of jurisprudence: the meaning of law, the source of law's authority, the status of the unjust law, the relationship of law and positive morality. Yet they are not. Because they are not, an entire family of questions about the criteria that lawyers use or should use in determining or debating the goodness or the justice of laws has been slighted, over the past half century or so, in the very field of legal studies to which those questions should be central. Jurisprudents do not ask themselves or one another or the rest of us particularly probing questions about the nature of justice or of what I will call for shorthand the "legal good" – by which I mean the quality or qualities of goodness that a good law possesses and a bad law lacks. In fact, we are in flight from these normative questions, and our jurisprudence as well as our critical practices are the worse for it.

It clearly was not always thus. At different times through the century just ended, both jurisprudents and legal philosophers routinely asked these questions. In our own time, however, although our three major contemporary jurisprudential traditions – natural law, legal positivism, and critical legal theory – ask jurisprudential questions that are surely related to these, they have nevertheless for the most part quite explicitly turned their backs on questions regarding the requirements of justice or the nature of the legal good. This has left a gap in each of these traditions, although in different ways.

The overriding purpose of this book is to explore the reasons that each of the three major jurisprudential traditions of North American legal theory – natural law, legal positivism, and critical legal theory – has abandoned normative inquiry and to urge that we change course. The purpose of this introduction is to summarize briefly some of the arguments I make in the chapters that follow. What is the goodness that a good law possesses? What does justice demand of law? These were once defining questions of jurisprudence, but they are no longer. Why?

Let me start with Natural Law. In *Natural Law and Natural Rights*,[1] John Finnis's great and greatly underappreciated 1980 jurisprudential work, Finnis developed what still stands as the most compelling twentieth-century Natural Law position that aims (partly) to answer precisely this question. The just law, Finnis argued, is the law that (in part) promotes the common good, which is itself nothing but the basic goods of the individuals affected by the law.[2] Those goods, in turn, include, in part, the value of play, of life itself, of friendship, of knowledge, of practical reason, and of autonomy. Both law itself, Finnis posited, and our basic legal institutions, such as contract, property, and marriage, are necessary conditions for the cooperation required among even benignly motivated citizens to secure these basic goods.[3] Thus, the just law promotes these basic goods of individuals, or the common good, whereas the unjust law does not. The good law likewise, then, is the law that promotes these goods. Criticism of law should reveal the relationship, or lack of relationship, between positive law and the human goods it ought to serve.

Finnis's decidedly substantive natural law theorizing, however, did not persuade late-twentieth-century American jurisprudents, including even those who embraced

---

[1] John Finnis, *Natural Law and Natural Rights* (New York: Oxford University Press, 1980).

[2] *Id.* at 154, 164.

[3] *Id.* at 231–33.

natural law, for several reasons, some internal to Finnis's work, some external. First, the method Finnis espoused was overly intuitionist – the basic goods were to be understood by people with experience, intelligence, and a capacity and taste for speculation – but against their grasp of the goodness of the basic goods, no arguments were germane. How do we know the content of the good, or the common good, that law ought to promote? The basic goods, Finnis argued, are simply understood as such by such good and intelligent people – they are good in themselves and need no further justification.[4] This is clearly unsatisfying, methodologically, for any who find Finnis's list incomplete or in some way wrongheaded. Second, by the 1970s, political liberalism itself, and eventually the constitutional jurisprudence built on it, had come to assume as axiomatic a theoretical structure that explicitly disavowed any reliance on any conception of the good life as the object of state action, politics, or certainly of law.[5] Finnis's work, and his approach, appeared to be illiberal when posited against a liberalism that claimed agnosticism toward all richly developed conceptions of the good life, and hence the basic goods. Third, Finnis's later writing and advocacy against same-sex marriage[6] seemingly validated the worry that his substantive natural law, targeted on a law that would advance a full conception of the good and the good life, would prove unduly conservative and moralistic. Finally, the secularized but loosely Thomistic approach he embraced in *Natural Law and Natural Rights* – the attempt to specify a universal account of human nature that would inform, although by no means define, the human good, and to place the value of law within that framework, came to embody, by century's end, an ambition that was unacceptable to a critical consciousness that worried not so much about parochialism and a good deal about imperialism. Any theory based on an account of human nature, even loosely understood, appears suspect. Finnis's early writing continues to influence, and heavily, the development of a Thomistic natural law tradition that views itself as decidedly outside the mainstream of the secular legal academy.[7] His writing on the moral duty to obey just law continues to attract attention from his positivist critics.[8] However, his developed substantive

---

[4] *Id.* at 92.

[5] *See* Ronald Dworkin, *Taking Rights Seriously* (Cambridge: Harvard University Press, 1977); Dworkin, *A Matter of Principle* (Cambridge: Harvard University Press, 1985) 191–92.

[6] *See* John Finnis, "Law, Morality, and 'Sexual Orientation,'" in *Same Sex: Debating the Ethics, Science, and Culture of Homosexuality*, John Corvino, ed. (Lanham, New York, London: Rowman and Littlefield, 1997) 31–43.

[7] *See, e.g.,* Robert P. George and Beth Elshtain, eds., *The Meaning of Marriage: Family, State, Market, and Morals*, (Richard Vigilante Books, 2006); Robert P. George, ed., *Natural Law and Moral Inquiry: Ethics, Metaphysics, and Politics in the Work of Germain Grisez*, (Georgetown University Press, 1998); –, In Defense of Natural Law, (Oxford: Oxford University Press, 1999); – , ed., *The Autonomy of Law: Essays on Legal Positivism*, (Oxford: Oxford University Press, 1999); – and Christopher Wolfe, eds., *Natural Law and Public Reason*, (Georgetown University Press, 2000).

[8] *See generally*, S. Aiyer, "The Problem of Law's Authority: John Finnis and Joseph Raz on Legal Obligation," *Law and Philosophy* 19.4 (2000): 465–89; Leora Batnitzky, "A Seamless Web: John Finnis and Joseph Raz on Practical Reason and the Obligation to Obey the Law," *Oxford Journal of*

natural law jurisprudence failed to significantly change the direction of natural law theorizing within the American liberal legal academy of the late twentieth century. By 1970, natural law, at least in the United States, had taken a dramatically different, far less substantive, and only purportedly more liberal turn.

In the 1960s, Lon Fuller, midcentury's foremost American secular natural lawyer, asked much the same question as that which engaged Finnis and his Catholic natural law colleagues but answered it by developing, in essence, a nonsubstantive, procedural alternative to natural law theories to which Finnis contributed: the goodness of a morally good law, Fuller argued, is to be found not in any relationship it might have to any substantive conception of the human good, the basic goods, or the common good but rather in its regard for what we now call process, or procedural justice.[9] Although the legal process school of the 1960s embraced, partially, his response, Fuller's so-called procedural natural justice did not prove particularly regenerative within jurisprudence proper over the next half century. The procedural notice, generality, transparency, and related process goals that Fuller demanded of law for it to be good, seem, collectively, not quite good enough – plenty of very bad laws possess all of these process virtues and more so. On the other hand, the analytic and philosophical claim Fuller insisted on – that legal regimes that fail to meet procedural criteria of goodness are not and ought not to be regarded as law – seemed, to many, far too stringent: plenty of regimes that lack the requisite goodness, defined by his criterion, seem to all the world except Fuller, perhaps, to be law nevertheless. Thus, Fuller asked the right question – what is the good that a good law possesses? – but his answer, procedural purity, notably failed to convince.

Ten years later, Ronald Dworkin offered a very different, albeit equally secular, natural law understanding of the legal good: perhaps the good law, or at least the good judicial decision, Dworkin[10] argued, is the one that most logically and politically fits within a pattern of institutional arrangements established by a prior web of such decisions and is at the same time consistent with some defensible conception of political morality. A judicial declaration that meets this two-pronged test might be properly called both just and law, whereas one that fails either prong is neither. Although it has had a longer shelf life than Fuller's account, Dworkin's account of the goodness of a good law as well – that legal doctrine, articulated by judges, is both law and good when it is consistent with past legal practice and not dramatically at odds with a decent conception of political morality – also seems to be waning in influence. Dworkin's reliance on integrity with past legal practice as the test of both

---

Legal Studies 15.2 (1995): 153–75; Joseph Raz, *The Authority of Law: Essays on Law and Morality* (Oxford: Clarendon Press, 1979); Raz, *The Concept of a Legal System: An Introduction to the Theory of Legal Systems*, 2nd ed. (Oxford: Clarendon Press, 1980); Kenneth Einar Himma, "Positivism, Naturalism, and the Obligation to Obey Law," *Southern Journal of Philosophy* 36.2 (1998): 145–61.

9 Lon Fuller, *The Morality of Law* (New Haven: Yale University Press, 1965).

10 Ronald Dworkin, *Law's Empire* (Cambridge: Belknap Press, 1986) 119–51; Dworkin, *A Matter of Principle*; Dworkin, *Taking Rights Seriously*.

the legality and the moral goodness of judicially created law struck many as unduly Burkean or tradition bound at best and pandering at worst – plenty of very bad laws will meet his test of goodness, if the historical web of traditional legal and political decisions have themselves been bad or unjust. Furthermore, as was true of Fuller's, the analytical jurisprudential claim at the heart of Dworkin's jurisprudence – that law consists only of those actual and potential and idealized pronouncements that meet these moral tests – like Fuller's, seemed both over- and underinclusive: it contains principles that do not strike anyone but Dworkin as the stuff of law, and it excludes ordinary legal pronouncements that may not meet the moral test but nevertheless seem to be law.

Both Fuller and Dworkin, for all their differences, put forward accounts of the legal good, but in both cases, the claims seem, and have seemed to their readers, too thin. Neither procedural purity nor institutional fit with the past are sufficient to ensure the goodness of law, and neither, perhaps, is even necessary. Perhaps more to the point, their moral claims about the content of the good that a good law possesses in both cases were overshadowed by their analytic claim: that a law that lacks goodness is therefore not law. The latter claim, which for different reasons also failed to convince their critics, captured the legal academy's attention more than either theorist's account of the goodness that good law (or simply law) possesses. For whatever reason, however, with Finnis's substantive natural law contributions largely influential only within Thomistic traditions, Fuller's influence discernible only in occasional traces, and Dworkin's influence on the wane, there is simply no secular natural law movement active in the legal academy that is putting forward a serious claim regarding the nature of the goodness that a good law exhibits – or an account of how we know it when we see it. For those of us who take seriously the importance of the moral question Finnis, Fuller, and Dworkin asked and who have a high regard for those natural lawyers in our history who have tried to answer it, this is a profound lack indeed.

What of legal positivism, once again the reigning philosophical and jurisprudential framework of the legal academy? Here, as well, we find little inquiry into the nature of the good law, at least since H. L. A. Hart's attempt to spell out the minimal natural law content of positive law.[11] There is a profound historical irony here: nineteenth-century positivists, at least from Bentham forward, insisted on the separation of law and morality, in large part, to facilitate a clearer critical posture toward the law that is – only by separating the is and the ought, Bentham and his colleagues thought, could we see the injustice or possibly the evil of some of the law that is.[12] Bentham's embrace of legal positivism, then, was clearly motivated by a desire to facilitate clearheaded moral criticism of law – that law is the command of the sovereign, and nothing more, permits the critic to put the rose-colored glasses

---

[11] H. L. A. Hart, *The Concept of Law* (Oxford: Oxford University Press, 1961) 189–95.
[12] Hart, *The Concept of Law* 270–71.

aside and adjudge its utility, and hence its value, or its goodness – apart from its claim to legality. Only by first seeing law as it is can we hope to evaluate its goodness. Understand clearly the law that is, so that one can better adjudge its utility – and then criticize it freely, and ultimately reform it.

H. L. A. Hart continued this Benthamic understanding of the critical root of legal positivism, although without the utilitarian overlay: Hart, too, developed legal positivism as a jurisprudence that would complement and facilitate liberal, and critical, political engagement with extant law. Post-Hartian contemporary positivists, however, have not followed through on the invitation to use legal positivism so as to clarify the basis of (and need for) the moral criticism of law – and hence pave the way for legal reform. Rather, contemporary legal positivists who inquire into various definitional accounts of law, including the relationship of law and a community's positive law or the relationship of law to true morality, do so, for the most part, to investigate the nature of the relationship of law to some moral standard, not to the content of the moral standard itself. The question for our contemporary legal positivist is how we determine whether some norm is a law and whether in answering that question we must first say something about its moral value. The question is not, however, the content of the moral good – or even how we determine that moral value or lack of it. Contemporary legal positivists, not unlike contemporary secular Dworkinians or Fullerians, have focused overwhelmingly on the analytic part of positivism – the claim that the content of law must be determined by a nonmoral metric – and have neglected the moral motive for doing so: to better subject the law that is to the light of critical reason.

Finally, critical legal theorists, their self-appellation notwithstanding, have for the most part likewise not sought to elucidate the nature of the legal good. Rather, critical legal theorists, since the 1970s, have asked probing questions about the relationship of law to power: Is law nothing but the product of power? If so, is that something to bemoan, celebrate, or simply acknowledge? What is the relation of law, some critical theorists ask, to patriarchal power, or, others ask, to the power of capital, or, still others, to white hegemony, or, recently, to heteronormativity? Does law legitimate these sources of cultural or social power; does law further the false and pernicious perception that these and other hierarchical arrangements are necessary? These are all good questions, but their answers do not imply anything one way or the other about the goodness or badness of the law so unmasked, revealed as contingent rather than necessary, or delegitimated. Rather, the focus of the contemporary critical theorist is relentlessly limited to the relationship of law to the power that perverts, produces, or constrains it, or alternatively to the social, cultural, or political power that is legitimated and mystified by the hegemony that is law's product. The nature of the legal good – what makes a good law good and what virtues a good law ought to have – is decidedly not the object of study, beyond showing the relationship of such a question itself to deployments of social or cultural or legal power.

Here, as well, this stands in contrast to the work of earlier generations of critical theorists who influenced the philosophical orientation of our critically minded peers and selves, notably the early-twentieth-century legal realists and American pragmatists, for whom questions of the nature of the human good that might ideally be served by law, and against which existing law ought be criticized, were real and pressing.[13] Likewise, the realists were not averse to explicitly moral critique of existing law and debate over the nature of the human good that good law ought to serve. Morris Cohen, John Dewey, and the architects of the New Deal had contestable but nevertheless articulable understandings of our nature and what law might do to contribute to human well-being. Contemporary critical theorists have in essence retained the realists' and the early critical theorists' insistence on power's pervasiveness, but they have dropped their constructive moral ambition: the ambition, that is, to specify a speculative account of human nature, from which one might imply an account of the good that law might do and then criticize law accordingly. From our critical jurisprudential traditions, we get a powerful critique of law's sometimes-hidden political basis. We do not get the basis for a moral critique of power or of the law that is its product.

In the absence of a jurisprudence specifically focused on questions regarding the nature of the legal good, how, then, *do* lawyers criticize law? For the most part, lawyers and legal scholars moving from the legal is to the legal ought tend to use, and to assume, values drawn very loosely, and for the most part nonreflectively, from some version of these three traditions. Thus, for many traditional legal scholars and likely for most lawyers, the goodness and the justice of a legal decision is a matter of its fit with prior decisions, in a manner not dissimilar to what Dworkin described forty years ago for his idealized Judge Hercules. For these lawyers, that a judicial decision is in accordance with law – that it has integrity; that it fits with prior precedent; that it is, in short, legally just – is all that need be said on the question of its goodness: if the decision is just, meaning in accord with prior institutional arrangements, then it is good, and if it is unjust, meaning that it fails to fit, then it is bad. Whether a decision is just depends on its fidelity to preexisting law. Ergo, legal doctrine itself, read in its best light and over an expansive period of time, exhausts the normative basis on which at least legal decisions, if not new law in its entirety, can be judged. The good decision is the just decision, and the just decision is the decision that accords in some deep and perhaps indiscernible way with past law. For other lawyers, the source of the value that accounts for the move from the legal is to the legal ought is roughly a tally of costs and benefits: that a law or regulation is efficient or inefficient, likely to create more wealth than costs, is all that one need know to ascertain the goodness of a law. Particularly for lawyers influenced by the normative wing of the

---

[13] Morris R. Cohen, *Law and the Social Order: Essays in Legal Philosophy* (New York: Harcourt, Brace, and Company, 1933); John Dewey, *Human Nature and Conduct: An Introduction to Social Psychology* (New York: Henry Holt and Company, 1922); Dewey, *Individualism Old and New* (New York: Minton, Balch and Company, 1930).

law and economics movement, that a law or judicial decision promotes efficiency or increases wealth is sufficient to establish its goodness. The lawyer's expertise, if any, is simply to complement that of the legal economist, to add legal acumen to the economic calculation where need be. And to the rest of us, that either a law or legal decision – and it does not matter which – does or does not entrench established structures of power is basically all we seek or need to know. If a law can be shown to legitimate power, promote hegemonic values of various dominant political groups, mystify the nature of the contingent and socially constructed world we live in, or create an illusion of false necessity, it is therefore a bad law. If it delegitimizes power, complicates the hegemonic power of dominant groups, demystifies what appears to be necessary as contingent, then it is good.

One can easily see the influence of natural law, positivism, and critical theory, respectively, in these common ways of evaluating law: the traditional doctrinalist echoes the Dworkinian natural lawyer's understanding that the good decision is the just decision that accords with the past; the legal economist echoes the classical legal positivist's insistence that welfare or utility, and not tradition or past decisions, ought to be the metric against which new law is judged, and the egalitarian echoes the critical legal scholar's focus on uncovering the politics behind both law and mainstream criticism. The legal community quite generally has embraced these three criteria – integrity, efficiency, and equality – for the moral evaluation of law and legalism. Jurisprudence proper, however, has eschewed the careful and dialogic consideration of precisely the questions that generated them.

Yet these criteria – criteria pertaining to the institutional fit, efficiency, or politics of law – and the possible answers they suggest do not exhaust the criteria we do or should use in debating or pondering law's goodness. That a decision is just – perhaps because it fits well with prior rules or decisions raising comparable facts – neither implies nor disproves the goodness of the rule with which the decision comports. As truly countless scholars have pointed out, that a law is efficient, maximizes wealth, or leads to a net increase of benefits over costs does not make it, therefore, a good law. Many of us can imagine or point to laws that are efficient, wealth maximizing, or conducive to more benefits than costs that we would nevertheless regard as travesties, and those who cannot so readily imagine nevertheless tend to concede the validity of the exercise. There is a gap between the goodness of a law and its efficiency, just as there is a gap between human welfare and wealth. Finally, that a law or decision or body of law, legitimates, mystifies, reifies, or reflects social power does not imply that it is therefore a bad law; its value depends entirely on the value of the use to which that power is put. Likewise, a law that furthers hegemony or that legitimates the power of patriarchy or capital or the state or corporations may or may not be bad – or good – by virtue of those facts.

There are reasons, internal to each strand of jurisprudence, for the diminishment in importance of the inquiry into the legal good. Both Dworkin and Fuller, our secular natural lawyers, invited an identification of constitutional with moral criteria of evaluation, thus conflating the legal is and the moral good, thereby conflating as well the determination of law with the determination of its merits. This has the effect, desired by both Dworkin and Fuller, of morally enriching the legal craft, but it also had the effect of subjecting the law only to internal legal – albeit higher or constitutional – critique, but legal all the same, thus muting both the purely moral criticism of law and jurisprudential inquiry into law's potential goodness. Within legal positivism, some (not all) utilitarians, many economists, and like-minded legal theorists have tended to embrace uncritically an identification of the good with the desired, and hence of human welfare with the product of choice and preference, thus conflating the moral inquiry into law's goodness with various empirical questions regarding the relation of legal constraints with market and democratic outcomes. Within critical theory, legal critical theorists tend to identify the project of critique with the project of unmasking power and to equate goodness with egalitarian outcomes, thus neglecting the work of identifying and promoting the human good. All of these intramovement trends have occurred over the past half century or so, and all have left our jurisprudence remarkably hollow. The nature of the good, and hence the good law, has been equated within secular natural law with constitutional norms (both procedural and substantive); within positivism with desire, preference, and choice; and within our critical jurisprudential movements with either the celebration or the eradication of power. Although other interdisciplinary movements – law and economics, law and humanities – have to some degree filled the gap, we have no sustained jurisprudential inquiry, within natural law, legal positivism, or critical jurisprudence, into the nature of the human good that law, a law, or the rule of law might do.

This book argues that we need a rejuvenated normative jurisprudence that centralizes, rather than marginalizes, the concept of the individual, common, social, and legal good and the varying accounts of human nature that might inform such understandings. Why? First, we need to be able to ask what social or private or political injustices might prompt us to desire new law, where such law is absent, and when we should create law rather than simply how we should interpret the law we have. We need to be able to ask whether a law might improve a less regulated or unregulated social environment. We cannot do this with a jurisprudence that is court-centered and focused on the virtue of maintaining continuity with the past rather than on legislative creativity and the virtue of meeting social need. Second, we need to be able to ask whether our most basic legal institutions are good or bad and why. We cannot do this with a normative jurisprudence that looks at most for integrity with past legal practice, tabulates cost and benefit that assumes current preferences as given, or asks too minimally whether a legal institution furthers or promotes social hierarchy. Third, we need to be able to ask whether the conceptions of human nature that current critical practices implicitly assume, or that implicitly inform our conception of the good and the good human life, are true or false, under-inclusive of our human community, or denying of aspects of our nature – whether, for example, a myopic fixation on our autonomous individualism has blinded us to the universality and centrality of our dependencies on others, our vulnerability to calamity and disease, even our mortality. We cannot do that with a jurisprudence that resolutely denies the relevance or the appropriateness of inquiry into human nature and the human good, as does much of our critical jurisprudence. Briefly, we need to ask, as a matter of both jurisprudence and political philosophy, what good law can do and all the questions that basic inquiry implies: What does it mean for human beings to flourish, and how can law and legalism contribute? In what way does law or a particular law or a legal regime or a field of law increase our well-being? When and where is law needed? What makes a good law good, and what makes a law necessary, and what makes it inefficacious or worse? These questions have in the past been central to jurisprudence and to its philosophical forefathers, in the writings on human nature and well-being from Aristotle to Aquinas, and in the writings on human happiness and welfare from Jeremy Bentham to John Dewey. They lurk in the writings of some of our contemporary public philosophers, notably the neo-Aristotelian and neo-Marxist writings of Martha Nussbaum[14] and the theorists of the capabilities approach to moral and political philosophy. However, questions regarding the good, and hence the legal good, have been sadly absent in our contemporary jurisprudence, and we are all the worse for it.

[14] Martha Nussbaum, *Women and Human Development* (New York: Cambridge University Press, 2000).

1

Revitalizing Natural Law

Modern liberal and progressive American lawyers are more than a little squeamish about the Natural Law tradition in jurisprudence. It is no wonder. In the United States, during the twentieth century alone, the Natural Law movement has been the intellectual home for a Catholic law school–led revolt at mid-century against New Deal lawyers and theorists;[1] an overwrought identification of Justice Oliver Wendell Holmes, legal realism, and American pragmatism with fascism;[2] a late-twentieth-century critique of gay rights and gay life that rests on little more than disgust with noncoital sexuality;[3] and an attack on the separation of church and state

---

[1] The antirealist Natural Law movement sought to replace the currents of legal thought that tended toward positivism and realism with scholastic, Catholic, Natural Law teachings and hence check the danger of a drift toward totalitarianism. The story is well told in Edward Purcell Jr., "Crisis in Jurisprudence," in *The Crisis of Democratic Theory: Scientific Naturalism and the Problem of Value* (University Press of Kentucky, 1973) 159–234.

[2] *See* particularly the writings of Francis Lucey, S.J., of Georgetown University School of Law; Paul L. Gregg, S.J., of Creighton University; and Father John C. Ford of Weston College, all of whom identified legal realism with political skepticism, an absolute state, and totalitarianism, and Holmes with fascism and frequently with Hitler. *See, e.g.,* Francis Lucey, "Jurisprudence and the Future Social Order," *Social Science* 16 (1941): 211–17; Francis Lucey, "Holmes, Liberal, Humanitarian, Believer in Democracy," *Georgetown Law Journal* 39 (1951): 523–62; Paul L. Gregg, "The Pragmatism of Mr. Justice Holmes," *Georgetown Law Journal* 31 (1943): 262–95; Ben Palmer, "Hobbes, Hitler and Holmes," *American Bar Association Journal* 31 (1945): 569–73, 571; John C. Ford, "The Fundamentals of Holmes' Juristic Philosophy," *Fordham Law Review* 11 (1942): 255–78; *see generally,* David Skeel, "The Paths of Christian Legal Scholarship," *Green Bag* 12 (2008): 169–83.

[3] This is now widely associated with the work of Robert George and Gerard Bradley. *See, e.g.,* Robert P. George and Gerard Bradley, "Marriage and the Liberal Imagination," *Georgetown Law Journal* 84 (1995): 301–20; Robert P. George, "What's Sex Got to Do With It? Marriage, Morality, and Rationality," *American Journal of Jurisprudence* 49 (2004): 63–85; *see also* John Finnis, "Law, Morality, and 'Sexual Orientation,'" *Notre Dame Law Review* 69 (1994): 1049–76; John Finnis, "The Good of Marriage and the Morality of Sexual Relations: Some Philosophical and Historical Observations," *The American Journal of Jurisprudence* 42 (1997): 97–134.

that threatens hard-won civil liberties for nonbelievers and religious minorities.[4]
All of this strikes many liberal and progressive lawyers as not only misguided but
decidedly beyond the pale – an assault on positions that perhaps at one time were
controversial but are no longer so, and on legal figures that, for many, are now iconic.
The Administrative State; the legacy and liberal credentials of the decidedly complex
figure of Oliver W. Holmes, a bland but clear-cut policy of nondiscrimination against
gays and lesbians; and a cleanly separated establishment of state versus church strike
most lawyers as relatively unassailable liberal and legal achievements. A *Lochner*-
era rigid libertarianism that precludes administrative softening of market excesses,
a punitive stance toward victimless sexual variation, and an aggressively Christian
nation, by contrast, strike most liberal American lawyers as a politics of religious
chauvinism at worst and of distraction from more pressing political dangers at best.
Any jurisprudence that flirts with *all* of these views – and in the century just closed,
natural law clearly has – seems to be, in a word, spent: a thoroughly discredited and
indeed regrettable strand of thought that is perhaps still of interest to legal historians
but the central claims of which are, however, best left in the dustbin of history.

In this chapter, I argue for a revitalization of a secular, natural law jurisprudence
among progressive and liberal American lawyers and legal intellectuals. First, however, I want to make a basic definitional point that is not at all controversial but that
is central to my argument and often unnoted in discussions of natural law: there are
now (whether or not there have always been) two quite distinct natural law movements. The first, which I call, following Jonathan Crowe's helpful terminology, the
ethical Natural Law movement, or "natural law ethics,"[5] is focused on the nature
of the "common good," the human good, "basic goods," intrinsic goods, or, most
simply, the good that may be furthered by law and the ethical ideals that law should
embody, given human nature. Natural law, understood in this way, takes as its starting
point a dictum from Aquinas's *Summa Theologica*: the just law, Aquinas counseled,
is the law that furthers the common, human good.[6] Natural law jurisprudence, then,
is (in part) the inquiry into the nature and content of the "common good" that the
just law does or should promote, sustain, facilitate, or protect.[7] The second natural

---

[4] *See, e.g.*, Tom West, "God and Man in America: A Review of *The Separation of Church and State*, by
Phillip Hamburger," *Claremont Review of Books* 3 (Spring 2003): 28–30 ("Let us hope that Hamburger's
useful book will encourage today's legal elites to abandon their erroneous understanding of the
Constitution's religion clauses and return to the American Founders' sensible awareness that belief in
a just God is not only *not* in conflict with political freedom, but is, as Washington said, its 'indispensable
support.'").

[5] I am adopting with some modification terminology introduced by Jonathan Crowe in "The Core
Claims of Natural Law Theory," in *Natural Law Revisited* (forthcoming, on file with author).

[6] Thomas Aquinas, *Summa Theologica*, Pt. I–II, ques. 96, Art. 4.

[7] Contemporary Natural Lawyers who understand the movement in this way include, most prominently,
John Finnis, Germain Grisez, Robert George, Gerard Bradley, and Mark C. Murphy. The philosopher
Henry Richardson calls this group the "new Natural Lawyers" and identifies the common ground
between them as consisting of their identification of "basic goods" as the target, or goal, of a just law.

law movement, which I call the jurisprudential natural law movement or natural law jurisprudence, has, for several centuries now, been focused on a particular claim about the definition of law: that there exists some necessary connection between law and moral truth or, put differently, that law must meet some minimal moral criteria for it to be truly law. This philosophical natural law movement also takes as its starting point a dictum from Aquinas's *Summa Theologica* – to wit, that "an unjust law is no law at all."[8] Although susceptible to various interpretations, all jurisprudential natural lawyers take seriously this seemingly counterexperiential claim.[9] A law by positivist criteria that fails to meet minimal moral criteria may result in the imposition of undesirable sanctions by powerful people on the less powerful or less fortunate, but it does not deserve the appellation "law." "Law," rather, is the word we should reserve for those positivist laws that are deserving of our respect.

What I argue for in this chapter is a reengagement of liberal and progressive lawyers with the ethical natural law movement – the ethical inquiry into the nature of the common good furthered by just law. Liberal and progressive lawyers, I argue, ought to engage the natural lawyer's ethical concern with what the law should be, what our ideals for it should be, how those ideals relate to our own understanding of both human nature and the human good, and how or whether actual law can be brought into alignment with the ideal. I do not mean to suggest for a minute that conservative or libertarian lawyers should not – only that they already do. In contrast, liberal lawyers and – for different reasons – progressive lawyers as well have aggressively eschewed this project, and the result is a rather severe political distortion of our natural law jurisprudence. To engage those questions, liberal and progressive lawyers must indeed challenge the relatively conservative and libertarian conceptions of both liberty and sexuality that have dominated natural lawyers' answers to them over the last century. We need to do so, however, in a way that retains the integrity of the questions that motivated those conceptions and not by assailing their coherence. What needs to be shown is that the claims underlying the various illiberal positions laid out earlier – the impossibility of gay marriage, the immorality of the New Deal,

---

Richardson faults the new Natural Law theory for holding simultaneously two positions he regards as incompatible: the "source thesis," which holds that all reasons for action derive entirely from a small set of basic goods, and the "thorough incommensurability" thesis, which holds that "every instance of a basic good is evaluatively incommensurable with every other wholly distinct instance." *See* Henry Richardson, "Incommensurability and Basic Goods: A Tension in the New Natural Law Theory," in *Human Values: New Essays on Ethics and Natural Law*, David Oderberg and Timothy Chappell, eds. (New York: Palgrave MacMillan, 2004).

8 Aquinas, *Summa Theologica*, Pt. I–II, ques. 96, Art. 4 (quoting Augustine: "A law that is unjust seems not to be a law"). More generally, see *id.* at ques. 93, Art. 3, reply 2; ques. 95, Art. 2.

9 Contemporary secular writers who understand the "Natural Law movement" in this way include most prominently Ronald Dworkin, Lon Fuller, and David Luban. *See* Ronald Dworkin, *Taking Rights Seriously* (Cambridge: Harvard University Press, 1977); Lon Fuller, *The Morality of Law* (New Haven: Yale University Press, 1969); Lon Fuller, *The Law in Quest of Itself* (Boston: Beacon Press, 1966); *and* David Luban, *Legal Ethics and Human Dignity* (Cambridge: Cambridge University Press, 2007).

and so forth – are false and that the moral claims built on them for the direction of law are unfruitful, not that the question that prompted them is nonsensical.

I also argue, however, that liberal and progressive positivists are correct to be skeptical of the analytical claim at the heart of the jurisprudential natural law movement – that "an unjust law is no law at all." At least since H. L. A. Hart's influential early essays on positivism and natural law,[10] liberal positivists have voiced the worry that the natural law equation of true law and justice expressed in this Thomistic axiom carries an unduly conservative subtext – to wit, that "the law that is, is therefore just, solely by virtue of its existence." To be sure, that reactionary claim is not the only possible interpretation of Aquinas's famous phrase: it was obviously not the interpretation intended by Martin Luther King, Jr., when he cited it so prominently in his "Letter from Birmingham Jail."[11] Nevertheless, it is an available interpretation, if an unfortunate one, and it, too, has had its celebrants, particularly in the legal academy. What I suggest in the first part of this chapter is that when expounded in academic legal texts – rather than in letters from jail cells – the natural law theorizing that takes this claim seriously has tended to laud, rather than criticize, existing law and has tended to equate the law that is with the demands of justice, even while also putting in doubt the legal status of the thoroughly unjust law or legal regime. Positivists, liberals, and liberal positivists are right to be skeptical.

Let me put these two halves together. What I want to argue in this chapter, perhaps counterintuitively, is that liberal and progressive legal scholars ought to seriously engage the ethical Natural Law movement even though, in the twentieth century, that movement has been the home of profoundly conservative and even fringe-conservative claims. I also argue, however, that liberal or progressive legal positivists – a group David Luban has dubbed "progressive positivists"[12] – are right to be skeptical of the jurisprudential natural lawyer's conviction that law requires a "moral minimum" – even though, at moments of crisis in the last two centuries, that conviction has given counsel and comfort to men and women of conscience in movements of revolution and civil disobedience. Both of those claims may seem counterintuitive, even reckless. I hope not. Minimally, however, I want to assert the logical possibility of the position. Positivists are right to insist on the separation of law and morality, if by that is meant that no logically necessary connection exists between the two. Ethical natural lawyers, however, are entirely right to ask what the content of the justice is that a just law ought to promote and to answer that question, in part, by inquiry into the content of the human, common good. The answers they have

[10] H. L. A. Hart, "Positivism and the Separation of Law and Morals," *Harvard Law Review* 71 (1957): 593–629; H. L. A. Hart, *Essays in Jurisprudence and Philosophy* (New York: Oxford University Press, 1984); H. L. A. Hart, *Essays on Bentham, Jurisprudence and Political Theory* (New York: Oxford University Press, 1982).

[11] Martin Luther King, Jr., "Letter from Birmingham Jail," in *Why We Can't Wait* (New York: Signet Books, 1963) 76.

[12] Luban, *Legal Ethics and Human Dignity* 122–24. Luban identifies Fred Schauer, Jules Coleman, and myself.

produced over the past one hundred years have not been attractive or conducive to liberal sensibilities. What follows, however, is that liberals and progressives should engage the inquiry and respond, rather than dismiss the question out of hand as incoherent, incomprehensible, authoritarian, or imperialistic. It is none of that.

The chapter is structured as follows. In the first section, I look briefly at the definitional claim central to jurisprudential natural law – to wit, that an "unjust law is not a law at all." Echoing suggestions made two centuries ago by Jeremy Bentham,[13] I argue that the claim is politically – and perniciously – ambiguous: it either implies that unjust laws are not binding, or it implies that all the law that exists is therefore just. In the United States no less than in Britain, emendations of this claim have served the ends and needs of power holders far more than the ends of civil disobedients or revolutionaries, particularly when it has emanated from the legal academy or the bench. Again, Hartian, progressive positivists are correct to be skeptical.

In the second and third sections, I suggest that – contrary to conventional wisdom – it is the ethical Natural Law movement, and not the jurisprudential, that is the apple ripe for liberal and progressive picking. Thus, in sections two and three I put forward some reasons that liberal lawyers should be more engaged than they currently are with the ethical natural lawyers' core projects: exploration of the common good that law can do, what human goods law can promote or protect or serve, what those goods are, and what justice requires of law. These are the natural law questions that call out for engagement across the political spectrum rather than where it currently resides, which is on the social conservative (and occasionally, the libertarian) right. *All* lawyers interested in the quality of justice, and not just jurisprudents and certainly not only Catholic intellectuals and social conservatives, should engage these questions. Yet we have not. Because of the neglect, we now have, in effect, a "missing liberal jurisprudence" of inquiry into the human good, the common good, and human well-being that just law ought to serve. I try to describe how our jurisprudence would be different if liberals and progressives took this Thomistic definition of the just law seriously. I then suggest some reasons why our failure to do so is a serious loss, both for our politics and for our jurisprudence.

First, however, let me stress again my introductory and least contentious point spelled out earlier: such a rejuvenated jurisprudential project – inquiry into the human good and the common good that just law ought to further, in part by reference to human nature, human well-being, and human flourishing – is by no means incompatible with positivist conceptions of the relation of law and morality

---

[13] *See* Jeremy Bentham, "Anarchical Fallacies," *The Works of Jeremy Bentham* vol. 2, ed. John Bowring (Edinburgh: William Tait, 1843) 486–531; *and* Jeremy Bentham, *Comment on the Commentaries: A Criticism of William Blackstone's Commentaries on the Laws of England,* ed. Charles Warren Everett (Oxford: Clarendon Press, 1928). Hart explores this two-pronged Benthamic attack on Natural Law in general, and Blackstone in particular, in Hart, "Positivism and the Separation of Law and Morals."

or positivist understandings of the nature of law. Indeed, several thinkers routinely identified as "natural lawyers" – including Thomas Aquinas himself[14] and in our own time, arguably, John Finnis[15] – have likely held some version of this understanding regarding the moral value of law but held what appear to be positivist conceptions of law's definition. Likewise, at least a few legal positivists – H. L. A. Hart among them – have contributed to this strand of natural law theorizing.[16] It is a fair question, then: in what sense can the view I am endorsing here be called a "natural law" view at all? I take up that and related objections in the concluding section.

"AN UNJUST LAW IS NO LAW AT ALL": DEFINITIONAL AMBIGUITIES

Natural law is described variously, but central to almost all definitions is some reference to Thomas Aquinas's claim in the *Summa Theologica* that "an unjust law is no law at all." This claim, as any number of positivists have argued, is ambiguous. What Aquinas meant by this, virtually without question, was that a law that violates God's law, or "natural law," is not binding *in conscience*,[17] or, to put it differently and in a more secular key, that a positive law that is unjust implies no moral duty of obedience on the part of citizens and, perhaps, no moral duties on the part of state officials (such as judges) to apply it as well. When understood in this way, as John Finnis has ably argued, the claim that an unjust law is no law at all points to the absence of a moral duty to obey laws that are unjust and, perhaps, a moral duty to obey laws that are not. It does little more, and the reams of positivist critique of natural law that assume it stands for the patently false proposition that all laws are just, or that laws that are unjust are not really laws, do nothing but attack a strawman.[18] Thus, John Finnis's long-standing complaint: the positivist attack on natural law, from Austin's own through that of Coleman and Leiter, is nothing but a massive, two- or three-century-long and running, historical misunderstanding.[19]

Finnis's protestations notwithstanding, however, the more literal way to read Aquinas's famous statement (although only once the sentence is yanked from context) is that for a law to create a binding *legal* and not just moral obligation, it must first meet some minimal moral requirement of justice. A norm that is promulgated by a powerful sovereign in accordance with accepted procedures, or with a rule of

---

[14] Aquinas distinguishes – he does not identify – human law with Natural Law, and then argues that only those human laws that are in accordance with the dictates of Natural Law command a moral duty of obedience. This is fully consistent with Hart's separation thesis, in turn definitive of the positive law tradition. *See* Aquinas, *Summa Theologica*, Pt. I–II, ques. 90–96.

[15] John Finnis, *Natural Law and Natural Rights* (Oxford: Oxford University Press 1980) 18–29.

[16] H. L. A. Hart, "The Minimum Content of Natural Law," in *The Concept of Law*, 2nd ed. (Oxford: Oxford University Press, 1994) 193–99.

[17] Aquinas, *Summa Theologica*, Pt. I–II, ques. 96, Art. 4 ("And laws of this sort are acts of violence rather than laws, as Augustine says. . . . 'A law that is unjust seems not to be a law.' Such laws do not bind in conscience, except perhaps in order to avoid scandal or disturbances.").

[18] Finnis, *Natural Law and Natural Rights* 25–37.

[19] *Id.*

recognition, or an originating Constitution, or whatever other test of pedigree positivism might require of law is nevertheless not truly "law" – in the stronger view – if it is so palpably unjust as to not, in effect, earn the appellation. The word "law," in effect, is reserved for that subset of commands and edicts that meet positivist requirements *and that* meet moral conditions. Palpably unjust "laws" that fail to meet these criteria need not be obeyed by citizens; whether or not we do so is entirely a matter of prudence or, in the extreme case, of personal bravery. They also *need not be enforced by courts*, however. Again, neither citizens *nor courts* are morally *or legally* required to obey, enforce, or uphold these legal nullities. An unjust law is truly not a law at all.

This ambiguity in the natural lawyer's definitional claim is much noted by positivist critics, and for good reason. If understood in the first way, as just suggested, it seems true but not something legal positivists would be inclined to contest; most of us agree, at least after the fact, that unjust laws impose no duty of obedience on people of conscience. If understood in the second way, it seems more interesting but patently untrue: surely, there are as many unjust laws around as there are brown blades of grass in my drought-stricken backyard. Natural lawyers (such as Finnis) who argue for the weak but not the strong interpretation have responded to the first positivist argument with the rejoinder that the weak claim is more interesting than it appears: it might suggest, for example, the existence of a robust duty to obey those laws that are not terribly unjust.[20] Natural lawyers who accept the second, stronger view – and contra Finnis, this is not a null set – have responded to the second, with the claim that the Thomistic insistence on law's moral minimum is not as implausible as it looks at first: our own Constitution, arguably, likewise requires that law be minimally just. The resulting arguments back and forth (Hart–Fuller[21]; Hart–Dworkin[22]; Dworkin and all his critics) have dominated legal philosophy since the 1960s.

There is, however, a second and, I think, ultimately more important ambiguity in Aquinas's utterance, one that is political rather than conceptual. It is present, furthermore, *regardless* of whether the natural law claim is interpreted in the weak or strong conceptual ways spelled out earlier but easiest to see, perhaps (and most pernicious), on the stronger view. So, to restate only slightly, the strong view that an "unjust law is not a law" might mean that any seemingly authoritative pronouncement that an individual might view as contrary to conscience is therefore not only immoral but not even a law to boot. It is binding in no sense whatsoever. Interpreted

---

20 *Id.* at 23–32.

21 The Hart–Fuller debate refers to a set of now-canonical jurisprudential texts. *See* Hart, "Positivism and the Separation of Law and Morals" *and* Lon Fuller, "Positivism and Fidelity to Law – A Reply to Professor Hart," *Harvard Law Review* 71 (1958): 630–72.

22 The Hart–Dworkin debate includes Dworkin's critique of Hart's positivism in Ronald Dworkin, "Model of Rules I," *Taking Rights Seriously;* Hart's response in his postscript in H. L. A. Hart, "The Nature of Legal Positivism," *The Concept of Law;* and Dworkin's response, in Ronald Dworkin, "Legal Theory and the Problem of Sense," *Issues in Contemporary Legal Philosophy: The Influence of H. L. A. Hart,* Ruth Gavison, ed. (Oxford: Oxford University Press, 1987) 9–20.

in this way, the axiom gives comfort to the civil disobedient of conscience. The antigovernment "constitutionalist" who refuses to pay taxes; the draft-card-burning civil disobedient who refuses enlistment, citing the unconstitutionality of the draft law; the antiabortion trespasser who intentionally interferes with the rights of clinicians and patients to egress and exit from abortion clinics, citing the moral necessity (and hence the legality) of the trespass; and the lunch-room-sitting civil rights activist who defies segregation laws, in part on the grounds that those laws are themselves unconstitutional – *all*, by reference to Aquinas's maxim so understood, are justified in viewing their moral views as giving them sufficient legal (as well as moral) grounds to ignore these laws *and, at the same time*, to claim their allegiance to "law." *They* are the true legalists, they are not anarchists at all. *They* respect *true* law more than their adversaries do; they are the devotees of good legal values; and they are the followers and obedients to a true rule of law.

Change the syntax, however, and the same thesis – that "an unjust law is not a law" – suddenly means something that is not just different but, in fact, *opposite* in meaning to the claim explicated earlier. That "an unjust law is not a law" might also mean that every single positive legal pronouncement – every law that *is* a law by positivist criteria – is *therefore*, by virtue of its legalism, a moral and just pronouncement, as well as a legal one. Because unjust laws are not laws, then all laws that actually exist are therefore just. A law that is promulgated by a true sovereign will not only dictate behavior but will also be, by definition, necessarily right, good, and just. Law is a demand of *justice* as well as the product of force. That a positive law exists, in other words, *is alone* sufficient grounds for its moral justification. The legal right and wrong is likewise the moral right and wrong. If the law exists, it must be just – because unjust laws simply do not exist. What the sovereign decrees is both necessary and good.

If that is a permissible interpretation of the axiom at the heart of the jurisprudential natural law movement, then that movement gives us a "looking glass" kind of problem: the same principle that counsels the *authority of conscience*, and hence the legitimacy of disobedience, to the disobedient or revolutionary also counsels to the king, president, or ruling majority the *conscience of authority*. If the sovereign commands it, that "it" that he commands must be a just command, as well as lawful one. If we take this political ambiguity seriously, then it appears that jurisprudential natural law thus lends its hand not only to the civil disobedient, bent on radical change through extralegal means but also to the authoritarian sovereign, bent on squelching dissent. The king's authority is just and good, no less than it is all powerful, precisely because the king is the lawmaker. An unjust law, after all, is no law at all. Because the king makes the law, whatever the king makes must therefore be fully just as well. For there is no denying that the king makes law.

What should we make of this authoritarian undertow? Is it just wordplay? In a recent book, David Luban has suggested that it is simply a "mistake" to interpret the natural lawyer's claim (that an unjust law is not a law) in this second way – as an obsequious apology for power, rather than as a jurisprudential handmaiden to those who would challenge it.[23] It is, he argues, just a positivist "misunderstanding," or misreading, of the Thomistic claim, to suggest that it might be read to imply the morality of existing authority rather than the illegality of abuses of power. Therefore, he suggests, the protestations of a group he calls "progressive positivists" (such as Fred Schauer and I) – that natural law has an unpleasant and illiberal authoritarianism – is an attack on a strawman (note the parallel: Finnis makes the same claim regarding positivist critics of the strong natural law thesis across the board). If he is right, then the entire legal positivist tradition, and not just Schauer and a few other modern writers, has built its philosophy on a straightforward – and simpleminded – mistake.

But is Luban right? Let me give just two examples, one historical and one modern, that suggest that whatever is at stake between natural lawyers and positivists is not just a "misreading" of the former by the latter. First, and as noted earlier, Jeremy Bentham found and objected to this political ambiguity – not the conceptual ambiguity that has so absorbed the attention of the modern philosophers – in the natural law traditions and ways of speaking of his day. Rights movements, he famously complained, exploited the revolutionary or anarchic interpretation – rights being "nonsense upon stilts."[24] Less famously, perhaps, he criticized the jurisprudence of William Blackstone – and, more specifically, Blackstone's natural law tendencies – as reactionary. Blackstone, recall, defined civil law as "a rule of civil conduct prescribed by the supreme power in a state, commanding what is right and prohibiting what is wrong."[25] Although the first Austinian part of the definition – that law is the command of the sovereign[26] – became a defining and central tenet of legal positivism, and grist for antipositivist criticism for two centuries following, the less-often-noted second half – that law "commands what is right and prohibits what is wrong" – echoed natural law themes rather than positivist, and was the target of Bentham's critical gaze.[27] Clearly, with regard to the second part, Blackstone did not mean that whenever the supreme power commands what is wrong or prohibits what is right the result is not law, such that citizens are morally free to disobey the errant commands and that courts have no duty to enforce them. Blackstone's definition (as well as his equation elsewhere of human law and God's law[28]) was not intended to give cover to the

[23] Luban, *Legal Ethics and Human Dignity*, 120–26.

[24] Bentham, "Anarchical Fallacies," *The Works of Jeremy Bentham* vol. 2, 501.

[25] William Blackstone, "Of the Nature of Laws in General," *Commentaries on the Laws of England* vol. 1, sec.2 (Oxford: Clarendon Press, 1765–69) 44 (digitized original edition available at http://avalon .law.yale.edu/subject_menus/blackstone.asp).

[26] John Austin, *The Province of Jurisprudence Determined*, 1832, Wilfrid E. Rumble, ed. (Cambridge: Cambridge University Press, 1995) 18–37.

[27] Jeremy Bentham, *Comment on the Commentaries: A Criticism of William Blackstone's Commentaries on the Laws of England*, Charles Warren Everett, ed. (Oxford: Clarendon Press, 1928). *See generally*, Felix S. Cohen, "Transcendental Nonsense and the Functional Approach," *Columbia Law Review* 35.6 (1935): 809–49, 838, *and* H. L. A. Hart, "Positivism and the Separation of Law and Morals."

[28] In *Commentaries*, Blackstone writes: "This law of nature, being co-eval with mankind and dictated by God himself, is of course superior in obligation to any other. It is binding over all the globe, in all

morally righteous civil disobedient – to absolve him of legal and moral guilt for disobeying lawful commands that do not prohibit the wrong and mandate the right. Although, no less than Aquinas's dictum, it is surely open to that interpretation. Nor was it a *declaration* of the sovereign's power to decide, Humpty-Dumpty style, right from wrong. Rather, and as Bentham complained, its function was to provide an apologia for power. In contemporary terms, it was a legitimation of power, and it was rendered in the language of natural law and natural rights – terms no less available, and familiar to conservative devotees of the British Constitution and the English common law, as to the American revolutionaries. It confidently equated political power with the moral goodness and the moral astuteness that one would want in rulers charged with the task of civilizing the untamed beasts of the British lower classes.[29]

countries, and at all times: no human laws are of any validity, if contrary to this; and such of them as are valid derive all their force, and all their authority, mediately or immediately, from this original." Blackstone, "Of the Nature of Laws in General," *Commentaries on the Law of England* 41. John Austin gave this passage a generally positivist interpretation: "But the meaning of this passage of Blackstone, if it has a meaning, seems rather to be this: that no human law which conflicts with the Divine law is obligatory or binding; in other words, that no human law which conflicts with the Divine law is a law, for a law without an obligation is a contradiction in terms." Austin, *The Province of Jurisprudence Determined* 158.

[29] On Bentham's subversive relation to legal authorities of all sorts, there is perhaps no better authority than John Stuart Mill. *See* John Stuart Mill, "On Bentham," *Utilitarianism and Other Essays* (London: Penguin Classics, 1987) 133–34 (originally published in *The London and Westminster Review*, 1838):

> Bentham has been in this age and country the great questioner of things established. It is by the influence of the modes of thought with which his writings inoculated a considerable number of thinking men, that the yoke of authority has been broken, and innumerable opinions, formerly received on tradition as incontestable, are put upon their defence, and required to give an account of themselves. Who, before Bentham . . . dared to speak disrespectfully, in express terms, of the British Constitution, or the English Law? He did so; and his arguments and his example together encouraged others. . . . Bentham gave voice to . . . those . . . who found our institutions unsuited to them [but] did not dare to say so, did not dare consciously to think so; they had never heard the excellence of those institutions questioned by cultivated men, by men of acknowledged intellect; and it is not in the nature of uninstructed minds to resist the united authority of the instructed. Bentham broke the spell. . . . If the superstition about ancestorial wisdom has fallen into decay; if the public are grown familiar with the idea that their laws and institutions are in great part not the product of intellect and virtue, but of modern corruption grafted upon ancient barbarism; if the hardiest innovation is no longer scouted because it is an innovation – establishments no longer considered sacred because they are establishments – it will be found that those who have accustomed the public mind to these ideas have learnt them in Bentham's school, and that the assault on ancient institutions has been, and is, carried on for the most part with his weapons. It matters not although these thinkers, or indeed thinkers of any description, have been but scantily found among the persons prominently and ostensibly at the head of the Reform movement. All movements, except directly revolutionary ones, are headed, not by those who originate them, but by those who know best how to compromise between the old opinions and the new. The father of English innovation both in doctrines and in institutions, is Bentham: he is the great *subversive*, or, in the language of continental philosophers, the great *critical*, thinker of his age and country.

See also H. L. A. Hart, "The Demystification of the Law," *Essays on Bentham: Jurisprudence and Political Theory* (Oxford: Oxford University Press, 1982).

Bentham's complaint about natural law was thus twofold; it was not limited to his famous insistence that natural law and natural rights nonsensically make the individual conscience the test of legality. Rather, the natural lawyer's definitional insistence that only just laws are truly "law," he thought, was politically ambiguous and destabilizing: it served the ends of both authoritarianism *and* anarchism (and he found both obnoxious, in more or less equal measure). If law is necessarily just, then it might follow that the unjust law is not law, but it also might follow that all the law in the books is therefore just. Interpreted in this second way, power, empire, and sovereignty are all morally legitimated. To Bentham, this political ambiguity rendered natural law the enemy, rather than the handmaiden, of responsible and coherent criticism and reform of law. The responsible citizen, Bentham opined, should "obey punctually and censure freely."[30] The natural law movement seemed to counsel precisely the *opposite* on both scores: if only just laws are laws, then the conscientious critic is free to disobey. There lies anarchy. Alternatively, if all the sovereign's utterances are therefore just, then all laws are beyond moral critique. There lies Blackstonian quietism, smugness, undue loyalty to the status quo, and the correlate intolerance of dissent that comes with it. Virtually by definition, or so it would seem, natural law counseled both disobedience on the part of the citizen and the censure of critique on the part of the sovereign. Natural law is a home, then, Bentham thought, to both reactionaries and revolutionaries. It is the natural home to all those who share nothing but their contempt for the liberal, reformist (and quintessentially Benthamic) mind-set: "obey punctually, censure freely" that should be definitive of responsible citizenship. This mind-set is precisely what natural law undermines.

What of contemporary interpretations of natural law, however, and of the American scene? Is David Luban right to complain that it is simply a "mistake" to interpret the twentieth-century American natural lawyer's definitional claim in the second, reactionary sense that Bentham found in Blackstone? It is easy enough to see why one might think so. If we look at America's record with this idea, it might seem that Bentham's worry that natural law can be employed as an apology for power, no less than a green light for civil disobedience, at least on first blush, looks misguided. After all, the American Revolutionaries claimed both right and law to be on their side – and they used natural law arguments to make the case. They were revolutionaries – no apologists for power there. A hundred years later, abolitionists argued both in and outside the courts that laws supporting slavery, such as the Fugitive Slave Act, were unjust, therefore not true law, and therefore not binding, either legally or morally, on people of conscience, including judges.[31] In the twentieth century, Reverend King

[30] Jeremy Bentham, *A Fragment on Government, Being an Examination of What Is Delivered, On the Subject of Government in General in the Introduction to Sir William Blackstone's Commentaries* (London: Athlone Press, 1977) xiv.

[31] Lysander Spooner, *The Unconstitutionality of Slavery: A Contemporary Legal Argument Against Slavery*, 1845 (New York: B. Franklin, 1965; *see generally* Randy E. Barnett, "Was Slavery Unconstitutional Before the Thirteenth Amendment? Lysander Spooner's Theory of Interpretation," *Pacific*

quoted Aquinas in his famous letter, concluding that it was the civil disobedient sitting at the lunch counter or waiting in jail, and not the armed policeman making arrests, that exhibited true respect for true law – badges, dogs, billy clubs, and other indicia of authority notwithstanding.[32] The draft protestor, Dworkin argued in the 1970s, was likely not breaking a law at all – the draft law itself was likely unconstitutional, because unjust.[33] In the 1990s and the aughts, the tax protestor and the trespassing abortion clinic protestor have claimed likewise.

Thus, is it a mistake, here and now, to worry that the Thomistic dictum and the philosophical movement it has inspired can be read as nothing but a brief for power and all the more insidiously so by seemingly giving comfort to the occasional civil disobedient? Again, I think not, and the issue might be sharpened if we look at the operation of natural law arguments in the academy rather than in the jails of Birmingham. Let me treat just one example. In the 1970s, Ronald Dworkin, surely one of the most generous and liberal secular natural lawyers ever to write on these themes, put forward two extremely influential sets of arguments, both of which were intended to refute Hartian positivism and both of which were fully resonant with at least the spirit, if not the letter, of the strong reading suggested earlier of Aquinas's dictum. First, Dworkin argued, American common law includes substantive moral principles that courts from time to time enunciate and that are themselves implied by our past legal practice understood in its best light.[34] Second, he argued, in a piece aptly titled "On Civil Disobedience," that at least many of the laws in the U.S. system that are patently unjust – meaning unjust in the light of past legal practice and decent moral belief – likely are not constitutional for just that reason; and if they are not constitutional, then they therefore are not law at all.[35] Taken collectively, the essays on the common law in *Taking Rights Seriously* argued the loosely Thomistic point that "law," properly understood, includes various moral principles, whereas the constitutional law essays in the same volume argued that some morally unjust laws, because they are unjust, are not true laws at all – they not only are not binding in conscience, but because of their likely unconstitutionality, they are likewise not binding in courts of law. At least American law, then, as Dworkin convinced two generations of law students and many of their teachers as well, is both more and less inclusive than positivists believe it to be. It is more inclusive by virtue of its inclusion of moral principles enforced as law by courts in deciding ordinary common-law cases. It is less inclusive by virtue of the nonlegality – the nullity – of laws that are so unjust as to be unconstitutional. For both reasons, the sphere of justice and the sphere of law are more nearly aligned than is believed by legal positivists. Law includes mandates

---

    Law Journal 28 (1997): 977–1014; J. M. Balkin and Sanford Levinson, "The Canons of Constitutional Law," *Harvard Law Review* 111 (1998): 964–1024.

[32]   Martin Luther King, Jr., "Letter from Birmingham Jail," *Why We Can't Wait* (New York: Signet Books, 1963) 76.

[33]   Dworkin, "Civil Disobedience," *Taking Rights Seriously* 207–8.

[34]   Dworkin, "Model of Rules I," *Taking Rights Seriously* 62–75.

[35]   Dworkin, "Civil Disobedience," *Taking Rights Seriously* 207–8; Dworkin, "Model of Rules I," *Taking Rights Seriously* 62–75; *see also* Dworkin, "Hard Cases," *Taking Rights Seriously* 81–130.

of justice, and unjust enactments that bear the positivist indicia of legality may not in fact be law, by virtue of their probable unconstitutionality. Prosecutors ought not to push aggressively for the arrest and conviction of the violators of conscience of the unjust-and-therefore-possibly-unconstitutional laws, and judges and jurors ought not to convict.[36]

In a moment, I'll suggest that Dworkin's purportedly liberal jurisprudence unintentionally validates rather than rebuts Bentham's worry about the illiberal political valence of natural law. First, however, let me review what have become the somewhat standard positivist objections to Dworkin's powerful revival of the natural law tradition in American jurisprudence – in part to distinguish them from the Benthamic objection I want to press but also in part because they clarify it. Dworkin is surely right that the moral principles that courts from time to time enunciate and the force of which sometimes account for judicial outcomes, such as the maxim that "no man may profit from his own wrong," do occasionally work their way as premises into judicial logic. By what evidentiary criteria, however, does Dworkin reach the conclusion that these moral principles, which we all agree are not law by positivist (or commonsensical) criteria, are in fact principles of *law*? (They don't look, walk, or talk, like law: who really thinks that it's a "law" that no man may profit from his own wrong?[37] People profit from their own wrong all the time, without even a pang of conscience as a sanction. It might be more accurate to say that no one ever profits without having committed a wrong, maybe *that's* a law.) Dworkin's answer: we know these maxims are legal principles (and not just moral principles) because they are the sort of thing that are or may be invoked by "courts of law" in arguments. They are law, in other words, because judges themselves consider them such; judges *act* as though they are binding. Courts treat moral principles as binding, and therefore, these moral principles are legal principles. However, these moral principles are not law by positivist criteria, therefore, positivism fails.[38] Now, put this in context. This large, powerful, influential argument against Hartian styled legal positivism is completely dependent not only on the claim that courts do from time to time invoke moral principles but also that *because* they do, those principles are therefore legal principles – a part of our law. Our "law," then, for this argument to work, must include the array of principles that courts treat as binding or determinative; that array includes moral principles not referenced by positivist criteria of law.

Dworkin's positivist critics have responded that both of these assumptions are pretty weak. First, as "inclusive positivists" have argued, it's not that hard to generate a rule of recognition that expressly proscribes judicial resort to moral principles implied by past legal practices when more immediate legal materials seem inadequate to resolve

---

[36] *See id.* Dworkin, "Civil Disobedience," *Taking Rights Seriously* 215.

[37] Famously, Dworkin's example of a moral principle that operates as a legal premise of judicial arguments. Ronald Dworkin, "Model of Rules I," *Taking Rights Seriously* 76.

[38] *Id.* at 35.

particular cases. Dworkin's adjudicative methods can thus be absorbed easily enough into the larger fabric of positivist accounts of law.[39] Second, and more convincingly, as his exclusive (meaning "hard-core") positivist critics have argued, it isn't at all clear that the moral principles that are or could be invoked by judges to resolve hard cases are law, solely by virtue of their felt bindingness (even if they are felt to be binding).[40] Much that is binding or is felt to be binding on judges – rules of grammar or rules of logic, for example – are not, solely by virtue of that fact, therefore law. Judges feel compelled to apply basic rules of logic, grammar, and ethics to their decisions; that alone doesn't make logic, grammar, and ethics "law." There is likewise no reason not to think of moral principles that may be implied by past practices. Judges might be and feel bound to apply them, and that may be an important aspect of adjudicative practice; that doesn't, however, make them law. It isn't the case that whatever binds judges, whatever they feel to be binding, or whatever they may utter or claim in the future to be binding is therefore law.

If so, then what apparently follows from the positivist rejoinder is that Dworkin has produced a theory, or account, or description, or conception, of *adjudication*, rather than a theory of *law*, and it is a theory of adjudication, furthermore, that is fully compatible with positivist accounts of law.[41] Adjudication – judicial opinion writing – is a subtle, complex, interpretive activity. In the course of doing that activity, judges do a number of things. They often – if Dworkin is right, they *always* – interpret law in light of moral principle. They provide accounts of law that, if they're doing the adjudicative task well, are the best legal account that can be given in light of the best moral account that can be dreamed up of our best past legal and political and institutional practices. Those principles inform the judicial task of assessing what the law is in part by suggesting what the law should be. It doesn't follow from any of this, however, that "law" includes all that weighs on judges – logic, grammar, ethics, or moral principle – when doing so. Principles have weight, and courts sometimes resort to them when deciding cases. They have adjudicative weight. That doesn't make them law. Dworkin's claim to the contrary might just be a distortion and a somewhat arbitrary one of our usual meaning of the word "law." To be sure, it is a distortion that may come more or less naturally to a small class of elite Supreme Court lawyers and some judges. Nevertheless, whether it comes naturally or not to

---

[39] Inclusive positivists include Jules Coleman and Philip Soper, who argue for a form of positivism recognizing that law does often (but does not necessarily) incorporate moral principles. *See, e.g.,* Jules Coleman, "Negative and Positive Positivism," *Journal of Legal Studies* 11 (1982): 139–64, 143; Philip E. Soper, "Legal Theory and the Obligation of a Judge: The Hart/Dworkin Dispute," *Michigan Law Review* 75 (1977): 473–519, 495–98.

[40] The most important exclusive positivist is Joseph Raz. Joseph Raz, *The Authority of Law* (Oxford: Oxford University Press, 1979); Raz, "Postema on Law's Autonomy and Public Practical Reasons: A Critical Comment," *Legal Theory* 4 (1998): 1–20; Raz, *Practical Reason and Norms*, 2nd ed. (Oxford: Oxford University Press, 1999) 193.

[41] Raz, "Postema on Law's Autonomy and Public Practical Reasons: A Critical Comment" 4–6.

such a group, it is still a distortion, not only for most citizens but likely for most lawyers and judges as well.

These are relatively well-rehearsed objections within the positivist literature – the former more so, perhaps, than the latter. There is, however, another problem, not so readily noticed by his positivist critics: Dworkin's early jurisprudence not only turns on a distortion of familiar meanings of "law." It also turns on a distortion – and, more important, a diminution – of the meaning and content of the "moral principles" that are or ought to be of relevance to law – moral principles, that is, that ought to be of relevance not only to our interpretive attempts to make law the best it can be but also to our critical attempts to criticize it for what it is, on the basis of that which no amount of interpretation can make it. By conflating "law" and "adjudication," Dworkin makes plausible the claim that "law" includes normative, moral principles; that legal interpretation engaged by courts in the process of determining the law to apply to a set of facts requires an understanding of a web of practice that embraces both moral principle and legal rule. If he is right, then legal positivist tests of what does and does not constitute law fail, as does the positivist's defining claim that law and the moral principles by which we might evaluate law are distinct. As his positivist critics have urged, this may distort our understanding of the word "law" past the breaking point, and the error may well be (I think it is) in the Dworkinian suggestion (or premise) that whatever judges regard as binding on them when rendering decisions is itself a part of law. Whether or not that's the case, what is less noticed, but perhaps more consequential, is that Dworkinian jurisprudence shrinks our understanding of the moral principles, or moral truths, that might be germane to the criticism, rather than "best interpretation" of law. It morally enriches legal interpretation, but it does so at the cost of legal criticism.

To see this, look at what those Dworkinian principles are and then at what they are not.[42] They are not just any and all moral principles that might have some relevance to the evaluation, criticism, or development of law. They are, rather, the moral principles that are fairly inferable from past legal, political, and particularly adjudicative practices and that are fairly applicable to the adjudicative quandaries of the present. They are, furthermore, the moral principles deducible from past practice that can be applied to present dilemmas in such a way as to inspire confidence in today's litigants that their disputes are being resolved in ways that are not a departure from past law. They are the moral principles that have sufficient rooted-ness in past practice to count not only as ideals for law but as embedded within existing law and as sufficiently clear to satisfy a litigant that he or she has received formal justice – that his case has been decided in the same way as like cases brought in an earlier time. Again, they are the subset of all possible moral principles that might be of

---

[42] *See generally* Larry Alexander and Ken Kress, "Against Legal Principles," *Iowa Law Review* 82 (1997): 739–86.

relevance to the project of law, that are inferable from past legal practice, and that are in some way applicable and relevant to contemporary adjudicative problems.

So – what *aren't* they? Well, they are not the moral principles through which we might determine that an entire legal system is unjust or, for that matter, that a particularly sizeable chunk of one might so be. They are not the moral principles through which we might determine that the moral codes, intuitions, or ways of morally talking, that we inherit from past practice, might themselves be morally suspect. They are not the moral principles through which we might criticize adjudicative law understood in the capacious and generous way that Dworkin himself has aptly described. They are not the moral principles through which we might criticize social practice that is currently legally unregulated or underregulated – and through which we might determine that greater legal regulation might be called for where none had existed previously. They are not the moral principles through which we might determine that a new law might be necessary, authored by the lawmaking democratic branch, rather than a new legal interpretation by the adjudicative branch. They are not the moral principles that suggest when, if, and where legislators might have a duty to enact law toward the common good. They are not the moral principles that might guide the politics that generates new positive law.

Dworkin states this limit of "naturalism" thusly:

> Of course, naturalism is a theory about judicial rights, that is, about the rights people have to win lawsuits. It takes no position about how far the political order furnishes or constrains the rights people have to particular legislation in their favor, or their rights to revolt or otherwise to establish a very different political order. If the political order includes a constitution which, properly interpreted, disables the legislature from changing the present order in certain ways, then people do have judicial rights, under this order, that the courts not enforce legislation which contradicts these commands. But naturalism, as such, leaves the legislature otherwise free to improve the present order, both in detail and if appropriate, radically. The idea, that people have an abstract judicial right to the enforcement of the present order, imposes a kind of conservatism on politics; but this is a conservatism imposed on adjudication alone.[43]

The moral principles at the heart of Dworkin's natural law are those embedded in existing past political and legal practice, and which are necessary to ensure – in a common-law world rife with apparent gaps in rule-based decisional law – that each litigant in such a system receives an adjudicated disposition of his or her claim that does not depart from past practice, thus ensuring that there are no breaches of norms of formal equality. To paraphrase his own account: Dworkin's principles are thus silent with respect to some part of the community's right, or lack of right, to have a new law legislated or created "in its favor." They are silent with respect to the entire community's right to have a new legal system period. They are not based,

---

43 Ronald Dworkin, "Natural Law Revisited," *University of Florida Law Review* 34 (1982): 165–88, 180.

in the final analysis, on any particular set of moral virtues, other than the virtue of equal justice in courts of law. They are based in past practice and a commitment to equal treatment of equally situated litigants. This is indeed, as Dworkin remarks, a "conservatism imposed on adjudication." However, if our test of law is what courts turn to when deciding cases – if law is a matter of what counts in adjudication – then it is a conservatism imposed not *only* on adjudication. It is a conservatism imposed on law.

Much the same can be said of Dworkin's constitutional jurisprudence. The hard constitutional case, Dworkin has argued for several decades, requires the Herculean judge to synthesize the best interpretation he can render of our political morality, as he discerns it from past practice, and of our constitutional history; this must be done in such a way as to yield a correct constitutional outcome.[44] Thus, a good constitutional decision must both reflect a decent political morality and exhibit fit with prior constitutional precedent.[45] Such a Herculean judge, Dworkin has argued, has creative and demanding work to do, and he cannot do it mechanistically.[46] On the other hand, he is hardly the unhinged instrumentalist, deciding cases on the basis of policy, his own political preferences, or his judgment of what's best, all things considered. Rather, he is interpreting the Constitution, within the context of a current case, in such a way, ideally, as to fit a pattern of past decisions[47] and an idealized political morality that is itself likewise culled from past practice.[48] The constitutional decision thus rendered is attuned not to particular judgments of framers, earlier courts, or the judge's own politics, but rather to the political morality of the country writ large, over the centuries, that is both morally defensible and decent on its own terms and that meshes with institutional history.[49]

Again, however, what sorts of moral principles are these, which dictate the proper course of constitutional decision making? The Constitution is a bridge, Dworkin argues, between moral principle and our positive law. Assuming he is right about this, however, for *which* moral principles or for *what sort* of principles is it a bridge? Which principles cross the bridge, and which do not? What moral principles does the Dworkinian Constitution, in fact, serve? The answer, in brief: not many, and they are highly conscribed even under the best of circumstances. They are the principles generated from a morally generous reading of our past constitutional practice – a practice that has not been all that ennobling. Second, they are the principles, again, that might serve as a major premise of Supreme Court reasoning in actual constitutional cases. They must not only fit past practice, they must also

---

44 Dworkin, "Hard Cases," *Taking Rights Seriously* 118–28.
45 Ronald Dworkin, *Law's Empire* (Cambridge: Belknap Press, 1986) 366.
46 Dworkin, "Constitutional Cases," *Taking Rights Seriously* 117–18.
47 Ronald Dworkin, *A Matter of Principle* (Oxford: Clarendon Press, 1986) 158–59; *see also* Dworkin, *Taking Rights Seriously*.
48 *Taking Rights Seriously* 90.
49 *Id.* at 87.

be serviceable toward the end of resolving current conflicts through adjudicative means. Third, they must fit with our institutional history, both immediate and past. They are the principles – moral principles, no doubt – that our past dictates.

This is a generous account of the nature of constitutional adjudication. It is nevertheless a decidedly *ungenerous* accounting of both constitutional law and natural law. First, as a goodly number of theorists now argue, the Constitution may well contain or suggest principles of governance well beyond those a court might find serviceable.[50] The Constitution may be "underenforced," as long as we rely on courts to do the enforcing. Second, however, it is likewise an ungenerous accounting of natural law. Our public morality, and our not-so-public morality, may contain moral truths not countenanced by our constitutional tradition, whether in the courts or outside of them. Our constitutional tradition, again whether limited to adjudicated constitutional law or not, will not include those moral principles through which the Constitution might be morally challenged. It will not contain those moral principles with which the Constitution is unconcerned, such as, perhaps, the moral duties of state legislators to affirmatively provide for certain goods – education, housing, health care, or child care. It will not contain moral principles that dictate the duties of action of legislators, rather than constitutionally mandated duties of restraint. It will not contain moral principles that suggest the moral failings of the Constitution. It will not contain these principles not because they are false, but rather because the moral principles the Constitution does embrace will be those generated by adjudicative history. Again, the conservatism of this constitutional jurisprudence is imposed "on adjudication alone." However, adjudication alone, particularly in the constitutional context, cuts across an awfully broad swath of not only our constitutional consciousness but also our politics, and political morality, as well.

Dworkin is without question the most progressive of our major liberal legal jurisprudentialists. Yet even in the writing of this generous egalitarian liberal, the various moral principles he identifies that law purportedly embraces are drawn from the positive law of the past, used to demonstrate the overall justice of extant law, so long as the latter is generously understood and invoked to ensure that most conservative of judicial virtues: the like treatment of cases with the similar cases from yesterday. It is a "conservatism imposed on adjudication alone," yes, but it is a conservatism all the same. The "adjudication alone" on which it is imposed is extraordinarily outsized not just in substantive reach but also in its moral ambition: adjudication is, after all, where, according to our constitutional lawyers, we can and should expect to find virtue, reason, and justice, rather than the horse trading, interest-group politics, and whimsy that we can expect to find and do find in legislative lawmaking.

---

[50] Lawrence Sager, *Justice in Plainclothes: A Theory of American Constitutional Practice* (New Haven: Yale University Press, 2004) 187–88; Mark Tushnet, *Taking the Constitution away from the Courts* (Princeton: Princeton University Press, 1999) 160–61; Robert Post and Reva B. Siegel, "Popular Constitutionalism, Departmentalism, and Judicial Supremacy," *California Law Review* 92 (2004): 1027–44, 1036–37.

Adjudication – not legislation – is what gives us law, intertwined with moral principle. That principle is in turn grounded in our quite positive institutional history. The result is indeed a judicial conservatism – but not only or even primarily among the judges, or lawyers, who embrace it. It is a conservatism imposed on the political morality that defines the constitutional framework of the country. That political morality, in turn, might exhaust the supply.

Let me sum this up. Sometimes outside the courts, and occasionally inside the courts, philosophical natural law American-style has provided a language of conscience for the disobedient or revolutionary. Martin Luther King did indeed argue from Birmingham Jail that the segregation laws he broke were not truly law at all, and he did invoke Aquinas and the natural law movement in toto to make the point; the abolitionists did indeed argue that the Constitution's seeming embrace of slavery was a legal as well as moral nullity, because unjust. Inside the academy, however? Not so much so. Inside the pages of law reviews, antipositivist natural law reasoning has been the natural language of the lover of adjudication, of American constitutionalism, and of the common law; of legalists who value continuity with the past, of those who champion the primacy of horizontal equity across like cases as the primary, perhaps only, constituent part of legal justice; of principled and neutral judicial decision making; and, of course, of the existence of remarkably resilient duties to obey law. Natural law, as articulated by legal philosophers, does unquestionably give judges who respect or love adjudication, constitutionalism, and the common law a regard for and sensitivity to moral principle that they might well otherwise lack: the Dworkinian judge is moved to nudge the law in a way that makes it the best it can be, whereas the "positivist" judge or the "formalist" judge who denies the relevance or existence of such principle will not be. Natural law inside the courts gives the positive law inside the courts a moral light it might otherwise lack. This was precisely Dworkin's ambition; this was the result he wanted to see, as he urged all of us, but emphatically courts and judges, to "take rights seriously." By virtue of so doing, however, Dworkin's jurisprudential admonition is also a contemporary version of the natural law that was the target of Bentham's critique. The adjudicated law from the past that is so richly interpreted, that holds rights in such high regard, is essentially equated with moral principle. The result is a mighty restriction of moral principle.

That fact alone does not alone render Dworkin or the Dworkinian lawyer a Burkean conservative. He does not see the divine right of kings transposed onto the Constitution or its interpreters. The point is not that the Dworkinian judge will see so much value in tradition as to equate its perseverance with justice. Dworkin does not see the "hand of angels" or "heavenly balm" or a "golden crown" on the heads of Supreme Court justices. He does not equate the anointed king, or the amended Constitution, with "the deputy elected by the Lord."[51] The Dworkinian Herculean

---

[51] Shakespeare so described the divine right of Richard the II – a source of power and moral wisdom both, such that the king can truly do no wrong. William Shakespeare, *Richard the II*, Andrew Gurr, ed. (Cambridge: Cambridge University Press, 2003) 127.

judge, lawyer, law professor, law student, or citizen is, however, indeed inclined to see in extant common-law principles more wisdom than they contain and in the Constitution perhaps more of that audacious hope than was ever intended or expressed. All that legal light can be blinding. Skeptical legal positivists are right to respond to Dworkin's romance with law with a healthy splash of their own ironic detachment.

A MISSING JURISPRUDENCE: LAW, HUMAN NATURE,
AND THE COMMON GOOD

Let me turn now to ethical natural law movements. In *Summa Theologica*, Aquinas gives the following account of what justice requires of law:

> Positive human laws are either just or unjust. If they are just, they have the power of binding in conscience.... [L]aws are said to be just:
>
> 1. From the end, namely when they are ordered to the Common Good;
> 2. From the lawgiver, namely when the law passed does not exceed the lawgiver's authority;
> 3. From the form, namely when burdens are imposed on the subjects according to proportionate equality for the Common Good.
>
> Likewise, laws can be unjust ... by being contrary to human good:
>
> a. either from the end as when some authority imposes burdens on the subjects that do not pertain to the common utility but rather to his own greed or glory;
> b. or from the lawgiver, as when someone makes a law that is beyond the authority granted to him;
> c. or from the form, as when burdens are unequally distributed in the community, even though they pertain to the Common Good.[52]

Aquinas's suggestion that "the just law is the law that promotes the human good," or the common good, is foundational to ethical natural law. The question central to this school is not whether an unjust law is or is not truly law. Rather, the quest is to define the human good that the just law serves, or to give content to the common good that law, both real and idealized, promotes or protects. Different natural lawyers in this ethical tradition do so in different ways: by resort to practical reason, by the consultation of first principles, by identifying norms of reasonableness, by inquiring into the nature of the good life, by reference to human desire and human nature, and so on. What they share is a focus on the human good, the claim that the just law is the law that promotes it, and participation in a joint attempt to define the content of the common good that the just law serves in part by reference to our nature. What they are not interested in is any definitional relation of law and morality. Finnis draws the distinction, which he regards as the distinction between a strawman account of the

---

[52] Aquinas, *Summa Theologica*, Pt. I–II, ques. 96, Art. 4.

natural law tradition erected by positivist critics and the actual natural law tradition in this passage:

> The tradition of "Natural Law" theorizing is not characterized by any particular answer to the questions: "Is every 'settled' legal rule and legal solution settled by appeal exclusively to 'positive' sources such as statute precedent, and custom? Or is the 'correctness' of some judicial decisions determinable only by appeal to some 'moral' ('extralegal') norm? And are the boundaries between the settled and the unsettled law, or between the correct, the eligible, and the incorrect judicial decision determinable by reference only to positive sources or legal rules?" The tradition of Natural Law theorizing is not concerned to minimize the range and determinacy of positive law or the general sufficiency of positive sources as solvents of legal problems.
>
> Rather, the concern of the tradition . . . has been to show that the act of positing law (whether judicially or legislatively or otherwise) is an act which can and should be guided by "moral" principles and rules; that these moral norms are a matter of objective reasonableness, not of whim, convention, or mere "decision," and that those same moral norms justify (a) the very institution of positive law, (b) the main institutions, techniques, and modalities within that tradition. . . . and (c) the main institutions regulated and sustained by law (e.g., government, contract, property, marriage and criminal liability). What truly characterizes the tradition is that it is not content merely to observe the historical or sociological fact that "morality" thus affects "law," but instead seeks to determine what the requirements of practical reasonableness really are, so as to afford a rational basis for the activities of legislators, judges, and citizens.[53]

From this passage, we can see the size of the disjunction between ethical natural law and natural law jurisprudence. In the first paragraph, Finnis describes precisely the interests of secular natural lawyers such as Dworkin and his critics with the boundaries of positive law; these questions Finnis describes as not the concern or interest of the tradition. In the second paragraph, he explains the nature of the natural lawyer's quite different understanding of the relation of law and morality, as he understands it. The institution of law, he believes, is contingently justified (so long as it meets conditions of justice) by moral principle. Natural law is the attempt to articulate what those principles might be.

One can also see, however, in Finnis's developed writings, a modern, secular understanding of Aquinas's claim: that the just law is that law which, in its content, furthers the common good. Law, Finnis explains, must be justified by moral principles, which themselves are a matter of objective reasonableness, not of whim, preference, or mere decision. One such principle is that the just law is that law that furthers the common good. Although this requires, in part, that law further the *common* good – rather than the good of elites, of rulers, or of a class – it also requires

53 Finnis, *Natural Law and Natural Rights* 290.

that law furthers the common *good*, plain and simple. To know what justice requires of law, then, requires an understanding of the good that law might be instrumental in furthering.

What is the common good that the just law must further? First, Finnis argues, the common good is simply the summation of individual goods of affected persons.[54] There's nothing mysterious or mystical or religious about the common in the phrase "common good." Individual goods, in turn, are those basic aspects of well-being, that are good in themselves.[55] These basic goods, Finnis argues, are not known to us through anthropology or sociology but rather through our capacity for practical reason – although given a hefty boost from evidence borrowed from the social sciences.[56] They are the things that are good in themselves, rather than things that are good instrumentally (medicine, law, and the legal institutions of property, contract, and civil marriage are all examples of the latter). We come to know the content of these individual, basic, intrinsic goods individually, through reflection, tempered and informed by experience.[57] They are variously described as those things that are essential to our "flourishing,"[58] those things "valued in all societies,"[59] values suggested by "human nature,"[60] those things that are "basic to wellbeing,"[61] those things "anyone anywhere would find desirable."[62] They are not the sort of thing that lend themselves to precise definition (and the sketchy descriptions here are all disputed).

So, with all appropriate disclaimers, what are these basic goods? Finnis answers with a list (after disparaging the lists and the list-making tendency of other writers): knowledge, life itself (which includes the good of procreation), play (which includes leisure), religion (which includes nontheistic speculation on ultimate questions), aesthetic experience, friendship (which includes all aspects of sociability and intimacy), and practical reasonableness (which itself requires a degree of freedom with which to make basic life choices, to make a life plan, to decide what one should do).[63] These first things, as natural lawyers tend to say, are goods in themselves. The

---

[54] *Id.* at 216–19.

[55] *Id.* at 205.

[56] *Id.* at 3–18.

[57] *Id.* at 30.

[58] As discussed later, this formulation was introduced into the legal literature by Martha Nussbaum, in turn recalling Aristotle. Martha C. Nussbaum, *Women and Human Development* (Cambridge: Cambridge University Press, 2001) 31; Finnis, *Natural Law and Natural Rights* 126.

[59] Finnis, *Natural Law and Natural Rights* 82–83.

[60] Finnis disavows direct reliance on knowledge of human nature as the source of insight regarding the human good but nevertheless relies on it indirectly throughout. *See id.* at 33.

[61] This is the formula that Faden and Powers rest on, after surveying alternatives, in Madison Powers and Ruth Faden, *Social Justice: The Moral Foundations of Public Health and Health Policy* (New York: Oxford University Press, 2008) 6.

[62] Finnis, *Natural Law and Natural Rights* 66; Nussbaum, *Women and Human Development* 142; Powers and Faden, *Social Justice* 6.

[63] Finnis, *Natural Law and Natural Rights* 83.

very institution of law, and the phenomenal degree of cooperation it facilitates and requires, is necessary to render these goods within the reach of most of us – thus the considerable instrumental value of law, so long as it is basically just.[64] The most basic institutions of law – which Finnis identifies as property, contract, criminal law and marriage[65] – likewise are necessary to the individual's realization of these goods. Many other laws might also be required, although their forms might vary. These institutions, however – law, property, contract, criminal sanction, and marriage – are fundamental, and it is important although surely not determinative that every society recognizes them in some form.

Of course, Finnis's list of the basic goods might be under- or overinclusive, and the method of practical reasoning he suggests for its specification may be flawed. He might also be wrong to be so sanguine about the basic justice of our extant legal institutions, given the list of goods he believes just law must promote (and the considerable amount of redistribution of wealth he thinks justice requires[66]). Nevertheless, all I want to urge here is that the Thomistic question he poses – regardless of the answers he gives – is meaningful, important, and *largely unaddressed* by liberal and progressive jurisprudents, philosophers, and constitutional theorists all. What is the common good that law ought to promote, or that it must promote for it to be just? This is the natural law question that for a host of reasons, which I discuss in the next subsection, has in effect been lost to American liberal jurisprudence. Liberal legal philosophers do not typically ask or try to answer it. We do not invite inquiry into the nature of the human good that a just law must promote, either among ourselves or our students. Neither the question itself nor various possible answers to it have had a noticeable impact on the shape of contemporary liberal legal jurisprudence.

I think this is unfortunate, for reasons I discuss later, but first it is worth noting that the question is central to other corners of political and moral philosophy, even if not to liberal legalist jurisprudence. Martha Nussbaum in particular has spawned an entire approach to political philosophy that is centered on questions regarding those "human capabilities" that might be essential to human well-being.[67] Nussbaum's list is more extensive than Finnis's (it includes health, autonomy, family life, and capacity for the enjoyment of nature), her method is more empirical and less intuitionist, and it owes more to Aristotle than Aquinas, but nevertheless, the question at the heart of her political and moral philosophy (as it pertains to law) is not dissimilar to the one that Finnis posed: what are the fundamental elements of human well-being – the basic human goods, the basic human capabilities – that law ought to promote? More recently, a major new book on social justice and public health by Ruth Faden and Madison Powers of the Georgetown Public Health and

[64] *Id.* at 260–75.
[65] *Id.* at 290.
[66] *Id.* at 177.
[67] Nussbaum, *Women and Human Development* 70.

Philosophy Departments, respectively, puts forward an account of social justice that has at its heart a set of claims about "human well-being" that, in the authors' view, law, including the law of public health, ought serve.[68] Faden and Powers (unlike both Nussbaum and Finnis) posit six general categories of well-being: physical safety and freedom from fear, intimacy and family, autonomy, health and longevity, education, and culture. Again, there are significant differences in all of these approaches, which I do not mean to minimize: Madison and Faden, unlike Nussbaum, emphasize well-being rather than capabilities[69] and focus on issues of inequality and social justice as they arise in the context of possible conflicts between these values.[70] They also keep a special focus on the health of children, not because health is prior in some sense but pragmatically because of the dependence of all others on health.[71] Nussbaum, like Sen,[72] puts far more weight on autonomy, rationality, and individual liberty than Powers, Faden, or Finnis, reflecting their greater immersion in and debt to liberalism. (Thus, for example, Nussbaum stresses the importance of ensuring that individuals have available the choice to be healthy, as a fundamental capability that should be in some sense guaranteed by liberal states, whereas Powers and Faden argue for a state that guarantees some minimal level of health, relative to the state's ability to provide it.)[73] Powers, Faden, and Nussbaum all employ a method that is much more attentive to the evidence of experience and much less dependent on the evidence of deep reflection than that put forward by Finnis.[74] Finnis provides justifications, tied to the basic goods he identifies, of our more-or-less extant law of contract, property, criminal sanction, and civil marriage,[75] whereas Nussbaum and Faden and Powers, less interested than Finnis in the relation of positive and natural law, will have none of that; their bottom line is much more critical and far less self-congratulatory.

---

[68] Powers and Faden, *Social Justice* 90.

[69] *Id.* at 37.

[70] *Id.* at 39.

[71] *Id.* at 12.

[72] See generally Amartya Sen, *The Idea of Justice* (Cambridge: Belknap Press, 2009). *See also* Sen, *Rationality and Freedom* (Cambridge: Belknap Press, 2004).

[73] *Compare* Powers and Faden, *Social Justice* 132–33 ("There are three features of the U.S. system of employer-based insurance that make it different from other employer-based systems, and those differences largely explain why the U.S. system fails to meet the most minimum standards of justice in health insurance markets.") *with* Nussbaum, *Women and Human Development* 82 ("Some differences in health among nations or groups are due to factors public policy can control . . . political principles have done their job if they have provided people with the full social basis of these capabilities.").

[74] *Compare* Nussbaum, *Women and Human Development* 300 ("Philosophy can offer good guidance to practice, I believe only if it is responsive to experience . . . with insufficient experience we do not even know what questions we should be asking.") *and* Powers and Faden, *Social Justice* 41–42 ("In this style we start with some bedrock of shared experience within a culture and perhaps supplement that with experience accumulating across cultures as well.") *with* Finnis, *Natural Law and Natural Rights* 64 ("Yet such presuppositions and principles can be disengaged and identified, by reflection not only on our own thinking but on the words and deeds of others.").

[75] Finnis, *Natural Law and Natural Rights* 281–91.

Nevertheless, for all the differences, there are significant commonalities, and it is the common ground I want to endorse. All of these theorists – Finnis, Nussbaum, and Faden and Powers – provide a conception of well-being that, in their view, lawmakers should attend, when engaged in the act of positing law.[76] All rely, although to varying degrees, on descriptions of human nature, of the human experience, and of human universality in formulating their respective lists of basic goods.[77] All tie the basic goods to a conception of the good life.[78] All view politics, law, and the state, ideally, as a vehicle for securing these goods.[79] All concur that individual effort in a prelegal state will be terribly unavailing, and all view law as a good thing and as justified to the degree that it fulfills this potentiality.[80] Thus, all view the basic goods, elements of well-being, or human capabilities, as essential to the justice of just societies, just politics, and just law. All can be viewed as emendations of Aquinas's simple definitional claim regarding the ends of law: a law is just if it furthers the common good and unjust if it does not.

The Contours of a Missing Jurisprudence

Now again, my most basic point is that the liberal jurisprudence that would naturally flow from an exploration of Aquinas's definitional account of law's justice is largely (not entirely) missing from the contemporary scene, both in jurisprudence and in professional legal philosophy. Rather than try to prove that negative – with its own host of significant exceptions – let me try to describe what our jurisprudence might look like if it were present and prominent – centralized rather than marginalized – in liberal legal theory. What might we ask, and debate, if liberal legalists regarded laws as just so long as they further the common good and unjust if they do not, and if they took it as a part of their mission, both pedagogical and scholarly, to explore the contours of law on this premise?

First, we would be asking questions we currently do not ask about the moral obligations and duties of legislators to act, rather than focusing so relentlessly and with less and less return on the obligations and duties of judges. The Thomistic inquiry into the common good as the end of the just law invites inquiry into a

---

[76] Finnis is perhaps the most clear that his understanding of the common good is intended as a guide for legislators and not only a guide to adjudicative interpretation. *Id.* at 286–88.

[77] *Compare* Finnis, *id.* at 85 ("life, knowledge, play, aesthetic experience, sociability (friendship), practical reasonableness, and "religion") *with* Nussbaum, *Women and Human Development* 78–79 (list includes: "life," "bodily health," "bodily integrity," "senses, imagination and thoughts," "emotions," "practical reason," and "affiliation"), *and* Powers and Faden, *Social Justice* 16 ("Our list contains six core dimensions: health, personal security, reasoning, respect, attachment, and self determination.").

[78] Finnis, *Natural Law and Natural Rights* 82; Nussbaum, *Women and Human Development* 77; Powers and Faden, *Social Justice* 55.

[79] Finnis, *Natural Law and Natural Rights* 184–92; Nussbaum, *Women and Human Development* 98; Powers and Faden, *Social Justice* 39.

[80] Finnis, *Natural Law and Natural Rights* 167; Nussbaum, *Women and Human Development* 124; Powers and Faden, *Social Justice* 23.

profoundly undertheorized set of questions of American jurisprudence: what are the moral duties of legislators? What should legislators do? What is the conception of justice that should guide, or inform, or constrain, the creative, lawmaking legislative act? When should the lawmaker legislate? What injustice, in an unregulated world, ought the legislator respond to? When is the legislator required, by moral duty, to act? Is the legislator, prompted by his or her duty to promote the common good, required to legislate so as to protect the vulnerable against various medical risks? Or, is the ideal legislator required, by his or her duty, to promote the common good, to legislate in such a way as to protect the impoverished, or the unhoused, or the unfed against financial calamity, bankruptcy, unemployment, or the ravages of nature? The Thomistic inquiry directs the just legislator toward the common good: the legislator should legislate in a way that facilitates, secures, or promotes the basic goods for all individuals. This is obviously no more than a framing of the question – but it is that.

Note what it is not. It is not about what legislators ought *not* to do, and it is not about what legislators have the *power* to do. It does not ask what individual rights citizens have that legislators may not, or cannot, invade. It does not ask what policies legislators have the power to pursue, if the public choice calculus suggests it. It does not delineate a sphere within which legislators may or may not exercise power. It is not about legislative power, judicial power, executive power, or the separation of powers. Rather, it asks what the just legislator ought to do with the lawmaking power that he or she has. This question, within both jurisprudence and constitutional law, generally goes unasked, unanswered, and undebated – really in American jurisprudence across the board, but most consequentially in liberal and progressive jurisprudence. We do not have a way of even asking, let alone answering, what law that we currently lack legislators might have a positive moral duty to enact.

Why is that? I have argued elsewhere, and in more detail, that the reason for this is at least in part – maybe in large part – our constitutional structure. Our jurisprudential questions follow the path of our constitutional "may do's" and "musn't do's."[81] Thus, we do have a rich jurisprudence, both constitutional and ordinary, of legislators' duties not to act. Legislators have duties not to act that parallel the negative constitutional rights that citizens have against overly intrusive legislative action. As often noted, however, citizens have no positive constitutional rights to legislative protections. Therefore, legislators have no positive constitutional duties to protect citizens against anything at all – no duty to protect against private violence, for example, no duty to provide a police force, certainly no duty to provide shelter or food for the homeless – and so on. As Judge Posner once remarked, in an opinion explaining the lack of constitutionally based legislative duties to protect people from

---

[81] *See* Robin West, "Unenumerated Duties," *University of Pennsylvania Journal of Constitutional Law* 9 (2006): 221–62.

crime – it may well be "monstrous" for legislators not to pass laws that do so. It is not, however, unconstitutional for them not to do so.[82]

Now of course, Posner might have been wrong about that – there may in fact be constitutional grounds that he does not see for positive rights of citizens, and positive duties of legislators, to welfare legislation, to a police force, to antipollution measures, and so on. Perhaps his reading of the Constitution is too crabbed, too constrained by judicial pragmatic constraints, too conservative, too libertarian, or too whatever. My concern here, however, is not with his holding, *but with his aside*: that it would be "monstrous" for legislators not to take certain sorts of action (such as, enact a criminal law, and, fund a police force) to protect people against crime. What I want to highlight is the lack of jurisprudence behind *that* observation. Legal philosophers and jurisprudents do not ask or wonder, and certainly do not explain, why it *would* in fact *be* monstrous for legislators not to do so. We do not think much about that. There is no developed jurisprudence suggesting why Posner's aside is right, and why it is right, regardless of whether his constitutional holding is sound: why, that is, it would in fact be monstrous, were a legislator to decide not to protect people against the private violence that so puts their safety and well-being at risk, even if they are not constitutionally required to do so; why, in other words, they may be morally required to take these acts even if not legally required.

That lack of curiosity, in turn, has consequences. If we do not know, and are incurious about, why it is that it might be monstrous for legislators not to do this quite basic legal task – protect people against crime – a task that surely goes to the heart of the raison d'être of the liberal state – it is not surprising that we *also* do not know (and are incurious about) why it might also be monstrous, or immoral, or unjust for legislators not to do other legislative tasks as well that might promote the common good, such as protect against homelessness, unemployment, or the predations of sickness and age better than we do. It is not surprising, given that incuriosity, that we have so little constitutional jurisprudence on citizens' possible positive *moral* rights to legislatively provided protections. Again, we have no developed jurisprudence of legislative duties to act. As night follows day, we likewise have no developed jurisprudence of the positive moral rights of citizens – whatever might be the case for their constitutional rights – to those protections.

That lack, in turn, has political consequences. Dworkin is surely right to note that the source of our political morality in this country, for better or worse, is largely constitutional jurisprudence. We tend to identify – likely, we tend to

---

[82] *Bowers v. DeVito*, 686 F.2d 616, 618 (7th Cir. 1982):

> But there is no constitutional right to be protected by the state against being murdered by criminals or madmen. It is monstrous if the state fails to protect its residents against such predators but it does not violate the due process clause of the Fourteenth Amendment or, we suppose, any other provision of the Constitution. The Constitution is a charter of negative liberties; it tells the state to let people alone; it does not require the federal government or the state to provide services, even so elementary a service as maintaining law and order.

overidentify – political moral truth not just with constitutional law but, more fundamentally, with constitutionalism and with our Constitution. If it is true, as it appears to be, that the Constitution confers no positive rights on citizens (even to protection against violence), then it follows that it likewise confers no positive duties on legislators to pass law that might protect those nonexistent rights. If we then go the one step further – as Dworkin has so often urged us to do – and identify our constitutional jurisprudence with our political morality – then what follows is that legislators have no moral duty to pass such laws, and citizens likewise have no moral positive rights to such protection. The consequence of all of this is that citizens have no positive rights to much of anything from the state, and the state, and particularly the legislative branch of it, has no positive moral duty to do anything at all. The citizen only has negative rights not to be invaded by certain sorts of law, and the legislator only has positive duties not to do so. The nature of that nonexistent right, and correlative duty, then, is legal, constitutional, political, and moral – all.

Now it may well be that every single step of this chain of reasoning – from the lack of a constitutional positive right, to the lack of a legal right, to the lack of a political right, to the lack of a moral right, and finally from all of that to the lack of a political, legal, or moral legislative duty – is flawed. I believe every single step of it is flawed. I have argued as much elsewhere.[83] Here, I want to stress that whether flawed or not, it represents conventional wisdom in our constitutional jurisprudence, and our ordinary, nonconstitutional liberal jurisprudence provides no counterweight to it whatsoever. We have no jurisprudential discourse centering on the positive duties of state legislators to pass law toward the common good. The constitutional conclusion that there are no such constitutional duties – and implicitly, likewise no moral duties – therefore receives no challenge from our jurisprudence. So – this is the first lack that follows from the absence of a liberal-progressive natural law jurisprudence.

Now the second difference. If we had a progressive account of the common good, of individual goods, of basic goods, or simply of the good that is the end of the just law, we might thereby have a jurisprudential tradition that could ground a more robust moral and political critique of the Constitution, that references the ends of law presumed by constitutionalism, rather than its processes (judicial review) or its indeterminacy. We currently lack such a jurisprudential tradition, and we lack such a critical inquiry.[84] One might, of course, posit the just end of law by reference to the social contract, as do some libertarians, and might derive from that tradition natural rights which the existing Constitution – the one we've got – can sensibly be

---

[83] West, "Unenumerated Duties" 231–35.

[84] Exceptions are few but important: Charles A. Beard, *An Economic Interpretation of the Constitution of the United States* (New York: The Free Press, 1986); Sanford Levinson, "How the United States Constitution Contributes to the Democratic Deficit in America," *Drake Law Review* 55.4 (2007): 859–78, 876.

read as protecting.[85] Yet what if the common good that the just law ought to serve goes beyond the Lockean goods of property and personal security? To put this in social contract terms, what if we might enter hypothetical social contracts not only for the reasons Locke posited – to escape the state of nature, not only to secure our physical selves against criminal assault and our property against theft – but also (and as Tom Paine argued) to secure a number of further interests as well: secure our future against the risk of sudden impoverishment, for example, or our health against deprivation, and so on.[86] It might be that the just ends of government – and hence of law – go beyond those enumerated in the Constitution, and beyond those sensibly derived from the historical social contract tradition of which it is arguably a part. If so, we'll never know it, unless we broaden our jurisprudential sensibilities: we lack the jurisprudential tradition within which it would be possible to make such a case. Because of that lack, the Constitution we have is required, in effect, to do double duty: it is the source of justification of the laws we have and is also, largely, the source of critique of the laws we have. It is the baseline, or background norm, against which we both justify and criticize – as well as challenge – our positive law. Current movements to take the Constitution away from the courts hardly challenge this role, in effect, they underscore and expand on it: their basic message is that ordinary citizens, not only judges and lawyers, should likewise think of and use the Constitution as a source of moral critique. It is not at all clear, however, that the Constitution we have is up to the task. The Constitution does not enact Martha Nussbaum's human capabilities or John Finnis's basic goods any more than Sir Herbert Spencer's social statics.[87] Overreliance on the Constitution as the sole source of our Higher Law – whether inside or outside the Courts – unduly narrows, and limits, our critical capacities, simply because those critical capacities are then cabined to some understanding of what the Constitution itself does or does not require. We need a critical vocabulary and discourse sufficiently rich to embrace the Constitution, its history, all of its possible interpretations, and certainly all of its clauses, as the object of criticism and not the font of it.

Why do we lack such a discourse? Why is it not obvious to all of us, and not just to Sandy Levinson, that we – meaning, we citizens – ought to be much more fluent in the language of constitutional criticism – as in, criticism of the Constitution – than

---

[85] For a modern attempt to read the Constitution as basically enacting John Locke's social contract, *see* Randy E. Barnett, *The Structure of Liberty* (New York: Oxford University Press, 2000).

[86] Paine argued that the then-recent social contracts – such as the various state constitutions of the United States – failed to secure the well-being of peoples who had in fact been better off in the "state of nature," that civilization was for these peoples a bad bargain, and that as a consequence the states were under moral obligation to provide what we would today call welfare rights. Thomas Paine, "Agrarian Justice," *Common Sense*, 1776 (London: Penguin, 2004) 89; Thomas Paine, *Rights of Man*, 1791 (London: Penguin, 1984) 211; *see also* Robin West, "Tom Paine's Constitution," *Virginia Law Review* 89 (2003): 1413–62 (discussing this and other aspects of the Painean interpretation and criticisms of the United States' constitutional projects).

[87] See *Lochner v. United States*, 198 U.S. 45, 75 (1905) (Holmes, J., dissenting).

we citizens are?[88] I realize there are many reasons for this near-universally noted phenomenon, but the lack of a critical, jurisprudential discourse that targets rather than builds on the Constitution and its ancestral heritage is a big and too often unnoted part of the story. It is also a part of the story within our – meaning legal academics' – control and responsibility. We can actually fix this one. We need a jurisprudence that can at least facilitate questions regarding the moral worth of the constitution. A jurisprudence that posited the common good as the end of just law – and just constitutions – would surely be one. We do not have one now. We could produce it. So, that's the second lack.

And, the third lack: a jurisprudence focused on the common good as the end of just law would provide a way of talking about the legislative product that could stand as an alternative to public choice theory and to the tabulation of preferences, costs and benefits it invites. Our jurisprudence currently constructs the adjudicative process as one of reason, principle, and high moral purpose and the legislative process, by contrast, as one of horse trading at best. Legislators, at least according to our public-choice theorists and Dworkinian jurisprudents, when they are not being thoroughly corrupt, tabulate and act on constituent preference. However, this is a debased view of democracy; the point of democratic representation is not only to ensure that citizen preferences and desires are acted on but also to ensure that citizens' *interests* are furthered. The two are not the same thing. The just law furthers "the interest of the governed," as both Bentham and Aquinas put the point.[89] It does not only fulfill or satiate their desires. The content of their interest is in part a function of the basic goods. A jurisprudence that invited inquiry into the nature of the common good would in turn require thought – not just tabulation – regarding the interests of the governed, aside from their revealed preferences. It would invite a richer conception of the meaning of the good than that provided by our contemporary celebrants of the satiation of desire.

The fourth lack: a jurisprudence aimed at elucidating the common good, and informed by a description of human nature, of human well-being, or of human flourishing would provide a context within which liberal and progressive lawyers could propound challenges to prevailing views of our nature and the normative systems that spring from them. This is next to impossible, within the context of a liberal jurisprudence that resolutely denies any dependency on accounts of human nature, while simultaneously embracing one, *sub silentio*, so to speak. This is the current strategic status quo. Contemporary liberal jurisprudents more or less uniformly eschew

---

[88] See Sanford Levinson, *Our Undemocratic Constitution: Where the Constitution Goes Wrong (and How We the People Can Correct It)* (Oxford: Oxford University Press, 2006).

[89] Compare Bentham's insistence that government must be for the interest of the governed, with Aquinas's definition of the just law as that which furthers common good – meaning that which serves the utility of the people and not of the rulers. Jeremy Bentham, *An Introduction to the Principles of Morals and Legislation*, J. H. Burns and H. L. A. Hart, eds. (Oxford: Oxford University Press, 1996) 12–13; Thomas Aquinas, *Summa Theologica*, Pt. I–II, ques. 96, Art. 4.

reliance on human nature and on the idea of human goods that might be inferable from human nature, while simultaneously embracing a conception of our nature as individualistic, atomistic, differentiated, and so lacking in common attributes as to defy attempts to describe it. This "universal particularism" is a thin account of human nature to be sure, but it is nevertheless an account of human nature, and it leads to a particular liberal jurisprudence: it leads to a liberal jurisprudence that prioritizes the liberty and autonomy of the independent individual, shrouds such a person in rights, grants him extraordinary powers within a wide ranging sphere of action, and in essence valorizes his freedom from the ties and bonds of community. It relegates, in turn, the interests, concerns, and cares of those of us who are not quite so autonomous or independent – those of us who are children; those of us who are bound by caregiving obligations to the home; those of us for whom our humanity is a function of our ties to others rather than our independence from them; those of us who are old, sick, infantile, or frail; and those of us who care for the old, sick, infantile, and frail – to the realm of policy and political whim rather than the heightened airy domain of right, reason, and constitutional protection. However, the conception of human nature on which this hierarchy of values depends is about as obviously and blatantly false – and partial – as these things can ever be. If there is one thing we all know, it is that we are dependents for much of our lives, and we care for dependents for much of the rest, and in either status, we are far less autonomous, individuated, and so on, than the dominant conception of our nature within American jurisprudence asserts. (In fact, it is the mother of all big lies: there is not a soul living who does not know how dependent he is, was, and will be.) Put positively, our ties to our communities no less than our independence from them makes of us what and who we are. Communitarian, feminist, and social conservative thought since the 1980s has jointly produced compelling accounts of the partiality of the liberal conception of our nature, on which so much of our constitutional jurisprudence depends.[90] It cannot be heard in a liberal or progressive jurisprudential conversation that resolutely denies the relevance of accounts of human nature and the human good while likewise denying its own dependence on one.

Part of the value of a liberal and progressive jurisprudence explicitly aimed at elucidation of the common good, I think, would be simply this: when a view of human nature on which a political and legal theory is premised is wrong, it would be more clearly wrong. Its falsity would not be shrouded in the obfuscating claim that it does not exist, that the political theory it grounds is in fact agnostic on conceptions

---

[90] For an example of feminist critique, see Eva F. Kittay, *Love's Labor: Essays on Women, Equality and Dependency (Thinking Gender)* (New York: Routledge, 1999); Robin West, *Caring for Justice* (New York: NYU Press, 1999). For an example of a communitarian critique, see Michael J. Sandel, *Liberalism and the Limits of Justice* (Cambridge: Cambridge University Press, 1980); and for a social conservative critique, see Alasdair C. MacIntyre, *Dependent Rational Animals: Why Human Beings Need the Virtues* (Chicago: Open Court Press, 1999) and MacIntyre, *After Virtue: A Study in Moral Theory* (Notre Dame: University of Notre Dame Press, 1984).

of human nature, of the human good, of the good life, and so on. A jurisprudence explicitly and forthrightly premised on an understanding of our nature is one that can be challenged, changed, and improved on like ground. It would constitute a gain in forthrightness, if nothing else.

The fifth lack: a liberal and progressive jurisprudence so based would require legal educators to think through the relevance of legal thought, expertise, and judgment to the exercise of lawmaking rather than the processes of adjudication. We currently do not. We conceive of legal education as providing a sort of basic training in the art of judicial opinion writing, with some professional lawyering skills tangentially attached. However, to the (considerable) degree that our pedagogical practices reflect considered judgments regarding the point and moral valence of law, it is clearly adjudicative law we have in mind. At best – and it can no doubt be very good – we teach students how to help judges write educated, sophisticated, and morally ambitious judicial decisions. Eventually, our graduates put the skills we teach them to use as lawyers. However, they put the values we teach them – the lawyerly tolerance, the respect for the rule of law, the love of process, and at the highest level the hopes for liberty and equality – to use as judicial clerks, as judges-in-training.

There is nothing wrong with this, but it is odd that we do not also consider it within our educational mission to teach students how to help legislators write decent, sophisticated, and morally ambitious laws. Surely educated lawyers might have something to contribute to the processes of legislation, no less than to the processes of adjudication. Our students graduate from school knowing a good bit of law, and willy-nilly they acquire an appreciation of legal values along the way: the value of consistency, of rules, of principled decision making, of justice between and among peoples, of substantive and formal equality, of individual liberty, and so on. Surely, these legalistic values ought to inform the processes of legislation no less than the processes of adjudication. If they also emerged with some appreciation of the moral preconditions of just law, they might then be well equipped to apply legal expertise to the imaginative and creative exercise of legislation, no less than to the interpretive exercise of adjudication.

And a final lack: a liberal jurisprudence that would centralize questions regarding the content of the common good that a just law ought to further would quite literally "revitalize" jurisprudence. It would put human beings at the center of it. Law should serve the common good of natural human beings, not corporations, preferences, profit, satiated desires, or utility. People are not sums of their revealed preferences, and human beings are not fallen corporate angels. One truly horrific cost (among others) of rendering corporations "persons" for constitutional law purposes[91] is that the search for the meaning of "personhood" is badly distorted: if both human beings and corporations are "persons," and we're trying to figure out what a "person" is, well, then, we will have to find common characteristics of humans and corporations. One

---

[91] *Cf., Citizens United v. Federal Election Commission*, 558 U.S. 50 (2010).

such common characteristic of corporate and human persons is that both are, or might be, utility maximizers. Consequently, personhood is so defined, and we're off and running: what law should serve, even the just law, is the utility maximizer, and if cost-benefit analysis, or Kaldor-Hicks efficiency, or wealth, is the best proxy of utility, then so be it. The tragedy of all this, which should be pretty obvious by this point in our progress down this particular pathway of the law, is that people may maximize utility sometimes, but not all the time, and even when we do try to do it, we are not very good at it. Our happiness, our well-being, our capabilities, our flourishing, our functioning, and even our much-maligned pleasure cannot be reduced to the sum of the utilities we seek, whether the latter is measured by revealed, satiated, consumerist, citizen, first-order, second-order, or any order preferences. We can force the equation definitionally, of course, between happiness and the satiation of preferences, but we risk leaving humanity on the cutting-room floor when we do so. Again, a jurisprudence that follows on Aquinas's suggestion – that the just law is that which promotes the common good – would at least have this one virtue: it would centralize the human being as the object of law's regard.

All this is as plain as the nose on your face. So what happened?

THE MODERN AND POSTMODERN PATHETIC FRAGILITY
OF THE COMMON GOOD

In *Summa Theologica*, Aquinas made two famous declarations: the first, echoing Augustine, that "an unjust law is no law at all,"[92] and the second, that a just law is a law that promotes the common good.[93] The first declaration, despite its well-known limitations, nevertheless continues to engage the imagination, attract critics, and absorb the attention of the sizeable – and growing philosophical community interested in law's definition. The second claim, seemingly more promising – at least, seemingly more "natural"– since the mid-twentieth century, has fallen into near-total disrepute, among sizeable chunks of the jurisprudential academy. I think we can identify three reasons for the twentieth-century demise of natural law jurisprudence, if you do not mind military metaphors: friendly fire, self-inflicted wounds, and incoming artillery.

Let me start with the friendly fire. Both Lon Fuller, in the 1950s and 1960s, and then later Ronald Dworkin, in the 1970s and 1980s, our two hugely influential American secular natural lawyers, explicitly disavowed this entire tradition. Start with Fuller. Fuller's procedural natural law was both intended and heard as an *alternative* to, not an elaboration of, a substantive natural law tradition that would center questions regarding the nature and content of the common good, toward which a just law

---

[92] Aquinas, *Summa Theologica*, Pt. I–II, ques. 96, Art. 4.
[93] *Id.* at Art. 1.

must aim.[94] For Fuller, a good or just law is a law that meets certain minimal moral criteria, but those criteria are themselves shorn of any connection to conceptions of the human good, other than an understanding of people as sufficiently autonomous to make decent legal process a desirable value. This claim eventually ensnarled Fuller in a decade of debate with H. L. A. Hart, who found even this minimal claim regarding law's necessary procedure or process either baffling or preposterous.[95] The ensuing exchange between Hart and Fuller on the necessity of procedural norms of justice to true law set the terms of American jurisprudence for the four decades following.

What is often overlooked in this familiar telling of the story of American jurisprudence, however, is the substantial ground Hart and Fuller shared. They were both (for different reasons) utterly repulsed by the moralistic reasoning of the Thomistic, Catholic Natural Law scholars that they each, with equal vehemence, rejected. At least some of the reasons for Hart's antipathy to moralistic lawmaking were fully spelled out in his famous debates with Lord Devlin. And Fuller? Fuller made clear in *The Morality of Law* that he, too, had no truck with Catholic moral norms that might, for example, require the criminalization of birth control or find its liberalization contrary to natural law.[96] However, Fuller's disdain for the Catholic "schoolmen" went considerably deeper than his disagreement with them over sexual morality. He did not think it wise or appropriate for legal scholars – or for the law or the state – to specify the moral conditions of a good life – about sexuality or anything else – and enshrine it in law. As a result, the distance between Fuller's procedural natural law and the natural law of the schoolmen was huge – greater, in retrospect, than that between Fuller and Hart.[97] It was not any particular subset of moral purposes that rendered the purposivism of legal enactments a moral good. It was, rather, purposivism itself that did so. Fuller's view of the relation of law and morality was a natural law view – but not (in his words) a "substantive" natural law view.[98] Although there are moral values essential to law, Fuller argued, they are not values that impose, or specify, any particular conception of the good. Rather, they are moral values that protect the autonomy of the individual to formulate and act on his own such conception.[99] They are values, furthermore, that are central to the effective resistance against communitarian conceptions of the good – and to a resistance that enlists the state in the effort. They are not values that promote the common good. Again, the distance between Fuller and Thomistic Natural Law, or any substantive account, could not be wider.

---

[94] Lon Fuller, *The Morality of Law* (New Haven: Yale University Press, 1969) 96–105; *see also* Lon Fuller, *The Law in Quest of Itself* (Boston: Beacon Press, 1966).

[95] Hart, "Positivism and the Separation of Law and Morals," 627–29.

[96] Fuller, *The Morality of Law* 32.

[97] *Id.* at 132.

[98] *Id.* at 133 ("I suggest that many related issues can be resolved in similar terms without having to reach agreement on the substantive moral issues involved.").

[99] *See, e.g., id.* at 153.

Now, Dworkin. In a series of early essays on the nature of liberalism (reprinted twenty-five years later in *Sovereign Virtue*), Dworkin effectively elevated this agnosticism regarding questions of the nature of the good into a guiding principle of liberalism. Liberalism, Dworkin argued in these early essays, is committed to the proposition that the state must treat each individual with equal dignity and regard, and what that requires, in turn, is that the state must be rigorously neutral regarding all concepts of the "good life."[100] Furthermore, once we appreciate the centrality of this principle of agnosticism, we can better understand the otherwise confused relation of liberalism to individual liberty on the one hand, and equality on the other. Liberty and equality are often seen as in conflict, and a political philosophy committed to both as therefore incoherent; but they are not in conflict.[101] Rather, Dworkin argues, both the priority of equality and the role of liberty within liberalism can be understood as following from an even more basic agnosticism toward theories of the good and the good life.[102] The principle underlying liberal commitment to both equality and liberty is that the state must be rigorously neutral toward all questions of the good and all conceptions of the good life. That is part of what it means to treat people equally. The state may then redistribute resources to compensate for inequalities that are the end product of differing allocations that in turn result from luck, inheritance, or other factors over which individuals exercise no choice. However, the state must remove itself from all individual deliberations regarding how one ought to live one's life – including whether one prefers pushpin to poetry, leisure to labor, beer to fine wine, straight to same-sex sex, and so on. Differing distributions of goods that follow from these choices (particularly from the choice of leisure over labor) must be respected, even if the result is drastic disparities of wealth.[103] Disparities that follow not from choice but from fate, by contrast, must and should be treated as held by the community in common, and accordingly as subject to democratic distribution.

Thus, Dworkin argued, political liberals' simultaneous commitment to sometimes deep redistributions of wealth and individual liberty is not so inconsistent as it might first appear. Liberals value individual liberty and equality, but the equality so valued is an equal regard for chosen life plans, not an absolute equality of distribution.[104] That synthesis, in turn, rests on an agnosticism regarding the good – it depends on that agnosticism. Liberalism is thereby distinguished from conservatism, which is committed to a theory of virtue and a conception of the good to which all citizens ought aspire and which states ought to promote, and from socialism, which pushes harder for an equality of distribution that is likewise not premised

---

[100] Ronald Dworkin, "What Is Equality: Part Two: Equality of Resources," *Philosophy & Public Affairs* 10 (1981): 283–345, 332.

[101] *Id.* at 284–88.

[102] *Id.* at 343–46.

[103] *Id.* at 336–39.

[104] *Id.* at 344–46.

on agnosticism regarding the nature of the good.[105] This understanding can make sense of liberalism's current constellation of commitments: to some redistribution of wealth, near unlimited civil liberties, and so on, as well as its history – major liberal theorists of the past have at least on occasion expressed some version of this understanding of the desirability of state agnosticism toward the good. As noted, it distinguishes liberalism in a principled way from both conservatism and socialism. It is also an attractive and plausible understanding of what the state should and should not be doing with its considerable power.

Note: this is not a normative theory of politics generally. It is not even a defense of liberalism. Rather, it is a limited claim about how best to make sense of liberalism's basic commitments. It is a theory, that is, *of liberalism*, it is *not* a liberal theory of the state. Perhaps precisely because it was so limited, however, it proved to be both successful and eventually influential: it is, in fact, a readily recognizable account of quite publicly held, quintessentially liberal commitments as well as more privately held intuitions. Liberals *are* generally committed to substantial redistributions of wealth, but at the same time, liberals are indeed more than a little comfortable with redistributions that stop far short of equality – so long as it is true, or so long as we can convince ourselves that it is true, that the disparities are in some sense a product of choice rather than fate. Liberals likewise are committed to near-absolute civil liberties and are generally skeptical of claims that the state should mandate particular conceptions of moral virtue. Dworkin's attempt to synthesize all this through positing a quintessentially liberal commitment to state agnosticism regarding the good – combined with a mandate of equal regard and respect for individual conceptions of the good life – is attractive. It was a limited project with a limited reach. He did not aim to show that this liberal agnosticism is beyond reproach, or even that it is what an ideal political system would embrace. He only wanted to show that this commitment to agnosticism is consistent with liberalism's deepest impulses and makes sense of otherwise inconsistent liberal commitments. It did all of that, and it struck a deep chord.

Because it was so successful, however, it deepened the rift between ethical natural law jurisprudence and political liberalism – and hence legal conceptions of liberalism likewise. Natural lawyers identify justice with the common good, and the common good, generally, with individual good. They then specify the content of the good – qualifiedly, one would hope, and tentatively, one should insist, but nevertheless, the content of the good, and hence of the good life. A life that is rich in the basic goods – knowledge, play, friendship, and so on – is a good life, this life is unattainable without a considerable degree of social coordination, and that coordination is only possible with state action that takes the form of law; accordingly, the state must be very much committed to the project of defining and promoting the good life of its citizens. The liberal state, however, Dworkin argued, can have none

---

[105] *Id.*

of this. Liberalism and substantive Natural Law are thus deeply antagonistic. So, look where this leaves us. Dworkin's own account of liberalism, was definitionally antithetical to jurisprudential Natural Law. It is not at all surprising that the secular Natural Law tradition he sparked was so hostile to it.

That is the friendly fire. Our prominent Natural Law theorists – first Fuller, then Dworkin – identified, defended, and came to embody a liberalism that was definitionally incompatible with any state commitment to the promotion of the common good. This effectively ensured the incompatibility of jurisprudential Natural Law with liberalism. It also, however, ensured the incompatibility of a philosophical Natural Law tradition associated with liberalism – the Dworkinian and Fullerian American revival of natural law – with jurisprudential natural law, as inspired by Aquinas's dictum regarding the common good, and the duty of the state to further it through law. The American, philosophical, secular, natural law tradition cannot live side by side with the ethical Natural Law movement committed to an understanding of the common good the just law promotes. One or the other had to go. Liberalism was not going anywhere, a natural law committed to understanding the content of the common good – albeit not natural law in toto – is what went.

Now, the self-inflicted wounds. There were – or are, as this takes us to the present day – two self-inflicted wounds: one substantive, one methodological. Substance first. Within the basic forms of human goods, per Finnis, lies "sociability," within which, in turn, lies family and marriage, and therein lies the problem.[106] For a number of currently self-styled "neo-natural lawyers," including Finnis himself, the institution of civil marriage, as a state-regulated practice, is central to the securing of this basic human good.[107] Thus, the necessity, and the goodness, of state-regulated and state-defined marriage. Marriage itself, however, is not the civil institution. Rather, marriage itself is what the institution of marriage ideally protects. What is marriage itself?

According to Robert George, professor of Philosophy at Princeton, and Gerard Bradley, professor of Law at the University of Notre Dame, marriage is, by definition, a "two-in-one-flesh communion of persons that is consummated and actualized by sexual acts of the reproductive type,"[108] and as such, it is an intrinsic, basic, noninstrumental good. Because marriage so defined is a basic, intrinsic good, it provides a fully sufficient, and noninstrumental, reason for marital spouses to perform marital sexual acts "of the reproductive type" – and to do so, furthermore, whether or not they are capable of producing children and whether or not they receive any

---

[106] Finnis, *Natural Law and Natural Rights* 87–88.

[107] *See, e.g., id.* at 269; John Finnis, "The Good of Marriage and the Morality of Sexual Relations: Some Philosophical and Historical Observations," *The American Journal of Jurisprudence* 42 (1997): 97–134, 134; Robert P. George, "What's Sex Got to Do with It? Marriage, Morality, and Rationality," *American Journal of Jurisprudence* 49 (2004): 63–86; Robert P. George and Gerard Bradley, "Marriage and the Liberal Imagination," *Georgetown Law Journal* 84 (1995): 301–20, 301–2.

[108] George and Bradley, "Marriage and the Liberal Imagination" 305.

pleasure from those acts.[109] The significant fact about such marital reproductive sex acts, according to our now self-styled "neo-natural lawyers," is not that such acts do sometimes lead to the conception of new life or that they are sometimes conducive to pleasure. Rather, the significant fact about such sex acts is that they are *of the form* necessary to the biological species for the reproduction of life.[110] Engaging in these coital reproductive acts, within marriage, expresses as well as constitutes a fully integrative conception of the human being. Marriage itself is thus the basic good that justifies heterosexual, genital, coital intercourse within civil marriage.

This is a tight, closed argument against "same-sex marriage," as well as against same-sex sex, and unapologetically so. Marriage is what justifies heterosexual, coital sex, when it is justified, and those sex acts in turn constitute as well as define marriage. Sex, so long as it is of the reproductive type, is justified and can only be justified by reference to an ongoing marriage of which it is a part: the sex actualizes the two-in-one-flesh communion. When so engaged, the couple acts as a unity: only the union of the two of them can perform the single act. It brings them together as one flesh (Plato's *Symposium* style). Thus, the two-in-one-flesh defines the marriage and justifies the sex within it. Sex *outside* of marriage so conceived – whether noncoital, digital, anal, homosexual, oral, adulterous, whatever – is not justified, and any union that includes such sex is not a marriage. Thus, the irreducibly morally oxymoronic "same-sex marriage." It is unjustified, immoral nonsense.

From this claim, Bradley, George, Finnis, and now a host of fellow travelers have developed an argument against gay sex, gay marriage, sex outside of marriage, non-coital marriage, contracepted sex within marriage, contracepted or noncontracepted opposite-sex sex outside of marriage, and a wide range of other sexual behaviors easily imagined. Sex is intrinsically good, when it is good, and it is intrinsically good only when engaged in because it is of the reproductive type – meaning that it is the type of sex conducive to the reproduction of the species (rather than good for actually reproducing). The argument is worth working through:

> Though a male and a female are complete individuals with respect to other functions . . . with respect to reproduction they are only potential parts of a mated pair, which is the complete organism capable of reproducing sexually. Even if the mated pair is sterile, intercourse, provided it is the reproductive behavior characteristic of the species, makes the copulating male and female one organism. . . .

> Mating is mating, . . . because it is the reproductive behavior characteristic of the species, or in Finnis's words, the behavior which, as behavior, is suitable for generation. Mating is an irreducibly unitive activity . . . And, inasmuch as the interpersonal unity achieved in the mating . . . of spouses is intrinsically good, spouses have a reason to mate quite irrespective of whether their mating will, or even can, be procreative.[111]

[109] *Id.* at 310.
[110] *Id.*
[111] *Id.* at 312.

Instrumental sex by contrast uses one's own or the other's body as an instrument toward the end of some other purpose and for that reason is "disintegrative" and gravely immoral:

> [All nonmarital sex] suffers from at least one grave moral defect: Sex that is not for the intrinsic good of marriage itself – sex that is... wholly instrumentalized to pleasure or some other goal – damages personal and interpersonal integrity by reducing persons' bodies to the status of means to extrinsic ends.... To treat one's own body... as a pleasure inducing machine, for example, or as a mere instrument of procreation, is to alienate one part of the self, namely, one's consciously experiencing and desiring self, from another, namely, one's bodily self. But these parts are, in truth, metaphysically inseparable parts of the person as whole. Their existential separation in acts that instrumentalize the body for the sake of extrinsic goals, such as producing experiences desired purely for the satisfaction of the conscious self, disintegrates the acting person as such.[112]

This argument against gay marriage, and for the narrow justification of marital, coital, sex, has been targeted, perhaps needless to say, by liberals. The best rejoinder came in the mid-1990s from the liberal political philosopher Stephen Macedo.[113] Bradley, George, Finnis, and the other neo-natural lawyers, according to Macedo, are seemingly incapable of imagining that the friendship, intimacy, sociability, and love that is sometimes a part of committed homosexual unions might also constitute a basic human good actualized by gay sex. Macedo called this the "failure of the conservative argument."[114] Feminists have also weighed in: opining that the unpleasant coital and undesired marital sex that the neo-natural lawyers nevertheless valorize as a basic good activity in which married couples ought to participate might be considerably less desired and less wanted by wives than by husbands, who after all at least experience enough pleasure to sustain an erection and possible ejaculation.[115] That fact alone should give pause.

To these critics, and others, the neo-natural lawyers responded with a methodological claim – and it is this methodological claim I want to identify as self-inflicted wound number two. The way to understand the content of the common good, or the basic goods, or the human good, Bradley and George have written in response to Macedo, is through reflection.[116] There is, they explained, little to be said to one who does not grasp the essential goodness of marriage, or coital sexuality, and hence

---

[112] *Id.* at 313–14.

[113] Stephen Macedo, "Homosexuality and the Conservative Mind," *Georgetown Law Journal* 84 (1995): 261–300.

[114] *Id.* at 293.

[115] *See, e.g.,* Robin West, *Marriage, Gender and Sexuality* (Boulder: Paradigm Publishers, 2007) 57–69; Chai Feldblum, "Gay Is Good: The Moral Case for Marriage Equality and More," *Yale Journal of Law & Feminism* 17 (2005): 139–84, 163–64; Mary Becker, "Women, Morality, and Sexual Orientation," *UCLA Women's Law Journal* 8 (1997) 165–218, 202.

[116] George and Bradley, "Marriage and the Liberal Imagination" 306–7.

the essential wrongness of nonmarital sex. Such critics are just not sufficiently con-
templative, reflective, experienced, or wise. It is unfortunate, but that's the way it is.
This is not the sort of assertion that is susceptible to ordinary forms of proof:

> One either understands that spousal genital intercourse has a special significance as
> instantiating a basic, non-instrumental value, or something blocks that understand-
> ing and one does not perceive correctly. Our liberal friends... honestly do not see
> any special point or value in such intercourse.... By contrast many other people
> perceive quite easily the special value and significance of the genital intercourse of
> spouses.[117]

And, again, somewhat more elaborately:

> Intrinsic value cannot, strictly speaking, be demonstrated. Qua basic, the value of
> intrinsic goods cannot be derived through a middle term. Hence, if the intrinsic
> value of marriage... is to be affirmed, it must be grasped in noninferential acts
> of understanding. Such acts require imaginative reflection on data provided by
> inclination and experience, as well as knowledge of empirical patterns.... The
> practical insight that marriage... has its own intelligible point, and that mar-
> riage as a one-flesh communion of persons is consummated and actualized in
> the reproductive-type acts of spouses, cannot be attained by someone who has no
> idea of what these terms mean; nor can it be attained, except with strenuous efforts
> of imagination by people who, due to personal or cultural circumstances, have little
> acquaintance with actual marriages thus understood. For this reason, we believe
> that whatever undermines the sound understanding and practice of marriage in a
> culture – including ideologies that are hostile to that understanding and practice –
> makes it difficult for people to grasp the intrinsic value of marriage and marital
> intercourse.[118]

These confident assertions, both in content and method, are illiberal in the
extreme. I have argued against them elsewhere in depth, as have a number of others,
and will not repeat those arguments here. Here, I only want to note that the self-
appellation and the assurance notwithstanding, Robert George and John Finnis's
argument against gay sex and gay marriage (as well as their bizarre argument for
the moral obligatoriness of unwanted marital sex) should not be understood as "the"
natural law argument on the topic; it is, rather, at best "a" natural law argument, and
as such, it is "a" natural law argument that is wrong on its own terms.

It is important to stress, I think, that the wrongness of these claims shows nothing
of the rightness or wrongness of thinking through the rights and wrongs of civil
marriage by reference to intrinsic human goods or intrinsic human needs. Rather,
this might be a quite sound way of thinking about the contested value of marriage,
for progressives, liberals, devotees of same-sex marriage, and their many critics alike.
I think it is, in fact, a sound way of thinking about these questions. Marriage may

[117] *Id.* at 309–10.
[118] *Id.* at 307.

well be an intrinsic good, and if it is, it is important to our understanding of the civil institution and the laws that sustain it to understand it as such. Further, if it is, this may be a very good reason to extend, rather than restrict, the franchise.

George, Bradley, Finnis, et al., may be asking the right sorts of questions, even if their answers are wrong, and even if their method of argument is overly intuitionist, a tad too confident, has more than a whiff of authoritarianism, and is horribly wanting in imagination, experimentation, or simple humility. They may be wrong to regard reproductive-type sex acts as having intrinsic worth (or any worth) and wrong to define marriage by reference to those acts. They may be wrong to think that nonreproductive "mating" carries so much moral (mystical?) significance. They may be wrong to think that other forms of sexual behavior, expression, and activity are intrinsically degenerative of human integrity. They may be wrong to rely so heavily on their own reflection on these matters and wrong to ascribe to their critics failures of perception caused by cultural decay. It does not follow, however, that they are wrong to think that legal institutions ought to serve intrinsic human goods. It does not follow that institutions that are degenerative of human integrity are beyond the pale of criticism. It does not follow, even, that an awful lot of sexual activity is not morally problematic for just the sorts of reasons they claim. (In fact, I have argued that precisely the sexual activity they go to such extraordinary lengths to valorize – unwanted marital sex – is more unwanted by women than men and is therefore not only not of intrinsic worth but is in fact morally problematic, and for much the sorts of degenerative, integrity-attacking reasons they explain.)

Natural law arguments can and, I believe, should be made to the effect that marriage, as a civil institution, serves human needs and well frames intrinsic goods, and it does so in ways that go beyond the utilitarian arguments made by marriage's many sociologically inclined utilitarian defenders. Marriage does well serve our needs for stability in our intimate lives. It serves the human good of developed, mature, lifelong relationships that can sustain and protect us. It creates a context within which we can engage in our individual projects with a modicum of certainty that we will have the companionship of someone who loves us, who provides a haven for our fragile selves, who will be there for our children should we die prematurely, and so on, and so on, and so on. If all or any of this is right, then of course marriage so understood might also well serve precisely the same human needs and promote these same intrinsic goods for partners of the same sex as well as of opposite sex, and perhaps, for groupings larger than two likewise. Whether we call such arguments "natural law arguments" depends in part simply on whether natural law is identified as a set of concerns with intrinsic human goods or with a set of claims about the content of those goods. I see no good reason and plenty of not so good reasons to confine it to the latter.

More important, however, and aside from labels, there are plenty of good reasons not to eschew entire arguments about marriage, and hence about civil marriage, that make resort to claims regarding intrinsic human goods. Some of those reasons are just crassly political: if liberal defenders of same-sex marriage want to win this political argument, and not just the legal or constitutional argument, for broadening the marital franchise, they must convince nonbelievers that same-sex marriage shares in the moral good of marriage, and if they cannot make assertions about what the moral good of marriage might be, it will not be possible to carry the burden on the former. Less crassly, perhaps (or perhaps not), the goodness of marriage, at root, might just *be* that it well serves human needs (whether intrinsic or instrumental) and well frames as well as promotes our enjoyment of intrinsic, or basic, human goods. The natural law tradition, vocabulary, and habits of thought provide a way of understanding some of what is good in our lives, including, perhaps, the goodness of marriage, which cannot be quantified in utilitarian calculi. It fits our ordinary way of talking about what is good, what serves us, and what does not. It fits the ordinary way of talking about such things shared by our neighbors. It is a way of talking, thinking, and arguing over value that is foreign to liberal legal forms of valuation. However, it is not so foreign to quite ordinary ways of thinking and talking about value. We might profit from efforts to transport this way of talking into our arguments, claims, and counterclaims over the nature and value of law.

Thus: natural law has fallen into disrepute among liberals for at least two reasons. First, both political and legal liberalism, these days, are increasingly defined by their insistence that states ought to be rigorously agnostic toward conceptions of the good and the good life. Natural law, in toto, is an attempt to give content to the nature of the good and to harness law toward its promotion. Thus, the antipathy of substantive natural law and liberalism. Second, prominent contemporary natural lawyers have defined the good as embracing in part a conception of sociability, intimacy, family life, and sexuality that is inimical to liberal demands for equal treatment of same-sex couples. When pressed, the substantive view is defended by resort to a method of reasoning that unabashedly embraces arguments based on premises "not susceptible to ordinary means of empirical proof." This resort to authority, intuition, or secret knowledge is patently illiberal, and liberals are right to protest.

There is one last factor that accounts for the antipathy between not just liberalism and natural law but progressivism and natural law as well. (This is the incoming artillery.) Natural law arguments rely heavily, or moderately, or somewhat on claims regarding human nature. Thus, it is by virtue of our human nature, not our American nature, or class nature, or masculine nature, or feminine nature, and so on that we have various needs and pursue various intrinsic goods. It is by virtue of those facts, in turn, that our legal systems ought to facilitate these pursuits. That is the basic structure of a natural law claim. Arguments of this sort have long been regarded as suspect by some philosophers because of the danger that they will impermissibly derive value from fact; that they will commit some version of a naturalistic fallacy.

In the past half-century, however, these claims have attracted a different sort of criticism. Scores of postmodern scholars from all sorts of disciplines now argue that arguments from human nature are impermissible because they assert the existence of a chimera, and that is human nature itself. There just is no set of characteristics shared by all human beings; there is no universal human nature on the strength of which normative claims about what law ought to be doing or ought to be about can be based. As a consequence, claims that assume there is such a nature tend, either intentionally or willy-nilly, to elevate some partial accounting of some part of humanity – such as all white people, or all men, or all heterosexuals, or all First Worlders – or, they are simply ignorant – they hypothesize a shared nature with interesting implications where there is no such thing. Like phrenologists, astrologers, social Darwinians, or medievalists who insisted on their fabricated correlations of moods with bodily fluids and functions (bile with melancholia, and so forth), natural lawyers tend to find generality, significance, and knowledge where there is in fact nothing but partiality, politics, and power.[119]

Maybe this is right and maybe it is not, but there are significant and I think unappreciated costs of this progressive allegiance to these antiessentialist claims, which ought to count as pragmatic reasons to doubt them. I cite just two such costs here. First, as long as progressives, women, gay men and lesbians, poor people, nonwhites, working people, Third Worlders, and everyone who cares about them continue to boycott these debates, then false claims about our nature, that have real and harmful consequences for those wrongly described, go answered. Thus, if progressives refuse to debate the moral case for marriage, or to assert a moral case for same-sex marriage, resting instead on liberal arguments that rely on rights, autonomy, or privacy, false claims about the essential nature and goodness of both heterosexual marriage and heterosexual parenting go largely unanswered. Same-sex couples who wish to marry, or parent, and their children, among others, pay the price. If progressives refuse to engage essentialist descriptions of our nature, false claims about our essentially autonomous, independent, and anticommunitarian nature go unanswered. Dependents, and the caregivers that give care (overwhelmingly women), pay the price, because legal institution upon legal institution is built, layered, and developed on the false claim that people are best off when others leave off and that we are all thus best served by an inattentive non–nanny-state and a distracted community. If progressives refuse to engage claims of nature – if false claims about our imperviousness to private power, our invulnerabilities to sexual

---

[119] *See* Michel Foucault, "Power, Moral Values, and the Intellectual," Michael Bess, int., *History of the Present* 4 (Spring 1988): 11–13; Barbara H. Smith, *Contingencies of Value: Alternative Perspectives for Critical Theory* (Cambridge: Harvard University Press, 1988); Robin West, "A Review of *Contingencies of Value: Alternative Perspectives for Critical Theory* by Barbara H. Smith," *Yale Law Journal* 99 (1990): 1473–1502; *and* Robin West, "Desperately Seeking a Moralist," *Harvard Journal of Law & Gender* 29 (2006): 1–51.

violence, our taste for risk, our willingness to tolerate inequalities, and so on go unanswered – victims of violence, of economic oppression, of rape, and of severe impoverishment pay the price. It might be time to end the boycott.

Second: progressives forgo the opportunity to absorb, rather than splinter, claims of differences as well as those differently described, by resisting so rigorously claims of human nature as a premise of normative arguments about the way law ought to be and the good that law ought to serve. If women are different from men in important ways, then the account of human nature that structures decision making in ways that adversely affect women must be changed – not chucked – to reflect that. "Chucking it" simply means that women, yet again, will not register as human. If some parts of the national community suffer from subordination, then the account of our human nature must reflect that vulnerability, and claims for and of law ought to reflect it. With the claim that sufferance should not be understood as a reason to abandon the inquiry altogether on the grounds that it is all politics comes the unsurprising result that the subordinated will likewise be relegated to the nonhuman status. If children, the elderly, and their midlife caregivers who are burdened with the duty to care for them are all dependent in ways that are currently not reflected in accounts of our nature that insist so relentlessly on independence or autonomy as an essential human trait, then those facts of dependency must be incorporated into an account of human nature, rather than asserted as yet more proof that any such an account will be unconvincing, incomplete, or unavailing. Again, the alternative is that the cared-for and the caregiver are relegated to the margins. This is a simple enough lesson that progressive politics and some strands of postidentitarian critical theory have already absorbed. It is not, however, reflected in our jurisprudence, not the natural law side of it, the progressive, or, to date, the critical.

To sum up: the antipathy of liberal and progressive lawyers to natural law ethics is a sturdy stool that rests on three legs. The first is liberalism's commitment to state neutrality toward the good and the good life. The second is contemporary neo-natural lawyers' embrace of an illiberal understanding of sexuality and simultaneous insistence on a reflective method that defies ordinary forms of rebuttal. The third is progressive disdain for any and all debate regarding human nature, and inferences regarding the content of need, and the content of basic human goods that might be drawn from a tentatively held description. None of these are particularly good reasons for neglecting the development of a progressive or liberal interpretation of natural law claims. Liberalism's commitment to an agnostic state is a relatively newfound self-understanding: liberal commitments to limited redistribution and robust liberty can as readily be interpreted as resting on a specified and complex conception of the good and of the good life as by reference to neutrality. Natural law can be defined by reference to the sort of question it centers – the content of the good, and the claim that law should serve it – rather than by reference to any particular set of answers, socially conservative, libertarian, or otherwise. Progressivism can and should insist on the plasticity, diversity, and variety exhibited by human communities and individuals without reliance on disabling claims regarding the incoherence of questions regarding human nature.

There may be no good reason not to – but is there any good reason to do so? Why participate in these debates? Let me suggest a few reasons. First, the progressive boycott of natural law discussions has led to a politically skewed understanding, in the natural law canon, of the human good and of human nature: assertions are made without rebuttal when one side abstains from the fight. This can have quite real repercussions in the realms of politics and policy and, eventually, law – as it has in the political and legal debate over same-sex marriage. Second, both politically and pedagogically, we need a jurisprudence focused not so obsessively on adjudication and a bit more on legislative arts – a jurisprudence aimed at the moral obligations of the creative lawmaker rather than the constraints on law's interpreter. Such a jurisprudence, cognizant of law's potential as well as its limitations, could have within its purview the social injustices occasioned by too little law, rather than the current focus of progressive jurisprudence on the legal injustices occasioned by either too much law or law irrationally applied. Third, progressive participation in natural law jurisprudence could occasion a progressive move toward the articulation of universal descriptions of human nature, human need, and human goods that embraces and absorbs, rather than splinters, claims of difference tied to ethnic, sexual, and racial identity.

Lastly, such a jurisprudence would be the natural place to develop accounts of the good that really are "natural" – empirical as well as reflective, not reduced to costs and benefits, wealth, efficiency, or Kaldor-Hicks analyses – but also not reducible to deontological, nonconsequentialist rights. That there are intrinsic human goods that cannot and should not be traded off or reduced to benefits and costs is a widely shared intuition – not limited to the editors and authors of *First Things*. Some of the intrinsic goods are reflected in our ordinary understanding of rights – rights to speech, worship, privacy, and so on – that should not be part of policy-driven consequentialist trade-offs. Some of those intrinsic goods are not currently reflected in our understanding of rights and, perhaps, should not be. The goods demanded by calls for the recognition of so-called welfare rights might be of this nature. Shelter, food, health, caregiving, and protection against various risks might be better understood – more naturally – as intrinsic human goods, and if so, they might be better argued for in those direct and less mysterious terms. Whether or not they are "rights," the human need for them is deep and irreducible. Their goodness is intrinsic. The demand for them cannot be compromised away. They have some urgency. Were we to recognize them as such, it would not follow that courts should therefore strike down pernicious laws – the standard consequence of rights claims. Rather, what would follow would be a moral imperative for legislative action – action that would protect, or create, through law, institutions that would promote intrinsic human goods and facilitate the human projects designed to achieve good ends.

Concluding Doubts: Would a "Progressive Natural Law"
Be Progressive, Natural, or Law?

Let me conclude with brief thoughts on what strike me as the most likely objections. Is my suggestion – that we develop a liberal and progressive natural law jurisprudence – too political to be jurisprudential? Is it too jurisprudential to be political? Were we to develop one, would it have anything to do with law?

On the first: jurisprudence is deeply, profoundly, and inevitably political, no matter what the flavor. Legal positivism has its roots in an attempt to bolster a liberal reformist orientation toward existing law. Natural Law as discussed in this chapter more often than not devolves into arguments regarding the necessity and goodness of existing law, giving it a conservative tilt or, far more occasionally, into arguments regarding the illegality of extant regimes, lending its hand to radical and revolutionary movements. What's missing from this laundry list, basically, is a natural law jurisprudence of and for progressivism: a jurisprudence that asserts and defends the connection to human need, intrinsic human good, and the common good, of progressive legal projects, either existing or ideal. To assert the need for such a thing is *of course* a political assertion, but it is felt as such largely because of its absence, not because of its nature.

On the second – would it be too jurisprudential to be political? Would it be just another academic fad that would not matter one whit? Again, it seems to me that it is the absence of a progressive and liberal natural law movement that prompts the question, more than the impossibility or impotence of one. Natural law ideas and arguments have mattered hugely to socially conservative political movements over the past three decades. Furthermore, natural law sorts of arguments, regardless of whether they are called as such, matter to our students. Students do ask these questions and want at least a discourse, whether or not they get answers: what is the good that law can do, what should the law be, how can I think about that, and how can I contribute? The absence of clear, if tentative, answers from left, liberal, radical, and progressive perspectives is an acutely felt failure of contemporary American legal education. The indeterminacy thesis, the dissolution of the distinction between law and politics, and the partial idealism behind some identify claims that have been the major products of left academic life over the past thirty years go nowhere near filling the need for explicit discussion of moral value in the classroom. Students go on to become lawyers, judges, legislators, and, of course, voting citizens. They have absorbed in law school plenty of jurisprudential ideas, claims and counterclaims about the role of judges, the role and nature of judge-made law, the relative weight of rules and principles, the permissibility or impermissibility of judicial decision making that incorporates the judge's moral "preferences," and so on. They have also absorbed plenty of ideology not labeled as such: the priority of negative over positive rights, the natural goodness of contract and property, the irrationality and malignancy of politics as opposed to law, the idealized reasoned processes of adjudication, and so on. No one pretends anymore that these lessons do not have political weight. What we are loathe to acknowledge, still, is that the political tilt is so relentlessly conservative.

All I have argued here is that the conservatism of law school–driven legal ideology is partly a matter of neglect rather than intent. There is indeed an irreducible conservatism to adjudicated law, which is nothing to bemoan. Law is what it is, partly because we see value in stability, continuity, and fidelity to the past. That is part of law's value; it beats the chaos, violence, fear, and risk that the absence of law would bring in its wake. Stability, continuity, and fidelity to the past are essential to the protection of property, privacy, and life itself that render possible the individualized pursuit of intrinsic goods, in much the way that John Finnis so ably described in 1980.[120] There is also, however, another face of law that is profoundly liberal, and that is the legislative impulse and possibility. We can create new law, modify the old, or scrap it, and begin anew – we can do all of this, when and if social justice requires. Law makes this creation and re-creation of our social world, in light of demands of justice, possible; it is with law, and sometimes only with law, that we can respond to social injustices. This potential of law – that by creating it we can respond to social injustice – we also ought to treasure, theorize, argue over, and philosophize, but we do not. The result is an imbalance. We currently have a developed jurisprudence that underlies and underscores the interpretive adjudicative process. It is, as Dworkin says, a conservatism imposed on courts. We do not, however, have a developed jurisprudence that underlies and underscores the creative, legislative, lawmaking process. We do not have it, in part, because progressives have been disinclined to create it. We are disinclined to create it, in turn, for a host of reasons: the indeterminacy critique and deconstructive faiths counsel the lack of necessity, while a cynically realist view of judicial decision making, perhaps, counsels its futility. Judges can create it from whatever texts we give them, if indeterminacy is right, and judges will do what they do, regardless of the texts we give them, if the cynic is right. This particular conjunction of political commitment and idea – of liberal or progressive politics, with at most a jurisprudence that counsels indeterminacy – has proved to be profoundly inadequate, both to our politics and to our students' aspirations. For the most political of reasons, we need a broadened jurisprudential inquiry.

Which raises the third question: what of any of this is *law*, natural or otherwise? The good that law can do, the human goods it ought to promote, the common good it can and should serve – none of that is itself law. They are (at best) ideals for law or ways of talking about law's ideals. That is the vital insight of legal positivism. Yet what of it is natural law? What about this is natural law, as opposed to "ideas for good governance"? Why call this "natural law" rather than "ideals that should underscore our politics"? For John Finnis, Robert George, and Gerard Bradley, ethical natural

---

[120] Finnis, *Natural Law and Natural Rights* 110–25.

law is "law" rather than politics, because their goal is in part (in large part) to argue that not just law but also our established legal institutions – contract, property, and civil marriage – are congruent with the mandates of natural law – extant legal institutions are instrumental to the intrinsic goods that positive human law ought to serve. Thus, "natural law," for these conservative jurisprudential natural lawyers, consists not only of a set of ideals for law but a set of arguments that in turn justify the law we have, in light of them. Law is good, both ideally and actually, because the law we have *is* largely what it ought to be – not as a matter of definition, but rather as a matter of social fact.

What if one has no such confidence, and no such claim, in mind? Then, in what sense is a set of ideals for law, drawn from a conception of the human good, the basis of a natural law? Why isn't it simply a set of moral values, which might or might not correlate with the values explicitly endorsed in political party platforms? Finnis's list of goods looks like the platform of the Republican Party, whereas the ones espoused in Powers and Faden's list of the basic elements of human well-being or in Nussbaum's capabilities approach look like that of the Democratic Party. In what sense is any of this relevant to legal discussion, legal education, or legal scholarship?

The question assumes a dour – and unjustifiably bleak – view of our politics, but leave that aside. The short answer is that there is no reason that parts of the planks of both political parties should *not* mirror the content of the natural law. One would hope they would; in fact, it would be surprising and an indictment of the two-party system, as well as the two parties themselves, if they did not. There is no reason that natural law should not incorporate steadfast political ideals. The Democratic Party might, after all, be right about some things that law ought to do that it currently does not. It may be true – not just a Democratic Party plank – that law ought to protect human health more than it currently does. It might be that security in old age, or caregiving labor, or childhood well-being are human goods, the protection of which is part of law's basic raison d'être. We should not view as an aspect of the human good whatever the parties have proposed – whether it be traditional definitions of marriage or universal health care. Nor should we *not* view them as aspects of the human good simply because they have been so proposed. Law is deeply political in every sense of the word; that we have law at all is a function of the political fears, ambitions, and imaginations of people. Law is in part the product of politics. Natural law likewise is in part the product of politics. That should not count against it. Rather, it is a natural enough acknowledgment that some aspects of our political selves are deep and enduring and ought to be recognized as such.

2

Legal Positivism, Censorial Jurisprudence, and Legal Reform

The heart of legal positivism, according to Jeremy Bentham and his then-contemporary band of "radicals," as well as modern positivist legal theorists, was what is now confusedly called the "separability thesis": the law that is, is not necessarily the same as the law that ought to be.[1] That a law exists, positivists insisted, then as now, does not imply anything one way or the other about its merits or demerits, about whether it is just, or about whether it is a good law: laws are not necessarily good simply by virtue of the fact of their existence; some laws are unjust or unwise but nevertheless law.[2]

---

[1] Joseph Raz calls this the "moral thesis," distinguishing it from the "social fact thesis." Joseph Raz, *The Authority of Law* (Oxford: Oxford University Press, 2002) 37–38 ("In the most general terms, the positivist social thesis is that what is law and what is not is a matter of social fact.... Their moral thesis is that the moral value of law (both of a particular law and of a whole legal system) or the moral merit it has is a contingent matter dependent on the content of the law and the circumstances of the society to which it applies."); *see also* H. L. A. Hart, *The Concept of Law*, 2nd ed. (Oxford: Oxford University Press, 1997) 8 ("theories that make this close assimilation of law to morality seem, in the end, often to confuse one kind of obligatory conduct with another, and to leave insufficient room for divergences in their requirements"); John Austin, *Province of Jurisprudence Determined*, 1832, ed. Wilfrid E. Rumble (Cambridge: Cambridge University Press, 1995) 10, 13 ("A law set by opinion and a law imperative and proper are allied by analogy only.... Positive law and morality are distinguished by modern jurists into law natural and law positive."); Jeremy Bentham, *An Introduction to the Principles of Morals and Legislation*, J. H. Burns and H. L. A. Hart, eds. (Oxford: Clarendon Press, 1996) 293–94.

[2] Today, this claim is often put in terms of the conditions of legality. Positivists all hold that the morality of a norm is not necessarily a condition of its legality. They split, however, on whether the morality of a norm can be a condition of legality or whether the possible existence of some legal systems in which the morality of a norm is not a condition of its legality is alone sufficient to sustain the positivist thesis. Incorporationists, or inclusivists, such as Jules Coleman argue that the existence of a legal system in which its rule of recognition might incorporate moral standards as part of its criteria for legal validity, does not defeat the positivists' thesis: what positivism holds, he argues, is only that a legal system might exist for which its rule of recognition does not do so. This does not violate the separation thesis as long as the latter is understood to require only that a legal system does not necessarily contain a rule of recognition that incorporates moral validity. *See* Jules L. Coleman, "Negative and Positive Positivism," *Journal of Legal Studies* 11.1 (1982): 139–164; Coleman, "Incorporationism, Conventionality and the Practical Difference Theory," *Legal Theory* 4.4 (1998): 381–425. *See generally* W. J. Waluchow, *Inclusive*

Bentham's way of putting this familiar positivist point, however, was different from virtually all of these modern formulations. Whereas modern positivists speak of the "separability" between the laws we have and the law we should have, between actual law and ideal law, between human law and God's law, between legal norms and moral norms, or between law and justice, Bentham, presaging Austin and borrowing from Beccaria before him, spoke in terms of separate *projects*. What needed "separating," Bentham thought, was "expository" from "censorial" jurisprudence.[3] Expository jurisprudence, for all three men, meant the study of the law that *is*. If you want to know what the law is, one must study the social fact of the matter and not confuse the object of inquiry with what one wishes the law to be. Censorial jurisprudence, by contrast, meant not the study of the law that is but the *criticism* of the law that is. The point of expository jurisprudence was to understand the content of law. The point of censorial jurisprudence, however, was to criticize it, and to do so toward the end of legal reform, whether that could be achieved through legal persuasion or political action. To do either of these projects well required understanding the difference between the law we have and the law we should have, or ought to have, or would have in a perfect world, or would want to have if we were to want a just and good legal order.

Thus, Bentham's legal positivism, not unlike today's, rested on a version of the "separability thesis," but what followed from acceptance of that thesis, for Bentham, was not so much two kinds of entities – one actual, the other ideal – as two projects, the first of which was scholarly, and the second of which was most assuredly political. Both, however – the scholarly and the political – were professional *legal* projects, and more to the point here, both (not just the first) rested on a commitment to legal positivism at their core. Thus, "analytic jurisprudence" concerns what we must do, and what we must not do, to discover what the law is, and then what it is we know, once we know it. We must do a lot of things if we are to know the law, and one thing we must do is hold fast to the separability thesis: if our object is to learn the law, either of a particular subject or more generally, we should not confuse the law that we seek to discover with our own hopes, wishes, or predispositions regarding what the law should be.[4] However, the second project following from the separateness

Legal Positivism (Clarendon Press, 1994). Nonincorporationists (or exclusive positivists) such as Joseph Raz argue to the contrary, that positivism commits one to the view that a society's rule of recognition cannot contain a moral test of legal validity; a norm can count as a law only if its source is determinable by a study of social facts. Raz, *The Authority of Law* 37–52. For a good general discussion of the debate between inclusive and exclusive positivists, see Brian Bix, "Patrolling the Boundaries: Inclusive Legal Positivism and the Nature of Jurisprudential Debate," *Canadian Journal of Law and Jurisprudence* 12.1 (1999): 17–34.

3   Bentham, *An Introduction to the Principles of Morals and Legislation* 294; John Austin, *Lectures on Jurisprudence: The Philosophy of Positive Law* (London: R&R Clark Publishing, 1885) 771–72; Cesare Beccaria, *On Crimes and Punishment* (New Brunswick: Transaction Publishers, 2009) xxix.

4   If you want to know the law, say, of negligence regarding the potential liability of homeowners for accidents suffered by their guests, you should be careful not to confuse that project with the task of thinking through what you or others think the law of negligence should be on that topic. More

of the law that is from the law that ought to be, at least for Bentham, was censorial jurisprudence. Both the criticism of existing law itself, as well as the study of the ways in which we criticize existing laws, constituted Bentham's "censorial jurisprudence." If the legal *ought* is distinct from the legal *is*, then we can and should criticize the law that is, on the basis of what it ought to be.

And so, criticize – censor – he did, and for the better part of six decades of his long life. The informed citizen, Bentham declared, in a basically decent democratic regime, should "obey punctually" – no anarchist he – but "censor freely."[5] He should "question authority,"[6] to quote from many adolescents' favorite bumper sticker that unknowingly quotes the great utilitarian. In fact, it was censorial jurisprudence – not the articulation or defense of utilitarianism against its many critics (Mill did that[7]), and not the encyclopedic compilation or organization of positive law (Blackstone did that, although not to Bentham's liking[8]), and not the workings out of the conceptual apparatus of analytical positivism (Austin's project[9]) – that occupied the bulk of Bentham's lengthy engagement with law.

So, how should positive law be criticized? What is the test of a good law? What is the metric against which existing law should be measured? For Bentham, as college freshmen newly introduced to philosophy all learn, *every* individual act of will, notably including every act of lawmaking, should be subjected to the moral test of utility. The test for a particular law, then, follows: if on balance a law increases the misery, suffering, unhappiness or pain felt by all affected parties it is a bad law, if it increases happiness, pleasure, or well-being, it is a good law. What college freshmen do not so often learn, is that this basic test was important to Bentham not because of what it might teach us about the moral obligations of hypothetical or real individuals facing genuine or fanciful moral dilemmas, but rather because it yielded

---

generally, if you want to study an entire legal system, it would be wise not to confuse that project with the task of spelling out what you think a legal system should be. Justice Holmes, who followed Bentham in this regard, famously had various pithy ways of making the point: if we want to know what the law is, we should "wash the law in cynical acid" and look at it as would a bad man. Oliver Wendell Holmes, "The Path of the Law," *Harvard Law Review* 10 (1897): 457–78, 462. He could have meant by this, and perhaps did mean, several completely different propositions about the relation between law and morality, but minimally, he meant the austere but sensible Benthamic claim that if we are to learn the law that we actually have, we must abstain from confusing ourselves by mixing it up with the law that we wish we had.

5   Bentham, A *Fragment on Government*, 1776 (Cambridge: Cambridge University Press, 1988) 10 ("Under a government of Laws, what is the motto of a good citizen? To obey punctually; to censure freely.").

6   "Bentham has been in this age and country the great questioner of things established." John Stuart Mill, "On Bentham," *Utilitarianism and Other Essays* (Penguin Classics: 1987) 133 (originally published in *The London and Westminster Review*, 1838).

7   *See* John Stuart Mill, *Utilitarianism*, 1861 (Chicago: University of Chicago Press, 1906).

8   *See* William Blackstone, *Commentaries on the Laws of England* (Oxford: Clarendon Press, 1765–1769) (digitized original edition available at http://avalon.law.yale.edu/subject_menus/blackstone.asp); *but see* Jeremy Bentham, *Comment on the Commentaries: A Criticism of William Blackstone's Commentaries on the Laws of England*, Charles Warren Everett, ed. (Oxford: Clarendon Press, 1928).

9   John Austin, *Province of Jurisprudence Determined*.

the content of Bentham's massive, encyclopedic body of censorial jurisprudence. Large swaths of England's then-existing law, Bentham believed, failed the moral test of utility: it led to misery aplenty and not much happiness, and it did so for no good reason. Some laws, particularly those backed by churchmen, failed the test because they perversely aimed for the maximization of *pain* rather than pleasure. They were driven by a "principle of asceticism" that seeks to inflict pain on people in the name of virtue, rather than a hedonic principle of pleasure, because they seemingly presupposed the moral value of suffering or, at least, the moral value of other people's suffering.[10] Other nonutile laws, Bentham believed, were simply misguided or foolish: criminal laws or penalties that were overly punitive, for example, because unduly retributive, prompted either excessive punishment or unwarranted acquittal and hence underenforcement.[11] Either way, they inflicted unnecessary pain on either past offenders or future victims.[12] Some laws failed the test because of their rabid inequality: they discounted – sometimes to zero – the pain felt by some people or some sentient creatures but not others. Slave laws in the American states and elsewhere did so totally, but so, too, did laws that permitted the cruel treatment of animals.[13] Some, particularly those that maintained drastically unequal distributions of wealth, failed the test because they rested on a denial of the shrinking utility of the marginal pound for the monied or privileged classes, and therefore perpetuated a crippling, and disutile, economic inequality across large

---

[10] Bentham, *An Introduction to the Principles of Morals and Legislation* 18 ("There are two classes of men of very different complexions, by whom the principle of asceticism appears to have been embraced, the one a set of moralists, the other a set of religionists. . . . The philosophical party have scarcely gone farther than to reprobate pleasure: the religious party have frequently gone so far as to make it a matter of merit and of duty to court pain.").

[11] Bentham, *The Principles of Morals and Legislation* 182–84. Bentham critiques the effect of disproportionately severe punishment on the defendant as *needless* (p. 183), and deems such punishment *unfrugal*:

> The effects of unpopularity in a mode of punishment are analogous to those of unfrugality. The necessary pain which denominates a punishment unfrugal, is more apt to be that which is produced on the part of the offender. A portion of superfluous pain is in like manner produced when the punishment is unpopular: but in this case it is produced on the part of persons altogether innocent, the people at large. This is already one mischief; and another is, the weakness which it is apt to introduce into the law. When the people are satisfied with the law, they voluntarily lend their assistance in the execution: when they are dissatisfied, they will naturally withhold that assistance; it is well if they do not take a positive part raising impediments. This contributes greatly to the uncertainty of the punishment.

[12] *Id.*

[13] *Id.* at 283:

> It may come one day to be recognized that the number of the legs, the villosity of the skin, or the termination of the os sacrum are reasons equally insufficient for abandoning a sensitive being to the same fate. What else is it that should trace the insuperable line? Is it the faculty of reason or perhaps the faculty of discourse? But a full grown horse or dog is beyond comparison a more rational, as well as a more conversable animal, than an infant of a day, or a week, or even a month old. But suppose the case were otherwise, what would it avail? The question is not, Can they reason? nor, Can they talk? but, Can they suffer?

groups of people.[14] Other laws, particularly secondary rules of procedure, evidence, and what we would today call professional responsibility, failed the test because they transparently sought not to maximize the utility or well-being of all, but rather the profit, position, power, and hence the pleasures of legal professionals, both judges and lawyers.[15] Their ornate complexity, if nothing else – the elaborate legal fictions, the baroque pleading requirements, the overuse of Latin, the mystifications, the pretensions toward universality, nature, reason, or divinity; in short, all of the various masks, thin or otherwise, that the common law courts used to blanket power with words – was nothing but a monopolistic attempt to protect the dominance of the legal establishment and the smug, self-satisfied judiciary from the encroachments of reform.[16] All of it served the interest of only legal professionals and all of it, as a result, was on balance disutile. Most disutile laws, however, failed the test of utility, Bentham argued, because they were simply self-serving: they maximized and sought to maximize not the "greatest good of the greatest number" but rather the greatest good of the powerful few who possessed the authority to make them.[17] They were, in a word, undemocratic, by which he meant *not* that they lacked a democratic mandate (although many did that) but that they were not conceived, passed, promulgated, or enforced "in the interest of the governed." They were, rather, conceived, passed, promulgated and enforced "in the interest of the governors" or of the governing

---

[14] Jeremy Bentham, "Pannomial Fragments," *The Works of Jeremy Bentham*, ed. John Bowring (Edinburgh: William Tait, 1843) vol. 3, 229:

> Of two people having unequal fortunes, he who has most wealth must by a legislator be regarded as having most happiness. But the quantity of happiness will not go on increasing in anything near the same proportion as the quantity of wealth:–ten thousand times the quantity of wealth will not bring with it ten thousand times the quantity of happiness. It will even be matter of doubt, whether ten thousand times the wealth will in general bring with it twice the happiness. The effect of wealth in the production of happiness goes on diminishing, as the quantity by which the wealth of one man exceeds that of another goes on increasing: in other words, the quantity of happiness produced by a particle of wealth (each particle being of the same magnitude) will be less at every particle; the second will produce less than the first, the third than the second, and so on.

[15] Jeremy Bentham, "View of the Rationale of Evidence," *The Works of Jeremy Bentham*, vol. 6, 173. ("In this, as in every other quarter of judge-made law, the advancement of the sinister interest of the makers: – the interest of the scepter, the interest of the purse, and the interest of the pillow; – the increase of power to the judges, – the putting of money into the pocket of Judge and Co. – and the saving of trouble to the judges."); Bentham, "Principles of Judicial Procedure," *The Works of Jeremy Bentham* vol. 2, 454 ("As to the Judicial Establishment, so intimate is its connexion with the system of procedure, that in any explanation given of the former, it is not possible to avoid bringing into view, to an extent more or less considerable, the intended purport of the latter").

[16] Bentham, "Principles of Judicial Procedure," 454 ("Having for its superordinate end, the maximization of the security afforded by the services of the functionaries belonging to the judiciary system, it sets before itself in the first place two conjunct subordinate objectives, namely maximizing the number of those to whom the benefit is imparted: and rendering and keeping at all times, adequate to that purpose, the number of the functionaries employed in the imparting of it.").

[17] *See id.* at 456. (He later refers to the motivation of judges to obfuscate judicial procedure as a "sinister interest.")

class. They maximized, and they aimed to maximize, the pleasures, happiness, or well-being of a small, empowered, and elite group of people – the people who passed or found them – rather than the pleasures, happiness, or well-being of all. Because they did so, they were disutile, and because they were that, they were immoral as well.

Through the entirety of Bentham's lifelong commitment to legal reform, the connection between his censorial jurisprudence and the legal positivist premise on which it all rested was never obscure. Far from it. Unlike the substantive and political particulars, the basic *logic* of censorial jurisprudence – the logic of the Benthamic project that takes as its "point" the criticism of the law that exists, on the basis of the law that ought to be – rested neither on his distrust of the common law, his faith in codification and legislation, his abolitionism, his political radicalism, his utility calculus, his democratic politics, nor his feud with Blackstone. Rather, the logic of censorial jurisprudence rested on the same straightforward analytic insight that is still at the heart of contemporary legal positivism in virtually all its forms: existing law – whether articulated by common law judges, by Blackstone, by magistrates, Lords, Chancellors, or priests – is not, simply by virtue of its existence, its longevity, the reverence in which it may be held, or its pedigree, *therefore* just. Bentham reiterated some version of this insight repeatedly in his encyclopedic writings, and he viewed the heart of the academic resistance to it – emanating largely but not only from Blackstone and his followers – as at the heart of much resistance to reform generally, and his own suggested reform projects specifically. The academic or Natural Lawyer's antipositivist's idealist claim, in other words, that a "true law" is therefore a "just law," coupled with the reactionary political claim, or predisposition, that all existing laws are of course true laws, he thought, just *was* the basis of illiberalism: the refusal to grant even the possibility of the need for reform. Thus, he insisted, throughout his life, not only on the utility calculus as the best way to evaluate law but more basically on the academic separation of analytic from censorial jurisprudence as key to an articulation of (as well as appreciation of) the *need* to evaluate it. Further, it was positivism – the separation of analytic from censorial jurisprudence – not utilitarianism – that illuminated that need, against all sorts of mystifying and legitimating claims to the contrary. Contra Blackstone, the Church, the Crown, and the Lords, the law that is, is not the ideal law, whether the latter is rooted in our nature and awaiting discovery or interpretation by fallible judges, or is a body of truths we might, but have not, yet uncovered, and whether the former is blessed with the authority of the Crown worn by a half-god–half-man king or with the authority of time encrusted common law principles inherited from a glorious past.

So, to emphasize, simply because this is the point that has been so utterly lost over the past century of our academically housed jurisprudential debates over the merits of positivism: what Bentham thought was needed, analytically, for his progressive and critical broadsides against the forces of unwarranted conservatism to be heard, was *not* increasingly robust or increasingly subtle theories of utilitarianism itself, but rather what we now call legal positivism or, more specifically, a broad-based appreciation of the separation thesis that was then and still is at its heart. The laws that govern us or that we issue to govern ourselves or others might, but certainly need not, and often do not, rest on truths that are self-evident, principles that have shown their value simply by virtue of their endurance over time, or moral codes that speak to our better nature. Whether or not our law from time to time, or a part of our law from time to time, can accurately be claimed to "rest on" or be "informed by" such truths, principles, or codes, law does not consist of those truths. Whatever may be true for contemporary legal positivists, for Bentham, the *reason* to insist on the "separation" of the legal is from the legal ought, and therefore of analytic from censorial jurisprudence, was through and through *political*, not solely analytic (as it sometimes seems to have been for Hart[18]), or pedagogical (as it was for Austin[19]) or professional (as it was for Holmes, at least as expressed in "The Path of the Law"[20]). The separation of analytic from censorial jurisprudence, Bentham believed, was indeed necessary for a coherent or clear headed understanding of the law, by either student or lawyer, but it was not only that. It was also necessary to the generation of meaningful moral *criticism*, both liberal and radical, of the law that is. Understand that the law we have is not the ideal we should have – and understand that, so that you might better reform it.

If this accounting of the motivations behind at least Bentham's commitment to legal positivism is correct, then there is a truly stunning discontinuity – one which cries out for explanation – between Benthamic positivism on the one hand and both American understandings of, and practice of, legal positivism on the other. Let me begin with American understandings. Legal positivism, in this country, has garnered a modern American reputation among nonpositivist legal philosophers and even more so among legal scholars outside jurisprudence that is now diametrically at odds with its critical and politically liberal Benthamic roots. In direct contrast to Bentham's insistence that the reason positivism matters, so to speak, is that it is the

[18] Hart wrote quite eloquently of Bentham's own reformist career and of the centrality of positivism to that career, in his essays on Bentham. *See* H. L. A. Hart, *Essays on Bentham: Jurisprudence and Political Theory* (Oxford: Oxford University Press, 1982). He did not, however, seem to value modern positivism, or even his own positivism, for its potential to ground legal criticism and reform. *The Concept of Law* only briefly suggests that positivism might be of value for this reason. H. L. A. Hart, *The Concept of Law* 210.

[19] John Austin, *Province of Jurisprudence Determined.*

[20] Holmes, "The Path of the Law." "The Path of the Law" contains Holmes's endorsement and reinterpretation of positivism, and the separation of law and morals, but does so confusedly and never with an eye toward reform. We should wash the law in cynical acid and view law as the bad man would – but not, apparently, so as to better reform it, rather, simply so as to better convey its content to our client. We should strip law of moral concepts, but the "moral concepts" to which Holmes refers are simply the positive moral beliefs of a community, and the reason for stripping them from law is to make the commands of law clearer, and thus better understood and followed – not to make the commands of law better to reform.

only sensible foundational jurisprudence for the criticism (and reform) of existing law, legal positivism, for at least three-quarters of a century, has been perceived in this country as the jurisprudential foundation for an undue conservative acceptance of law *as it is*. The American indictment of positivism as unjustifiably conservative or as the jurisprudential handmaiden of reactionary politics is both broad and deep; it has persisted across generations and across a surprisingly wide range of American jurisprudential movements. Thus, and to take just a few of the most salient examples, in the past half century alone (positivism's reputation was, if anything, worse in the first half of the twentieth century), legal positivism has been characterized by our most deeply reform-minded and prominent radical and liberal American legal theorists as the jurisprudence behind a Nixonian insistence on law and order[21] and a concomitant hostility to both civil and judicial disobedience.[22] It has been said to harbor a Borkian hostility to living or evolving constitutions;[23] to have at its heart an inadequate understanding of human rights and constitutional liberties.[24] Most famously, it has been accused of being the philosophical attitude behind judicial complicity in the worst imaginable legalist evils, from Nazi-era laws mandating genocide[25] to U.S. laws regulating slavery.[26] More generally, it is routinely characterized as the philosophical excuse for a hide-bound insistence on law-as-law whatever

---

[21] Ronald Dworkin, "The Jurisprudence of Richard Nixon," *New York Review of Books* 18.8 (May 4, 1972) 27–35. Judicial passivity, Dworkin argues, can be based on either moral skepticism (either of moral rights generally or of their applicability to law) or deference (to those who are politically accountable). Dworkin puts Nixon in the second camp, and not the first:

> The policy of judicial activism presupposes a certain objectivity of moral principle; in particular it presupposes that citizens do have certain moral rights against the state, like a moral right to equality of public education or to fair treatment by the police. Only if such moral rights exist in some sense can activism be justified as a policy based on something beyond the judge's personal preferences. The skeptical theory attacks activism at its roots; it argues that in fact individuals have no such moral rights against the state. They have only such *legal* rights as the Constitution grants them, and these are limited to the plain and uncontroversial violations of public morality that the framers must have had actually in mind, or that have since been established in a line of precedent.... These theories are so different that an American politician, like Nixon, can consistently accept the second [deference], but not the first [moral rights against government].

[22] *See* Ronald Dworkin, "On Not Prosecuting Civil Disobedience," *New York Review of Books* 10.11 (June 6, 1968): 14–21; Robert M. Cover, *Justice Accused: Antislavery and the Judicial Process* (Yale University Press, 1984).

[23] *See* Ronald Dworkin, "The Bork Nomination: An Exchange," *New York Review of Books* 34.15 (Oct. 8, 1987); Ronald Dworkin, "The Bork Nomination," *New York Review of Books* 34.13 (Aug. 13, 1987); Ronald Dworkin, "Reagan's Justice," *New York Review of Books* 31.17 (Nov. 8, 1984).

[24] John Mikhail, " 'Plucking the Mask of Mystery from Its Face' ": Jurisprudence and H. L. A. Hart," *Georgetown Law Journal* 95 (2007): 733–780.

[25] Lon Fuller, *The Morality of Law* (New Haven: Yale University Press, 1969); David Luban, "Fairness to Rightness: Jurisdiction, Legality, and the Legitimacy of International Criminal Law," in *The Philosophy of International Law*, Samantha Besson and John Tasioulas, eds. (Cambridge: Oxford University Press, 2010) 569–88, 578 (citing Robert K. Woetzel, *The Nuremberg Trials In International Law* [New York: Praeger, 1960]).

[26] Cover, *Justice Accused* 1.

the cost to justice;[27] as legitimating a blind and formalist refusal to grant the potential for play in the joints of legal rules;[28] as the jurisprudential view behind the quietest claim that even unjust laws, solely by virtue of their legal validity, entail a moral duty of both civic and judicial obedience;[29] and as both harboring and perpetuating an ignorance of the temperate and tempering role of equity and equitable doctrines in legal systems far and wide. It is the judiciary's commitment to *positivism*, American scholars have in various ways charged – and not just occasionally charged, but repeatedly and even *routinely* charged – rather than the judiciary's (or a particular judge's) commitment to its or his or her own class or professional interests, or its or his or her own latent racism, or even just its or his or her own overwrought commitment to the rule of law that accounts for the judiciary's unwillingness, across time, to bend the law so as to interpret it humanely,[30] or even to contemplate judicial resistance as a morally required or permitted response to legal evil,[31] just as it is the prosecuting state's (or the prosecutor's) commitment to positivism, that renders it or him incapable of interpreting law so as to exercise leniency toward the morally motivated civil disobedient.[32] In the eyes of contemporary American legal scholars, and perhaps more broadly, legal positivism is perceived to be the jurisprudential foundation not of a reformist and critical stance toward law but of an illiberal acceptance of law's evils, and of judicial complicity in those evils as well. The idea that a censorial jurisprudence – the criticism of the law that is, on the basis of stated ideals regarding what the law ought to be – follows on the heels of positivism has almost entirely disappeared – at least from American legal positivism's *reputation*.

So the reputation of positivism, in the minds of most American legal theorists, is directly opposed to what at least for Bentham was its political reform-minded heart. That alone is interesting, and again, requires explanation. But what might be even more striking, and certainly more consequential, is that Bentham's "censorial jurisprudence" has also disappeared from American legal positivist *practice*. Again, for Bentham, legal positivism grounded two legalist projects: analytic jurisprudence – the study of law – and censorial jurisprudence – its criticism. Contemporary legal positivists, to some degree in Britain but even more thoroughly in the United States, have taken up the call for a positivist analytic jurisprudence, but they have for the most part simply ignored Bentham's call for a censorial jurisprudence. Legal positivists almost never *laud*, and only on occasion even *refer to* positivism as the necessary foundation of legal criticism. The connection, and again even the idea that there *is* a connection – the idea, that is, that criticism of the law that is on the basis of the law that ought to be, is a distinctly positivist project reflecting a distinctly positivist approach to legal criticism – has been lost. Rather, positivism is today understood

[27] Ronald Dworkin, *Taking Rights Seriously* (Cambridge: Harvard University Press, 1977).
[28] Lon Fuller, *Anatomy of the Law* (London: Pall Mall Press, 1968) 177–78.
[29] John Finnis, *Natural Law and Natural Rights* (Oxford: Oxford University Press, 1980).
[30] *See generally* Cover, *Justice Accused.*
[31] Dworkin, *Taking Rights Seriously.*
[32] Dworkin, "On Not Prosecuting Civil Disobedience," *New York Review of Books.*

by its practitioners as the jurisprudence requisite to a clear *understanding* of law, and particularly of law at its most foundational, principled level – and not as the jurisprudence requisite to its criticism and reform. Legal positivism, in other words, has become almost entirely identified with what Bentham would have called its analytic project: understanding the law that is. Contemporary positivists do not seemingly embrace the second half of Bentham's famous mandate – to "criticize freely" – as a commendable stance of responsible citizens toward law, much less one that is freed by, or in any way even affected by, a positivist insistence that we should all recognize the difference between that which is and that which ought to be. They are most decidedly not devoting the bulk of their professional legal careers to the criticism of law, or even to the study of or articulation of the basis for it. Criticism of law and its reform, in other words, is simply not regarded as a part of the positivist project. Bentham's "censorial jurisprudence" – criticism of the law which is, on the basis of the law that ought to be – is no longer a part of legal positivism, or even a project that is viewed as following on its heels.

The absence of a distinctively positivist censorial jurisprudence matters. It shows in our general legal theory and more importantly in our general legal scholarship. Most glaring, and as has been much remarked over the last century, we do not have a body of positivist jurisprudence that is critical of constitutional law, or even more serious, of the Constitution itself. There are a few exceptions, of course – Charles Beard,[33] Sanford Levinson,[34] Mary Becker[35] – but for the most part, the libraries of constitutional scholarship (much of it deeply critical of social and legal practice) in this country is profoundly nonpositivist and even antipositivist in its stance toward the Constitution itself: it assumes the goodness and rightness of the Constitution and then proceeds to argue either the unconstitutionality of various laws or legal regimes, assuming the Constitution as the baseline of criticism, or against particular interpretive glosses on the Constitution, emanating either from judges or fellow scholars, assuming a correct understanding of the Constitution as the baseline of criticism. There is, by contrast to both of these critical-constitutional ways of thinking, little constitutional scholarship that views the Constitution positivistically and as the object of censorial jurisprudence rather than its metric: that assumes, that is, that the Constitution is simply a social fact, properly subjected to criticism, and then mounts a criticism of it pressed toward the end of its reform. This is just not how we think about the Constitution, to state the obvious.[36] The absence of positivist censorial jurisprudence might be part of the reason we do not have a censorial jurisprudence

---

[33] Charles A. Beard, *An Economic Interpretation of the Constitution of the United States* (New York: The Free Press, 1986).
[34] Sanford Levinson, "How the United States Constitution Contributes to the Democratic Deficit in America," *Drake Law Review* 55.4 (2007): 859–78.
[35] Mary Becker, "Towards a Progressive Politics and a Progressive Constitution," *Fordham Law Review* 69.5 (2001): 2007–56.
[36] This is clear in part from the widespread resistance to even the idea, much less the possibility, of constitutional amendments, particularly on the progressive left. For a striking example, see Kathleen Sullivan, "Constitutional Amendmentitis," *American Prospect* 20 (September 21, 1995).

focused on the Constitution – although, as I argue later in the chapter, the causal arrow may go in the other direction as well: the insularity of the Constitution against reform-based critical commentary may be one reason we lack a censorial jurisprudence across the board.

What is so obviously true of constitutional law is also true, although not as noticeably or relentlessly, in other fields of law. We have plenty of critical jurisprudence – most of our ordinary legal scholarship is critical, or normative, in some way, although this may be changing – but we tend to think of the fundamental premises of a body of law as the baseline of criticism, not as the social fact that is itself in need of critical assessment and possible change. Thus, for example, we have a wealth of critical tort scholarship, but little that asks whether the body of law in its entirety might be misguided, whether its goals might be better met by a combination of decently humane compensation schemes for accidents and regulatory or quasi-criminal sanctions for negligent misconduct, regardless of whether that misconduct proximately causes compensable harm (although there is certainly more critical tort scholarship of this sort than critical constitutional law scholarship).[37] Rather, the massive amounts of tort scholarship we do have criticizes some part of tort doctrine on the basis of the bulk of tort doctrine, assuming the latter as the baseline of criticism of the former, or alternatively, criticizes or asserts some claimed moral theory of tort law, against the baseline of the extant bulk of judicial tort decisions. What is true of tort is generally true of common law subjects, and also, albeit to a lesser degree, of regulatory subjects as well. To generalize, we have massive amounts of ordinary legal scholarship that is critical of law, but almost all of it criticizes some piece of doctrine against the baseline of other aspects of law and legal doctrine. This piece of doctrine does not fit with that piece of doctrine, that piece of doctrine has or should have priority for various reasons, so this piece of doctrine requires reform. "Traditional" doctrinal legal scholarship, which is still the bulk of our scholarship, as Dworkin argued some time ago, is in fact of just this deeply antipositivist form: the value, or goodness, or justice, of an overarching political settlement regarding some swath of law is assumed, and some part of the law is then criticized on the basis of that settlement.[38]

This kind of criticism can be done well or badly, and it can be a worthy project. Particularly if the "law" that is taken as the baseline of critique is morally capacious in the way Dworkin described, the resulting body of critical jurisprudence need not be particularly Blackstonian, and it obviously need not represent unwarranted complacency or complicity with extant law.[39] It does not invariably and fatally

---

[37] Richard Abel's scholarship is a striking exception. *See* Richard Abel, "Judges Write the Darndest Things: Judicial Mystification of Limitations on Tort Liability," *Texas Law Review* 80 (2002): 1547–75; Abel, "Questioning the Counter-Majoritarian Thesis: The Case of Torts," *DePaul Law Review* 49 (1999) 533–58; *see also* Abel, "The Real Tort Crisis: Too Few Claims," *Ohio State Law Review* 48 (1987): 443–67.

[38] Dworkin, *Taking Rights Seriously* 66–68.

[39] *Id.* at 15–16.

confuse the is and the ought; some part of the law we have is criticized on the basis of a better understanding of a broader swath of law that in turn includes a clearer articulation of the moral principles at its heart.[40] This kind of critical engagement with law might, and often does, push the law in the direction of justice. However, "censorial jurisprudence," it is not. It is not the critique of the law that we have, on the basis of some moral metric outside of law. It is, rather, a critique of some law on the basis of a moral metric deduced or inferred from some other law. It is what lawyers and judges do in brief and opinion writing and at least arguably what they should be doing when they are writing briefs and opinions. It is not so obviously, however, what the rest of us should be doing when we engage in critical thinking about law.

This chapter concerns, largely, the disappearance of censorial, positivist jurisprudence, and a plea for its reenlivening. In the first two sections below, I suggest two reasons for the disappearance of censorial jurisprudence from American legal positivism, both stemming, in various ways, from distinctively American arguments against the separation thesis. In the third and fourth, I take up two apparent counterexamples to my thesis that censorial jurisprudence is absent from American positivist practice. Thus, in the third subsection, I argue that rights discourse and rights consciousness has not emerged as a positivist mode of legal criticism – although it could – and in the fourth I argue the same, although for different reasons, with respect to "cost-benefit analysis." Finally, I suggest in the concluding part of this chapter that the failure of positivists either to embrace censorial jurisprudence or at least to note it as a distinctively positivist project is unfortunate. Censorial jurisprudence – the criticism of the law that is, on the basis of the law that ought to be – should be a part of positivism and a part of our general jurisprudence. It is not, and we are the worse for it.

THE DISAPPEARANCE OF CENSORIAL JURISPRUDENCE FROM AMERICAN LEGAL POSITIVISM

At least on first blush, the connection between the separation thesis and Bentham's censorial jurisprudence – the connection, that is, between understanding the difference between the law that is and the law that ought to be, and clear-headed criticism, and hence reform, of the former on the basis of the latter – is nothing but a straightforward, and by no means counterexperiential, bit of common sense. It is reflected in countless clichés, fables, old wives' tales, and bits of folk wisdom. If we think the king is God's representative on earth, we will not see the evil he does; we will be blinded by the light of the sun's rays that stream down upon his crowned head. The king, after all, can do no wrong. Whatever he does, then, if he is a true king, must be right. True law – if it is true – must be just. If we love the

---

[40] *Id.*

law, and if we tend to think our beloved is touched with divinity, we will not see her flaws. We therefore will not be inclined to reform it. If we think our common law is by definition ideal, because encrusted with the eternal and universal moral wisdom and virtue of the ages, we will not see its shortcomings. We will stick with it through thick and thin. If we think the Constitution's framers were Godlike in their wisdom, beneficence and foresight . . . and so on. Basically, to switch clichés, if we look at either the law or the world or our beloved through rose-colored glasses, we will not see their horrors. We can keep going with this. If the low-hanging rotten grapes are all you can reach, you may develop a taste for them, which might make you happy, relatively speaking, of course, but you will not be much of a wine critic. Turns out, you cannot actually make a silk purse from a pig's ear no matter how hard you try, but you *can* manage to confuse yourself mightily about the value or worthiness of the materials at hand, if you think that is what you are doing. And so on. All of these clichés and bits of pop or Shakespearean wisdom were true enough and widely embraced when Bentham wrote, and all are true enough now. So, in the face of this all-too-human tendency to see things as better than they are, or even as perfect – particularly those things we likely cannot change, but more important, for those few things we can change but for reasons of self-interest or complacent (or bored) lack-of-interest would prefer the luxury of not bothering – came Bentham's positivist's rejoinder, which has remained the heart of legal positivism ever since. The law we have is not necessarily the law that we should have. If we wish to make it better, we must first see that it is not, simply by *being*, already *best*.

So what happened? Legal positivism is *not*, today, either in the United States or in Britain, broadly identified with an outpouring of criticism freed by a clear-headed, no-rose-colored-glasses appreciation of the difference between the legal world as it is and the legal world as it ought to be. In the United States (although not in Britain), it *is* identified, rather, with a judicial reluctance, in the face of powerful moral arguments, to interpret law in a way that avoids moral catastrophe, or even simply tilts it toward more just outcomes. Why this difference?

Part of the reason, I believe, for Benthamic positivism's poor reception in the United States has to do simply with confusion over definitions, and part of that has to do, in turn, with the ill-chosen phrase "separation thesis." Never has a turn of phrase so badly served the movement for which it was coined. The basic legal positivist proposition required to ground censorial jurisprudence is that the law that is, is not necessarily as it ought to be. Censorial jurisprudence hardly needs the near absurdly counterfactual claim that the law that is, is *never* as it ought to be, or that at least some bits and pieces of our law are not fully consistent with the demands of justice. Nor need it rest on the depressing realpolitik claim that the point of law is something other than the achievement of justice, societal well-being, the happiness of the greatest number, the greatest liberty possible for each individual consistent with that of others, some other credible moral ideal or set of ideals. Nor need positivism, or the censorial jurisprudence that Bentham thought it grounds, require the claim that legal rules never aim for or converge with conventional moral rules: that prohibitions against homicide, for example, have an entirely different or separate aim than widely accepted moral rules against killing people, or that legal rules sanctioning the breach of contract have no connection or overlap whatsoever with moral norms against breaking promises. The phrase "separation thesis," however, whether or not intended, at least pictorially suggests some version of all three of these dubious propositions: that "legal norms" and "moral norms" inhabit separate planes of existence, and because they do, never the twain shall meet; that the law never achieves or even aims to achieve justice or any other moral goal; that legal rules, once washed in cynical acid, have no overlap with either conventional or critical moral norms. All of these claims are baldly and demonstrably false and widely understood to be: plenty of existing law fully comports with the demands of justice and is quite satisfactorily just, exactly as it is. A lot of our modern law, whether that which prohibits discrimination or protects free speech or imposes strict liability in tort for badly manufactured products represents quite real and transformational moral victories that have made us a much more just society and of which the legal profession as well as the political actors that brought these regimes to fruition should take pride; plenty of our quite ordinary law, of criminal law, tort, and contract, but much of the rest of it as well, rest on the same sorts of prohibitions on immoral conduct as do our rules of conventional morality. Positive politics, through the efforts of good and courageous people, can yield positive law that is profoundly just; a legal system, positivistically understood, can be and should be aimed in its entirety at moral ideals, and whether this is true, even just willy-nilly or by Machiavellian design, will contain enumerable rules of primary conduct that prohibit much the same malfeasance and mischief as ordinary rules of conventional morality. Legal positivism – identified with the "separation thesis" and the latter wrongly but understandably then read to suggest the lack of any relationship, occasional, contingent, or otherwise, between positive rules of law on one hand, and rules of either critical or conventional morality, as well as ideals of justice, on the other – has suffered as a consequence.

The ill repute of legal positivism is not, however, all just one big misunderstanding. If it were, it would have been cleared up by now.

A second reason – and this pertains to contemporary British positivism as well as American – has to do with nothing more than a diversion of resources: drawn in by their critics, positivists have become defensively immersed in questions of law's *authority*, rather than law's value.[41] A commitment to legal positivism – that even unjust laws are nevertheless laws – when jointly held with the view that at least in well-functioning legal systems, citizens have a prima facie duty to obey the law,

---

[41] Joseph Raz is widely regarded as the most influential contemporary legal positivist, and his writing is almost entirely absorbed with explaining the reasons for and the (limited) nature of law's authority, and its limits. *See* Raz, *The Authority of Law*; Raz, *Between Authority and Interpretation: On the Theory of Law and Practical Reason* (Oxford: Oxford University Press, 2009).

seems to entail a moral obligation to follow immoral rules, which is odd to say the least. Positivists who adhere to the view that there is such an obligation to obey the law are therefore absorbed with the task of finding the source as well as the justification of law's authority.[42] I do not want to enter this debate or comment on its worthiness. All I want to suggest (and I do so primarily in the second part of this chapter) is that there are real opportunity costs to holding this debate at all. Whether an unjust law commands any authority, and if so, what is its source, is one question. What renders a law unjust, however, is a second. The first has absorbed the attention of contemporary positivists. The second has been neglected.

I think there are two additional reasons for the poisonous reception of legal positivism in the United States, as well as the abandonment of censorial jurisprudence as an American legal positivist project, which I address in more detail. The first stems from the much-noted difference between American and British jurisprudence: the former centers the judge as legal actor, interpreter, pronouncer, and critic, and the latter centers the legislator, or sometimes the citizen. This difference in focus has turned out to have far reaching consequences for both the meaning of the "separation thesis" at the heart of legal positivism and for the connection of the separation thesis to censorial jurisprudence. The second reason is cultural. Americans' view of law – and particularly of legal processes – is so capacious, and so generous, that American legal theorists often simply deny the *need* for censorial jurisprudence.[43] The denial is more often implicit than explicit, but not always. Either way, the claim is that any serious criticism of law can be and should be made within the institutions, premises, principles, and confines of existing American law, not outside it. I'll take these up in that order.

Judging through Rose-Colored Glasses

Start with the institutional differences, and the impact of that difference on the meaning and valence of the separation thesis itself. Contemporary positivists (and their critics) think of positivism as asserting the "separation" of actual and ideal law, or the difference between law as it is and ought to be, or the difference between law and our ideals for law, and so on. As suggested earlier, in terms of Bentham's projects, this mandate – to separate the actual from the ideal – makes good pragmatic sense, if we are engaged in either analytic or censorial jurisprudence. If we want to know what the law "is," we should indeed not confuse it with what it ought to be, and if we want to criticize the former on the basis of the latter, it is even more imperative to keep the two apart. Legal positivism is just the fancy name for the bit of common sense rehearsed earlier: if you want to clear-headedly appraise something,

---

[42] For a good, brief comment on this intrapositivist debate, see Brian Bix, "Legal Positivism and Explaining Normativity and Authority," *APA Newsletter on Philosophy and Law* 5 (Spring 2006).

[43] For an example, see Owen Fiss, "Objectivity and Interpretation," *Stanford Law Review* 34 (1982): 739–64.

best to keep wishful thinking out of the equation. Yet think of the sensibility, or lack of sensibility, of this bit of "common sense" as applied to the judge's distinctive tasks of adjudicative reasoning. Judges are charged with the tasks of interpreting and applying law – not simply "learning" what the law "is" or criticizing it against an ideal metric. Judges are law's interpreters, and by virtue of that role, they are part of the cake-making machine, so to speak, rather than being solely a member of the community of cake critics. The judge is *making* the cake, all the while criticizing, modifying, and reforming the recipe for it as she goes. She does not just study law – ascertain it in order to criticize it – she *makes* it. That means that she authors it. She ascertains the legal materials not *so as to* critique them, but *so as to* interpret them, refashion them if need be, and, if she has the institutional authority to do so and the intestinal fortitude, apply them. By so doing, she makes law in the process. The judge, that is, ascertains the law *to* reformulate it – not to criticize it, as would Bentham's censorial jurisprudent. That ascertainment quite naturally, then, will be, and should be, of law in its *best light*. Of course the judge, as author, has an investment in making the law the best it can be. She is remaking the legal materials, after all, to create a product from them and of them – but *better*. That better law she seeks to re-create through her interpretive labors will have to have some claim of continuity with and even identity with the law she discovered when she set out on the journey. Of course, she reads the law through rose-colored glasses, as well she should, if she has any moral imagination at all.

Furthermore, judges are not simply charged with the duty to remake the legal materials into some vaguely better form – more coherent, more crystalline, more aesthetically pleasing, whatever – they are, more specifically, charged with the work of doing so toward the end of doing *justice*. Doing justice is the point of their enterprise. Now, it may be that doing the work of "formal" or "legal" justice – narrowly understood, is simply the work of treating like cases alike and that it requires them to simply apply the law as it is, no interpretation required. However, few judges so construe their work, and even if they do, as the realists were at pains to show, that work is hardly syllogistic: treating like cases alike requires an ascertainment of similarity and difference across cases and attributes of cases that do not themselves inevitably come self-labeled, and the judge's application of general norms to those attributes therefore requires substantive judgments that are ethical at heart.[44] This case is like that case, and so this rule of law rather than that one applies, not for any old reason picked out of a hat, presumably, but because justice so mandates. Doing "justice," even if we narrowly construe the justice judges are charged with doing as "formal justice," requires ethical judgment, and it is in part because judges have interpretive latitude with respect to the legal materials that face them, that they can be sensibly charged with this task, rather than something less morally demanding

---

[44] Felix Cohen, "Transcendental Nonsense and the Functional Approach," *Columbia Law Review* 35 (1935): 809–49; Karl N. Llewellyn, "Remarks on the Theory of Appellate Decision and the Rules of Cannons about How Statutes Are to Be Construed," *Vanderbilt Law Review* 3 (1950): 395–406.

(such as administration).[45] A more accurate description of the judicial task, then, meaning a description that accounts for its moral center, should be something like this: judges should decide cases in accordance with law, interpreted in such a way as to make it as congruent with the demands of justice as it is possible to be. Doing anything less than that – bypassing an opportunity to interpret law in a way that is in accord with justice – looks like a breach of judicial duty, not a praiseworthy refusal to engage in activist judicial decision making.

Against the backdrop of this *judicial* project – to interpret and apply law in such a way as to bring it as close as possible to the mandates of justice – all of the clichéd truths rehearsed earlier that made the separation thesis at the heart of positivism seem so commonsensical, seem, instead, to be utterly inapposite. A judge seeking to make law its moral best *should* look at the law through rose-colored glasses. We *want* him to make the law the best it can be, and if making the law the best it can be means, in part, seeing the law as rosy rather than gray, than by all the means he should don the glasses so that he can do just that. Unlike the social scientist or even the hard-headed legal critic, we *want* the judge to cherry-pick the evidence as he tries to ascertain and then restate what the law is. He has clerks in his chambers and advocates in court and writing *amici* briefs, in fact, who are helping him do the cherry-picking. If there is a split in the decisional authority, and one fork of that road is just and the other unjust, then the judge should by all means regard "the law" as that which follows the more just path. If one set of principles underlies one line of precedent, and another set underlies another, and the former is stronger or better or more just, by all means choose it. If a set of cases can be rationalized by either of two principles, and one principle is notably more just than the other, again, by all means, pick the better. If the low hanging fruit is what is available, and it is better than the mushy stuff on the ground, pick the low-hanging fruit. The judge, after all, may actually have the power to turn that pig's ear into silk, so by all means we should let him try; of course we want him to try. Why settle for a pig's ear when we could have silk? If we want judges to ascertain and apply law in accordance with justice, then we will want the judge to do just what we cautioned against, when thinking of the Benthamic, censorial jurisprudent. The same positivistic directive – separate the law that is from the ideal it should be – that looks like such a natural prerequisite for censorial jurisprudence, looks (and is) utterly misguided for the project of adjudication.

We can see this even more clearly if we look at the consequence, should judges embrace the positivist mantra that, Bentham argued, underlies coherent legal criticism. The judge who looks at law in its worst light – all so as to avoid being a naïve idealist – is needlessly reaching unjust results. She is willfully refusing the

---

45 Thus, Holmes's mandate that social policy rather than logic drives law, and elsewhere, that experience rather than logic determines the path of the law. Oliver Wendell Holmes, *The Common Law* (Boston: Little, Brown, and Company, 1909) 312; *see also* Holmes, "The Path of the Law" 465 *and Lochner v. United States*, 198 U.S. 45, 75 (1905) (Holmes, J., dissenting).

opportunity to look at law in its best light, reinterpret it to render it authoritative, and apply it accordingly. She is passing up moral opportunities to make the world a more just place, and doing so, furthermore, through the inauthentic route of denying her power to do precisely that. This does not seem like hard-headed realism, it just seems morally perverse. In the most extreme cases, furthermore, such a judge is needlessly applying evil laws, and she is therefore complicit in the evil regime she is promoting. Thus – the indictment of the American positivist judge. The mid-nineteenth-century abolitionist judge (say, Judge Shaw) who ascribed to a positivist jurisprudence, just as Robert Cover charged, might be applying the fugitive slave law and sending men and women back to slavery *needlessly*.[46] Thus, shame on him, if Cover was right about that. With just a little moral imagination and a bit of courage – not even a lot of either – he could have interpreted the law in such a way as to avoid those horrific results. The Vichy-era judges, according to Richard Weisberg's provocative and moving intellectual histories, did likewise when facing challenges to the application of the "Race Laws" in Vichy France during the Nazi era.[47]

The indictment by both of these legal historians of legal positivism as the heart of the massive injustice perpetuated by at least these judges, then, is this: Positivism holds that law is law, regardless of its moral merits, and judges are charged with the task of interpreting, upholding, applying, and enforcing the law. There is no possibility for the *positivist* judge to fight his or her way out of this box. It is, after all, not open to the positivist judge to argue, as might the Natural Lawyer, that an evil law is not a law and that therefore the judge need not apply it. The immoral law is nevertheless law, and the judge's duty is to ascertain and apply it. The judge who refuses to be a mush-headed, naïve idealist will look at the evil law as it is, not as he wishes it to be, and apply it, because that is his duty. Positivism and its many commonsensical directives – law is law, bad laws are nevertheless law, take off the rose-colored glasses if you want to know what the law really is, do not be naïve – leads at least the judge, whatever may be true of the censorial critic, or the advocating lawyer, or the student, on a path away from morally directed interpretation, and hence on a path away from justice. Legal positivism, when embraced and employed by judges, as American legal theorists have claimed now for more than a century, does look like a path toward complicity with legally sanctioned evil.

Is this a paradox, or a telling counterargument, as Dworkin clearly believed it to be?[48] How can it be that the *same* pragmatic directive – do not let your desires for what the law should be color your perception of what the law is – that looks so

---

[46] *See* Cover, *Justice Accused* 169.

[47] *See* Richard Weisberg, *Vichy Law and the Holocaust in France* (Harwood Academic Publisher, 1997) 355; Weisberg, "Daniel Arises: Notes (such as 30 and 31) from the Schlagaground," *Georgetown Law Journal* 97 (2009): 857–64, 862.

[48] *See* Dworkin, *Taking Rights Seriously* 305; *see also* Dworkin, "'Natural' Law Revisited," *University of Florida Law Review* 34 (1982): 165–88, 169.

commonsensical and appealing, when viewed as the foundation of legal criticism, look so wrong, when viewed as the foundation of legal adjudication? Do not both the critic and the judge have a shared interest in having a clear-eyed, no-rose-colored-glasses view of what the law is? The short answer is that no, they do not, and Bentham's formulation of the *projects* that positivism facilitates – analytic and censorial jurisprudence – actually helps us to see why. Bentham himself, after all, never claimed *adjudication* as one of the projects that positivism grounds – and for good reason: adjudication really is different. The judge is adjudicating and the censorial critic is criticizing; the difference in their projects matters. The adjudicating judge is *responsible* – as author and lawmaker – for the moral quality of that law, and has some power to affect it, by reading it as the best it can be. It is entirely proper, then, and of course desirable, for the judge to regard the law (or the legal materials, if he prefers to so regard them) that he is discovering as relatively malleable, subject to multiple fair interpretations, and to re-form those materials as one might re-form (and therefore think of) clay, so as to create a more ethically pleasing product, or to re-form the relative measure of ingredients, if one is baking a cake. The judge as an interpreter after all is a lawmaker: perhaps not a legislator, but certainly not a stenographer. He is responsible for re-forming it, and how he "reads" it – what he claims it "says" – will largely determine that reformulation. We want him to read it generously, as Dworkin has insisted for half a century, so that it can be "the best it can be," not skeptically, not washed in acid, not viewed as a bad man views it. As Dworkin said in the early 1980s in one of his more exasperated defenses of what was at heart a pretty straightforward claim, why *wouldn't* we want the judge to read the law in its best light? To wish anything *other than that* would simply be morally perverse.[49]

Contrast, however, the position of the responsible legal critic: Bentham's censorial jurisprudent. The censorial jurisprudent, in contrast to the Dworkinian judge, is responsible to state the law clearly, so as to highlight what needs changing, and changing by other legal actors with the power to effectuate the change. She herself – no judge she – does not have the power to remold it as she does so. She is not the law's author. She is most assuredly not responsible for doing so, so as to make it more morally appealing. If she reads the law in its best light, making it the best it can be by her own rosy glasses, she does both herself and the rest of us nothing but a disservice. Her interpretive task does not embrace the directive to *do* justice through her interpretive reading. It embraces the directive to state the law clearly, elucidate its shortcomings, and suggest reforms.

This does, in purpose and function both, indeed lead to something like a bifurcation in their relative perception of the object of their gaze: the judge will see one thing when he looks at the preexisting law, the censorial jurisprudent, or critic, something quite different, even if they are looking at basically the same texts. This is neither cynical nor pernicious. Nor is it all that unique to law or judging: the critic

---

49 *See id.* at 168.

reviewing the cookbook will read the recipe for marble cake ungenerously, while the baker reading the same recipe will read it so as to make it the best it can be, even if that means reading it so as to invite his discretionary judgment that three eggs might be better read as meaning two, because that will make the best cake, and besides, eggs can be quite different sizes. The critic, by contrast, will not read three eggs to mean two; rather, the critic will complain that the recipe is bad. The critic and the pastry chef, then, see two different things when they look at the recipe, because of their different projects: criticism versus baking. Likewise, the judge and critic; the judge and censorial jurisprudent.

Nor does the claim that the difference between what the critic and judge see when they look at the law is a function of their differing role, purpose, and project rest on a nihilistic, relativistic, or deconstructionist view of the nature of law, morality, justice, or the judicial process. It rests, rather, on the simple observation that the judge and critic are doing two different things, with two different objectives, even though they are doing their work, at least initially, with what looks to be the same set of materials. The point is *not* that one has power and the other does not, and that therefore one carries a moral burden but the other does not. Of course the critic has some power, and of course the judge's discretion is not unlimited. Rather, they have two different projects, with two different goals, and, importantly, they have two quite different sorts of power – one legal and one social – and therefore, two different sets of responsibilities. The judge is an active participant in the process of rendering decisions and therefore making law, and he does so, in part, by regarding the law he seeks to apply as malleable material that is ripe for remixing. He has both the power and the authority to remix it, and he is expected to do so, and so there is surely no reason in the world, just as Dworkin states, that he should not do so toward the end of creating a more just legal system. Would we have him do this toward the end of creating a *less* just system? Do we want him to read the recipe in its worst light? What he creates, however, must have some measure of continuity with what he confronted – it must be a remix of ingredients and of the recipe he is reading, and not a re-creation. It has to be a cake he is making, and it has to be a marble cake from that recipe for a marble cake, and not a different product altogether. Therefore, the way he reads the law, and what he sees when he does so, will be influenced by a constrained moral directive: he will read the law as the best *it* can be, so that he can authoritatively pronounce *it* to be the best *it* can be – not the best some other imagined law could be. The critic has no such authority, and not that kind of power, and no similar incentive to exercise the power she *does* have in a way that tilts existing law toward justice. She is not a participant in the process of reading generously, interpreting capaciously, and remixing existing law toward a more just articulation. Quite the contrary: she may sensibly think that the political prospects of reform are better if she highlights the law's shortcomings, rather than airbrush them out of the public eye. However, whatever she thinks of the prospects for reform, her goal in reading the law is to understand it, and to understand it critically – not to understand it toward the end of stating it authoritatively in its best light.

Both the critic and the judge might overreach. The critic might be too dour and read the law as being worse than it would ever be held to be, by any sensible judge with even a modicum of conscience. If so, the critic is simply attacking a strawman and his suggested reforms, if he is urging them, are pointless because unnecessary or redundant. A critic who blasts a law for being overly formalistic without realizing that it contains unstated equitable limits that will be enforced by virtually any judge other than the most obtuse, for example, has simply missed the mark. A judge, on the other hand, might be too morally ambitious: a restatement or remixing that aims to make law the best it can be might in fact be a failed attempt to make it something it cannot be. Nonetheless, we should not overread the moral of either limit. That the judge and critic both might err does not imply that they are in fact engaged in the same enterprise, that they have the same amount or kind of power with respect to the materials at hand, or that they do or should read the law toward the same set of overriding institutional purposes. They are not engaged in the same enterprise. The critic – Bentham's censorial jurisprudent – who seeks to criticize the law needs to separate cautiously the law as it is from the law that ought to be, the law he seeks to criticize from what he thinks the law should be, so as to criticize the law as it is on the basis of what it ought to be. The judge who interprets the law so as to adjudicate should read the law in its best light, as *being* the best it *can be* – not just as being something she can disingenuously claim to be better than it in fact is. The critic should discard, just as the judge should don, the rose-colored glasses. Legal positivism, and the clean separation of the ought and the is that it mandates, is a necessary foundation for the first project – that of censorial jurisprudence. It is contraindicated for the second.

Despite four decades of often withering positivist critique,[50] Dworkin's jurisprudence convincingly showed as much, but that is also *all* it showed. Dworkin argued that positivism in its entirety fails, but what he showed was a different proposition: positivism is not a good foundation *for morally motivated adjudication*. What is odd, though, truly odd, is that the Dworkinian demonstration of the limits of positivism – it is not well suited to the work of adjudication – was taken so broadly to be the failure of legal positivism in general. That positivism will not well serve the project of morally decent adjudication just does not imply that it will not well serve the ends of either legal criticism or even legal education. A few of us – a *very* few of us – are judges, or clerks to judges, or were clerks to judges, or will be clerks to judges. Those few, when they are in those roles, and when they have the power to do so, should indeed,

---

[50] *See, e.g.,* Brian Leiter, *Naturalizing Jurisprudence: Essays on American Legal Realism and Naturalism in Legal Philosophy* (New York: Oxford University Press, 2007); Leiter, "The End of the Empire: Dworkin and Jurisprudence in the Twenty-first Century," *Rutgers Law Journal* 36 (2005):165–82; H. L. A. Hart, *Law, Liberty, and Morality* (Stanford: Stanford University Press, 1963); Hart, *The Concept of Law*; Symposium Issue, "Justice for Hedgehogs: A Conference on Ronald Dworkin's Book," *Boston University Law Rev* 90.2 (2010). *See also* Scott Hershovitz, *Exploring Law's Empire: The Jurisprudence of Ronald Dworkin* (New York: Oxford University Press, 2006).

as Dworkin suggests, keep those rose-colored glasses firmly in place and make the law we inherit the best it can be. Most of us, however, are not judges, and those of us who have been clerks are not always and forever clerks. Why have so many of us concluded that what Dworkin showed to be true of judging is true of anything else we might do with law, such as criticize it, follow it, disobey it, or seek to improve it?

There are obvious cultural explanations for this – namely, that those who have overread Dworkin's antipositivism do aspire to be judges, always and forever. I will address that in a moment. Another possibility, however, for this four-decade long overreading of the implications of Dworkinian antipositivism is a mistaken logical argument that goes like this: both the judge and the critic have to first know the law, meaning they must ascertain it, before they then go their separate ways. Both the cookbook critic and the chef have to first read the recipe. The "first step," then, in both of their different projects, is the *same* step – reading is reading – and it is that first step that requires, according to positivism, adherence to the separation thesis. So, if it will not behoove the judge of all people to adhere to the separation thesis when reading the law, then clearly this is true across the board, for anyone who has any other reason to learn the law, no matter what the purpose of the reading (lawyer, client, judge, critic, student, scholar). If positivism fails for the judge, then it fails, period.

This rejoinder, however, misconstrues the nature of law, of what the judge does with it, or both. Here again, think of what Dworkin has in fact *shown*, rather than what he has argued. The judge is adjudicating, and in the process of doing so, he seeks out authoritative and binding materials to guide the adjudication. Some of those materials will be the same legal materials the critic uses when engaged in criticism of law and some will not: to take Dworkin's most hoary example, the judge might, in some context, view the maxim that "no man may profit from his own wrong" as binding him.[51] But that hardly makes the maxim "no man may profit from his own wrong" a "legal principle," and therefore a part of the law, properly fit for the critical tools of censorial jurisprudence. The judge may feel bound by all sorts of things – grammar, ordinary morality, professional morality, common sense, custom, aphorisms. There's no harm, perhaps, in the judge thinking of any or all dictates that he feels bind him in some way as a part of our "law" if he so wishes, but there is no reason that the rest of us should follow suit. In fact, for the most part, we do not follow suit: really *no one*, other than, perhaps, Dworkin himself, thinks that "no man may profit from his own wrong" is a legal principle, whether or not an occasional judge sometimes regards it as binding (people profit from their own wrong all the time and do not regard themselves as violating laws by virtue of so doing; think of your own purchases of products that are priced low because of wage theft). Nonetheless, the point can be generalized. The judge seeks out a set of materials that will guide resolution of a case. That set of materials includes legal

---

[51] Dworkin, *Taking Rights Seriously* 305.

materials and much else. He then puts on his rose-colored glasses and cherry-picks the evidence, as, I have argued, well he should: the legal ideal does and should guide his judgment of what constitutes "the law" that he reads as authoritative. The judge doing his job well is pushing to remake the law to bring it as close to a moral ideal as it can be; he will naturally be, and should be, motivated, both in his initial determination of his legal materials and in his choice of method for reading them, to make that task doable. He can and should then re-form the whole ball of dough into something that is more pleasingly just. The "law" is both an underinclusive and overinclusive appellation for the materials he initially specifies: it does not include the moral principles, maxims, common sense, and so on that the judge may use or feel bound by, and it includes much that the judge may justifiably set aside – outdated precedent, morally unappealing lines of authority, and so forth. The judge's task of ascertaining the "law" is as guided by the morally enriched project of adjudication as is the task of reforming and applying it. If judges interpret the law so as to make it as just as possible, they do so from start to finish, not only after first finding the relevant materials. The critic – Bentham's censorial jurisprudent – does not. He interprets the law to highlight its divergence from the ideal, not to highlight its possible convergence. The materials he selects will and should reflect that end.

None of this is terribly subtle, and all of it has been noted by contemporary positivists (notably, most recently, Brian Leiter).[52] Why, then, to repeat the question, is the rejoinder unconvincing to so many? Why is Dworkin's demonstration that positivism is an ill fit for morally responsible adjudication so widely taken to be a refutation of positivism across the board?

The better explanation, I believe, for the overreading is quasi-sociological rather than logical. We have overgeneralized from Dworkin's demonstration of the inappropriateness of positivism to judging, the inappropriateness of positivism to all law-related projects, perhaps, because at least in this country, we have blended the persona of the judge with all others who may engage law: the judge is the quintessential student, critic, compiler, scholar, and philosopher of law.[53] This conflation of seemingly all roles and purposes with which just about anybody who might have an interest in engaging with legal materials is vividly reflected in American legal pedagogy: what all American law schools teach all law students, whatever else they teach, is the art (or craft) of judging. Everything else – the arts (or crafts) of legal criticism, of legal compilation, of negotiating or mediating, even of rendering legal counsel or lawyering, and certainly of legislating – is viewed as either peripheral to legal education, or as in the last case, utterly irrelevant to it, and has been so viewed now

---

52 *See* Brian Leiter, "Explaining Theoretical Disagreement," *University Chicago Law Review* (2009): 1215–50, 1221.

53 This is vividly reflected in realist jurisprudence, which held both that law is that which is produced by judges and that law is that which judges consult and find authoritative. The law that emerges from these jointly held beliefs is entirely judge-centered. *See* Holmes, "The Path of the Law" 466 *and* Leslie Green, "Positivism and the Inseparability of Law and Morals," *New York University Law Review* 85 (2008): 1035–1058.

for well over a century. What we teach, centrally, is the judicial opinion, and what we test on is their ability to write one. We do not teach how to ascertain the need for a law, write one, or pass one. We do not teach how to compile or criticize law, and we do only the most casual job of teaching how to advocate, negotiate, or mediate in or around legal materials. We treat the judge, in the law-school classroom, as the quintessential legal actor – not the encyclopedia writer, not the scholar, not the legal critic, not the lawyer, not the legislator, mediator or negotiator, and not the American Law Institute [ALI] drafter. This is, on its face, peculiar: all of these actors must master law before engaging it, and more students will engage law in the role of these neglected forms than as a judge. *Why* we do this is well beyond the scope of this chapter – in my view, it is a function of the combined legacy of Langdellian formalism and realism, which, collectively, yielded the result that both what the judge *does or produces* (the realist claim) and what the judge *regards as authoritative* (the formalist claim) collectively constitutes "law." Thus, if students can be taught to inhabit the shoes of judges and both learn to regard and produce law, they will know the "law." That is a complicated claim, however, and beyond my scope. All I wish to claim here is that we *do* so embrace this narrow understanding of legal education. Some students take clinics, and learn a different governing narrative about what law is and what it is not, but most students, alas, do not. Some students read ALI sections and encyclopedias and get a different sense from those sources of what law is and is not, but most are encouraged not to, and they do not. A very few students eventually intern for legislators, where they will get an as yet different understanding of what is, and is not, law, but most will not, and virtually none are encouraged to. Some students become law professors, but that hardly changes the pattern of what they are taught or will teach others. It reinforces it. Students at the gateway of the profession – after three years of law school – regard the judge as the lawmaker, law critic, and law scholar, because, quite simply, that is what they have been taught to do. Dworkin and others have shown quite conclusively, in my view, that legal positivism is a bad fit, even descriptively, but certainly morally, for what the judge does. Furthermore, students learn, in their formative educational experiences, that the judge is *the* legal actor: the judge masters, interprets, and reforms the law in a morally just direction. The judge, in short, does it all. Positivism is a bad fit, then, for understanding law, regardless of the context in which understanding is sought.

Our Perfect Constitution . . . and Our Perfect Law of Tort, Contract, and All the Rest of It As Well . . .

The focus on judging that is such a distinctive feature of American jurisprudence and pedagogy, cannot fully explain either positivism's current reputation or current practice. It cannot fully explain, that is, why positivism is regarded as little more than an excuse for judicial complicity in evil law or why legal positivists themselves do not regard censorial jurisprudence as a positivist project. It is, after all, increasingly recognized, particularly but not only by legal positivists, that Dworkin and other

American legal philosophers of the last quarter of the twentieth century criticized positivism largely on the basis of adjudicative practices – thus showing, at most, that positivism is not well suited for American-style adjudication.[54] Dworkin himself has not done anything to blunt this domestication of his antipositivist views in the cozy spaces of adjudicative law. His recent writings simply repeat it: he focuses on judging and then, on the basis of arguments that succeed in that context, proceeds to make broad claims about law.[55] Yet, this apparent concession – that the greatest antipositivist of the past half century has shown at most the ill fit between positivism and adjudication – has not slowed the critique of positivism as little more than an amoral excuse for judicial complicity in evil.

Second, and more significantly, even if we limit the jurisprudential focus to the project of adjudication, positivism, and its call for clear perception of legal evil, one would think, would be viewed as at least *sometimes* felicitous toward the end of identifying failings of justice that cannot be wished or interpreted away by even the most morally ambitious and bravest of all possible judges, and would at least *sometimes* be recognized as such, *particularly* by judges who one would think would have a professional and reputational interest in not being regarded as omnipotent. Assume *arguendo*, the truth of what Robert Cover argued in the mid-1980s: that the abolitionist judges of the mid-nineteenth century could have used their legal power to save escaped slaves by acknowledging and then using gaps in the Fugitive Slave Act,[56] and their discretionary authority to interpret those gaps in a way conducive to justice. Further, assume that it was, as he claimed, their commitment to positivism, coupled with a heightened sense of their judicial responsibility, that masked that possibility. Assume as well, as Dworkin has argued, that a similar myopia afflicts contemporary judges and justices, and in a much larger range of cases. If so, then Dworkin and Cover are right that legal positivism will not be a helpful jurisprudential orientation in cases in which the law is sufficiently flexible that a judge inclined to do so can and therefore should indeed steer it in a more just direction. Maybe they are right that positivism-on-the-bench blunts moral imagination of judges who might otherwise feel morally empowered to do the right thing, and in just the way they both charged. Yet surely, even if this is true, even if they are right, nevertheless, judges cannot *always* turn the pig's ear into anything even remotely resembling a silk purse; when they cannot, the difference between the hand they have been dealt and the hand they wished they had been dealt should be an important distinction to hold onto – even for judges normally inclined to use their interpretive powers to make the law the best it can be. Surely *sometimes* bad law just cannot be made "best," or even better. Sometimes, in fact, this has been explicitly and poignantly recognized. A few federal judges faced with mandatory sentencing laws during the 1970s,

---

[54] This is a recurrent theme in the vast literature rebutting Dworkin's jurisprudence. *See* Hart, *The Concept of Law* 263; Raz, *The Authority of Law* 205; Leiter, *Naturalizing Jurisprudence* 104–5.

[55] *See* Ronald Dworkin, *Justice for Hedgehogs* (Cambridge: Harvard University Press, 2011) 138.

[56] Cover, *Justice Accused* 170.

for example, said as much: they found the law they were compelled to apply unjust and as a consequence they faced a real conflict between their obligation to uphold the law and their obligation to do justice.[57] They were not suffering from a lack of legal imagination. They were suffering from a surfeit of bad law and no good choices. They contemplated, quite publicly, resigning in the face of this injustice, and a few did. Three strikes laws present another set of stark examples. Perhaps positivism sometimes present judges with a false choice – either apply the law or do the just thing – where the actual range of choices, given law's malleability, permits the alternative of doing both. When it does so, it should be faulted, but at least in *some* cases, quite the contrary. In those cases, positivism might well be a clear guide to a clear articulation, even for the judge, of the true nature of the moral dilemma she faces: follow and apply an unjust law, refuse to follow the law, or resign. If the judge, because of her office, is duty-bound to apply unjust law, then she faces a true, not just apparent, moral conflict. Who knows how she will resolve it. She will not even *see* it, however, if she cannot acknowledge the possibility of the existence of an unjust law. Positivism, one would think, would be a help, not a hindrance, in recognizing it as such. Yet, there is precious little discussion of any of this, among either positivists or their critics.

A second reason for both positivism's ill repute, and the neglect of censorial jurisprudence among positivists, is simply that American lawyers, both positivist and nonpositivist, seem to share not only an adjudicative orientation but also a commitment to law's essential *goodness*. *All of us* in law – not just judges and wannabe judges – tend to think American law does not have many of those inescapable dilemmas; it is basically sufficiently just, when read generously and capaciously, as always, somehow, to provide a path to the just outcome.[58] It is the *combination* of these two commitments – to the centrality of adjudication, and to the always present possibility of the just adjudicated outcome – that generates, I believe, positivism's disrepute in this country. Furthermore, American lawyers, by virtue of training, culture, and experience, are in some foundational way Blackstonian natural lawyers. Like Blackstone, we tend to hold the common law in high regard, as well as close to the chest. More important, following Blackstone, we tend to think that law, or at least American law, by hook or crook, does more or less "dictate what is right and forbid what is wrong." As Blackstone believed of English common law, so American lawyers believe of at least constitutional law, and perhaps all the rest of it likewise: it really is just that good and wonderful. It really does have that pleasing content. It has that content, furthermore, *not* by definition – not because the lawmaker just flat out has power over moral truth as well as the machinations of state – but rather, because

---

57 *See* Marvin E. Frankel, *Criminal Sentences: Law without Order* (New York: Hill and Wang, 1973); *see also* Frankel, "The Search for Truth: An Umpireal View," *University of Pennsylvania Law Review* 123.5 (1975): 1031–59.

58 The clearest example of this is Owen Fiss's piece "Objectivity and Interpretation." *See* Fiss, "Objectivity and Interpretation" 753.

American law, read generously, really is fundamentally just. We are fortunate, lucky, blessed, or maybe we are just preternaturally just and virtuous, but we have done it. We have created a terrifically just body of law. As the English law, for Blackstone, came from time immemorial, and acquired its virtue through that historical process, so American law, for American lawyers, comes from the framing, Reconstruction, and from various "constitutional moments," surrounding our constitutional history; through the process, it acquired its fundamentally just nature. The claim to the natural justice of our law is neither an analytic (and baldly self-serving and slightly ridiculous) claim nor is it the product of self-delusion. It is a hard-won moral victory of our nation. It really is just that good.

The claim that American law is fundamentally just, at least on first hearing, sounds pretty audacious, even ridiculous. Yet in some form, it is widely shared among lawyers, judges, legal academics, and surprisingly, in my view, law students (meaning, I always expect students to be more skeptical than they are about the fundamental rightness of virtually every case they come across in the first year curriculum, and they are always far more inclined than I think they will be to accept the law's goodness and justice and to argue for it in the face of professorial skepticism). This belief in the goodness of American law comes out in classrooms on *both* sides of the podium. One hears it particularly in the moral emphasis, or exclamation marks, implied in claims of constitutionalism: "that would be unconstitutional!" (with the implicit, no need to even say it, claim being that the "it" that is unconstitutional must therefore be bad). In his early writings, Dworkin made the point repeatedly that constitutional law in particular was in effect the "bridge" between morality and positive law; that American constitutional law is in effect suffused with political morality.[59] In his mature writing, he asserts far more directly that law simply is a "branch" of political morality: that what Pierre Schlag (and others) usefully calls law's "propositional content" is a part of the propositional content of political moral truth.[60] Legally true propositions, then, are morally true propositions. Legal truth and moral truth more or less converge. It is an audacious claim all right.

It is instructive to remember the evidence that Dworkin initially turned to, when he first made his audacious claim about the goodness of our law: the reason, Dworkin argued in *Taking Rights Seriously*, that we can be so confident that law has this relation to morality, lies in the way lawyers *talk*. Lawyers *talk* as though the law is just, lawyers *talk* as though legal propositions that are unjust are therefore false. The unjust legal proposition is a false claim and the just proposition of law is a true proposition. The claim, for example, that "Affirmative action is constitutional" asserts the justice of affirmative action programs as well as their legality, and if it does so falsely, then the claim is false; if affirmative action is unjust, then it is unconstitutional likewise, or so our patterns of talking seem to suggest about the way we think (and, for Dworkin, therefore the way things are). That antiabortion

---

[59]　See Dworkin, *Taking Rights Seriously* 105.
[60]　See Pierre Schlag, "Spam Jurisprudence, Air Law, and the Rank Anxiety of Nothing Happening (A Report on the State of the Art)," *Georgetown Law Journal* 97 (2009): 803–35, 816.

laws violate a constitutional right to privacy (if they do) asserts a moral truth as well as legal truth, and if it fails in one of those ambitions, it fails in the other. That a plaintiff can recover for negligent infliction of emotional distress is true if it ought to be true, and not true if it ought not to be. If it is true (well, if truly true) as a matter of law and pleading, than it simply must be the case that plaintiffs so injured *should be* entitled to recover. This antipositivist way of talking is, after all, the way lawyers talk – and that lawyers talk that way shows that they believe it.

It is, of course, also important to remember the context in which Dworkin made his audacious claim: Dworkin put forward his Herculean arguments about American law's basic justice at a point in time when it was not ridiculous to think that the Supreme Court would be moving the country slowly, but inexorably, and always wisely, toward a closer and closer convergence with Rawlsian justice: with the way the world should look, if we were designing it from scratch with no inkling as to our privilege, generating a fair distribution of resources for all freed of distributions brought on by luck or the accidents of history, shrinking the relative position of the most and the least fortunate among us, and providing maximal individual liberty for all along the way. Dworkin urged lawyers to read Rawls, and urged philosophers to take seriously the arguments of lawyers, and if he succeeded in no other way, he certainly succeeded in both of those ambitions.[61]

The claim, however, that we are approaching a Dworkinian convergence between Rawlsian ideal, and Herculean judicial precedent, either in Fourteenth Amendment jurisprudence or otherwise, is now not just a bad bet but is patently absurd: it will not be Herculean Supreme Court Justices that draw this society to a more Rawlsian understanding of justice, if anyone does. The law – all of those institutional settlements – is moving steadfastly against the direction hoped for and argued for by Rawlsian liberals of the time Dworkin first claimed this harmonic convergence. If *Rawls* is one's guide to what political morality requires – and in a rough way, it was Dworkin's guide to political morality – one must relinquish the dream that the Court's decisions map a course toward it.[62]

The rough sociological evidence – the way lawyers talk – for Dworkin's early claim – that law is what it ought to be and is widely regarded as such – has not changed substantially, or at least there is no indication that it has. Lawyers do still talk, sometimes anyway, as Dworkin claimed in the 1980s: sometimes, lawyers do talk as though the "propositional content" of law is either true or false and that its truth or falsity is in large part a function of its convergence or divergence with the demands of justice.[63] Lawyers do sometimes talk as though a just legal claim is more likely to be

---

[61] See Dworkin, *Taking Rights Seriously* 149.

[62] Dworkin's latest book, *Justice for Hedgehogs*, is moving in this direction. The Court, and judicial review, and constitutional law, have been seriously demoted; in that book, justice is much less tied to the binding precedents of the past as interpreted by Supreme Court Justices and much more tied to ideal social arrangements and rights to those arrangements – such as a right to health care that might follow from them, and quite independent of what prior cases have said on the matter or what current Justices might believe. See Dworkin, *Justice for Hedgehogs* 212.

[63] See Dworkin, *Taking Rights Seriously* 149.

a true legal claim by virtue of that fact, so a true claim of law is therefore more likely to be a just claim of law. Thus, if we think affirmative action is unconstitutional, we do tend to also think it is unjust, and if we view it as just, we are much more likely to argue that it is constitutional. If we think that the Constitution protects reproductive privacy, we likely think as well that it should, and if we think it should, then we tend to think the Constitution does . . . and so on. We tend to think, whatever our view of the Constitution's substantive content, that it converges with requirements of justice. If we are right in so thinking – if we are right in thinking the Constitution is perfectly just, or at least, if we are right in thinking that a right understanding of the Constitution's content is one that is perfectly just, even if we grant the possibility of our own fallibility – then obviously that fact alone evidences the failure of positivism. This is basically how Dworkin understood and presented that fact: that American lawyers tend to talk that way, at least about American constitutional law, evidences the failure of positivism.[64]

It might alternatively, however, evidence not the failure of positivism but rather evidence of the ways in which lawyers are acculturated. We teach law, so to speak, in a heroic and narrative way. Principles and rules are taught through stories, with real-life characters, and with judges as both heroic actors and fair-minded narrators – the judge narrates not just the story of the case but the story of the development of the law.[65] A sympathetic reader will indulge the storyline, and students for very good reasons tend to be sympathetic readers: the ambiguity or conflict in a line of cases is explained by a judge in a narrative fashion, and then resolved in a morally and legally pleasing way, with the judge emerging from his role as narrator into a heroic character in his own drama at the moment of decision. The positivist separation of law and morality is as antithetical to this heroic narrative as it could possibly be: the judge is at best, in a positivist version of this story, a cog in a banally evil legal machine. He may, with the help of positivism, better understand his position, and better understand his moral dilemma, when he faces a true conflict between the demands of law and the requirements of conscience. However, it is a position of relatively little power and even less nobility. It is not a position that underscores the heroism of the judicial role. It is no wonder that positivism is disfavored in a legal regime that is built on the pedagogical and scholarly centrality of the heroic judicial narrative.

The Role of Rights

In this country, at least much of the time, we criticize existing law, when we do, not on the basis of utility, as Bentham and his followers urged us to do, but on the basis of individual rights: a law that invades our rights is a bad law, one that follows from or enforces our rights is a good law. This is as true in the legal academy as

---

[64] *See id.* at 142.
[65] *See* Robin L. West, "Jurisprudence as Narrative," *New York University Law Review* 60 (1985): 145–210, 166.

outside it. When we object to law, whether as individuals or as a part of a political movement, or in our scholarship, it is far more often on the individualistic ground that a law, purportedly in the public interest, has been passed by a legislature or recognized by a court that invades the province of our individual rights, than on the collectivist ground that a law, purportedly in the public interest, simply is not so. We tend to rise up against a law that invades an individual right; in contrast, we only grouse about a law that is simply inefficient or unwise. The former elicits our deepest moral American inner self, the latter offends our inner policy wonk. Thus, if we feel that a law criminalizing abortion conflicts with our right to privacy, we tend to think that it is therefore a truly immoral law, not just, all things considered, one that is just not so good. If a law criminalizing the sale of organs conflicts with our right to bodily sovereignty, we believe it is therefore immoral, not just dumb. If a law criminalizing high-interest loans or low-wage employment conflicts with our right to contract, it is therefore wrong, not just unwise. If a law mandating separate schools for races or sexes conflicts with our right to be treated in a nondiscriminatory manner, it is deeply immoral, rather than unsound. If a law that forbids the sale or ownership of pornography or erotic literature or anarchist tracts or communist propaganda invades our right of independent thought, it is deeply wrong rather than annoying. And so forth. We have *rights* that protect our individual autonomy, privacy, and individual projects, and laws that invade those rights are therefore immoral, and deeply so. Rights-based critiques of law thus seemingly stand as a vital form of just the "censorial critique" Bentham called for, although they use a different critical metric than the utilitarian one for which he argued: the censorial rights critic criticizes on the basis of individual rights rather than on the basis of collective utility. Criticize, though, the rights devotee surely does, and often with profound effect. There is no reason to think that some of those rights devotees are not also legal positivists: the law that is, is different from the law that ought to be, with the law that ought to be being the law that is consistent with our rights. Is not the presence, and vitality, of rights-based legal criticism, therefore, both in the academy and the general culture, a counterexample to the claim made earlier, that censorial jurisprudence has virtually disappeared, at least in the United States, as a positivist jurisprudential project?

In the next chapter of this book, and elsewhere, I argue that as a genre of political critique, rights-based criticism of law comes with costs that are substantial and often hidden. Some of those costs were explored in the 1980s in the various critiques of rights that were produced by the critical legal studies movement[66] and by some communitarian legal scholars.[67] A full understanding of the effect of rights discourses, and particularly of rights-based legal criticism, I believe, is a part of the substantial unfinished business of both of those prematurely aborted critical movements in the

---

[66] *See generally* Mark Tushnet, "An Essay on Rights," *Texas Law Review* 62 (1984): 1363–1404; Morton J. Horwitz, "Rights," *Harvard Civil Rights–Civil Liberties Law Review* 23 (1988): 393–405; Mary Ann Glendon, *Rights Talk: The Impoverishment of Political Discourse* (New York: The Free Press, 1991).

[67] *See* Glendon, *Rights Talk* and Michael J. Sandel, *Democracy's Discontent: America in Search of a Public Philosophy* (Cambridge: Belknap Press, 1998).

legal academy. In chapter three, I address that unfinished business in some detail.[68] Here, I want to make a much more limited point, which is simply that rights-based legal criticism in the legal academy – the criticism of law on the basis of rights – has not thrived *as a positivist project*. It has not, in fact, developed as a form of censorial jurisprudence that simply uses rights as a deontological baseline for the criticism of law, rather than utility as a consequentialist one, against the law or legal regime that is the subject of the critique. It *could* – there is nothing about the nature of rights or the nature of legal positivism that precludes this partnership – but it has not. We do not have a body of scholarship arguing that laws criminalizing abortion or same-sex marriage or ownership of guns or of pornography violate the right of autonomy or dignity or equality, and so forth. We do, of course, have large bodies of scholarship arguing that those laws violate various constitutional provisions, and hence various constitutional rights, but that is not the same thing. The latter type of scholarship criticizes some particular law on the basis of some other more general, more foundational, higher, more permanent, more quintessentially American, or simply more basic law, but nevertheless, law. It is not, generically, exemplary of a body of thought, critical of law on the basis of a moral baseline. Thus, it is not generically an example of censorial jurisprudence, although it is plenty sufficiently "censorial" or critical. It is not, to put it as stated earlier, a part of a positivist critical stance toward existing law.

That a rights-based critique of law has not developed as a positivist (rather than constitutional) project, I urge in a moment, has had consequences for censorial jurisprudence quite generally. First, however, a prior question: why hasn't it? Why do we not have a body of positivist, legal scholarship that fits the parameters described earlier: criticism of positive law on the basis of a moral claim of right? The major reason, I believe, is this: a criticism of existing law based on a claim of right, here, seamlessly, and virtually instantaneously, becomes a criticism of existing law based not simply on a moral right, but also on a claimed *constitutional* right. Once that occurs – once the moral right has been folded into a constitutional claim – the criticism of law, whatever its merit, has lost its positivist valence: it has become, rather, a criticism of an ordinary law based on constitutional law.[69] In much of our discourse, both in the legal academy and outside of it, there is no "light," in other words, no space, between moral criticism of law based on a claimed right, and legal criticism of that law based on constitutional right. The claimed right is presumed to be grounded, somehow, even if the Court does not think so, in the Constitution – maybe in the lost Constitution, maybe in an evolving Constitution, maybe in the Framer's Constitution, maybe in the perfect Constitution, but somewhere, somehow, in the

---

[68] Chapter Three, *infra*.

[69] *See* Robin L. West, "Unenumerated Duties," *University of Pennsylvania Journal of Constitutional Law* 9 (2006): 221–261; Robin L. West, "Katrina, the Constitution, and the Legal Question Doctrine," *Chicago-Kent Law Review* 81 (2006): 1127–72.

Constitution. The rights critic in the legal academy is rarely content with the austere claim that the violated right stems from morality alone.

So, to return to the examples given earlier, if a "pro-choice" critic of abortion law notes, or just believes, that a law criminalizing abortion violates a right to privacy, and is for that reason a bad law, then she almost invariably believes, notes, or argues that the law violates the Fourteenth Amendment for that very reason; if I have a "right to privacy," then that right must be perfectly or imperfectly embedded in the Fourteenth Amendment, so if I have a right to privacy that is invaded by a law criminalizing abortion, then I have a constitutional right that is likewise invaded.[70] The law criminalizing abortion, then, is both a *bad* law, because it violates a moral right to privacy, and is unconstitutional to boot – and is therefore not a law at all. Thus, the criticism of the criminalization of abortion on the basis of the rights such criminalization invades becomes an argument about the Constitution's content, which, if one is correct in the constitutional assertion, invalidates the law.[71] What becomes crucial, then, to the pro-choice critic's argument is that the Constitution has this contested content. So, at that point, where that becomes the issue – what is the content of the Constitution, does it or does it not contain a right to privacy – the critique of the law that criminalizes abortion on the basis of the violation of privacy (or autonomy or dignity or equality), whatever its merits, is no longer a positivist critique: it is no longer a criticism of the law on the basis of a moral baseline (rights). It is instead a criticism of a law on the basis of a different law, the Constitution, which invalidates it. The problem is not the law. The problem is the erroneous assertion that law can inhibit one's choice to procure an abortion.

The same is true of the other examples recited earlier. The late nineteenth-century–early-twentieth-century libertarian critic of a minimum wage law or maximum hour law might well have believed that such a law violates a right to decisional autonomy, or freedom to contract, or personal liberty. That claim, however, not only in our constitutional case law but also in constitutional scholarship of the period, might well have in turn bolstered the claim that the law was unconstitutional because of that invasion. The actual argument, however, from that point forward, both on the Court and off the Court, became about whether the Constitution contained such a right, whether the Constitution embraced Mr. Herbert Spencer's *Social Statistics*,[72]

---

[70] For a recent example, *see, e.g.,* Reva Siegel's work on dignity as the grounds for abortion rights. She argues not only that the criminalization of abortion violates an interest in human dignity but that the interest in human dignity is also reflected in constitutional clauses, so that the criminalization of abortion likewise violates those constitutional rights. Reva Siegel, "Dignity and the Politics of Protection: Abortion Rights under Casey/Carhart," *Yale Law Journal* 117 (2008): 1694–1800.

[71] It is difficult, perhaps impossible, to find a pro-choice advocate who believes that the Constitution does not contain a right to privacy, even though the latter claim is quite conventional and probable, as a matter of constitutional interpretation, and the former political claim is entirely ordinary. *See* Robin West, "From Choice to Reproductive Justice: De-Constitutionalizing Abortion Rights," *Yale Law Journal* 118 (2009): 1394–1432.

[72] *See Lochner*, 198 U.S. at 75 (Holmes, J., dissenting).

whether it was based on an economic theory the country did not believe,[73] and so on. It was not about whether the Constitution should embrace those social statistics or should be based on that economic theory no matter what the country believed. Furthermore, for a couple of decades, the Court held that the Constitution did indeed contain such a right, until it quite famously or infamously found, in the late 1930s, that in point of fact it did not.[74] For the rest of the century, constitutional scholars continued to debate the proposition that the Constitution does or does not invalidate redistributive or paternalistic labor legislation.[75] That debate, however, whatever its merits, was clearly not about whether the laws that prohibit contracting for labor under a certain wage violate rights to personal autonomy, however described. The debate was about whether or not the Constitution prohibits such laws. The claim that such laws violate rights of autonomy, in other words, lost its positivist logic and its positivist valence once it became an argument taken over by the Supreme Court: it was not a claim about the value of a law – the minimum wage law – on the basis of a moral baseline of critique – a personal right to autonomy. It became, for virtually the entire century, an argument about the content of the Constitution.

The recently minted constitutional right to own firearms has the same history. Gun control laws may violate personal autonomy rights to own weapons, to defend oneself, to hold off an oppressive sovereign. The claim that they do just that, or at least one of those things, animated early political agitation by gun enthusiasts on this issue in the 1970s.[76] That claim, however, quite early in the evolution of this debate – certainly by the late 1970s or so – was quickly folded into a claim not about the importance of individual gun ownership but, rather, about the content of the Constitution: about whether the Second Amendment extends to individuals, rather than state militias, the right to own weapons.[77] For thirty years, a coalition of gun owners seeking to defend their property or selves, hunters seeking greater latitude

[73] *See id.*

[74] *Compare Lochner, Coppage v. Kansas*, 236 U.S. 1 (1915) (invalidating a Kansas statute that prohibited yellow dog contracts because the statute infringed on liberty of contract), *and Adkins v. Children's Hospital*, 261 U.S. 525 (1923) (finding federally imposed women's minimum wage requirements violated liberty of contract), *with Nebbia v. New York*, 291 U.S. 502 (1934) (upholding New York's regulation of the milk prices), *and West Coast Hotel Co. v. Parrish*, 300 U.S. 379 (1937) (upholding women's minimum wage legislation in Washington State).

[75] *See generally* Dworkin, *Taking Rights Seriously*; Richard A. Epstein, *Takings: Private Property and the Power of Eminent Domain* (Cambridge: Harvard University Press, 1985); Epstein, "A Theory of Strict Liability," *Journal of Legal Studies* 2 (1973): 151–204; Richard A. Posner, *Federal Courts: Crisis and Reform* (Cambridge: Harvard University Press, 1985); Elisabeth M. Landes, "The Effect of State Maximum Hours Laws on the Employment of Women in 1920," *Journal of Political Economy* 88 (1980): 476–94; Henry P. Monaghan, "Our Perfect Constitution," *New York University Law Review* 56 (1981): 353–96; Cass R. Sunstein, "Lochner's Legacy," *Columbia Law Review* 87 (1987): 873–918; Sunstein, "Naked Preferences and the Constitution," *Columbia Law Review* 84 (1984): 1689–1732.

[76] *See* Sanford Levinson, "The Embarrassing Second Amendment," *Yale Law Journal* 99 (1989): 637–60; Levinson, "The Historians? Counterattack: Some Reflections on the Historiography of the Second Amendment," in *Guns, Crime, and Punishment in America*, ed. Bernard E. Harcourt (New York: New York University Press, 2003) 91.

[77] *See* Levinson, "The Embarrassing Second Amendment" 644; Randy E. Barnett, "Foreword: Guns, Militias, and Oklahoma City," *Tennessee Law Review* 62 (1995): 443–60, 451.

in the weapons they could own, and politically radical right-wing militia enthusiasts argued that the Constitution's Second Amendment protects their individual right to own guns, in the face of a solid wall of Supreme Court and lower court decisional law to the contrary. That argument, however, was overwhelmingly about the content of the Constitution, rather than the merits of the rights-based argument. Again, whatever the merits of the latter argument, it was no longer a positivist one: it was no longer an argument about the value of a law as judged against an independent moral metric. It was and is no longer an argument about the value of the law as weighed against a moral right; it is, rather, an argument about the validity of a law as weighed against a constitutional counterweight.

The right to own and sell pornography, erotica, or obscenity has the same trajectory. There may be a moral right, based on personal autonomy, to own or sell sexually explicit materials, even in the face of state interests in forbidding it.[78] There may be, on the other hand, a moral right to be free of such material, if pornography has a substantial role to play in the subordination of women.[79] The debate over whether there are such individual moral rights to autonomy or equality, and which should trump the other as a matter of political morality, was quickly drowned out in this country (not in England) by the constitutional debate into which it was almost immediately folded, as soon as the debate hit these shores: whether there is a First Amendment right to own pornography that is broader or narrower than the Supreme Court had held in its earlier obscenity jurisprudence, or whether there is a Fourteenth Amendment equality right to be free of it that might inform and bolster the state's interest in forbidding it, or permitting a civil cause of action for damages in the face of it.[80] Whatever the merits of the latter argument, it is not an argument about the merits or demerits of a law, as measured against an independent moral metric: a right to autonomy on the one hand or a right to equality on the other, that a law prohibiting the sale or purchase of pornography might further or frustrate. It is, rather, an argument about the content of the First Amendment.

The same is true of debates over gay marriage. The claimed right that same-sex couples have a right to marry is now in the process of being constitutionalized, so to speak, by the claim that the Fourteenth Amendment contains such a right. The idea that we have such a right as a matter of political morality has become

---

[78] *See* David Copp, *Pornography and Censorship* (Amherst: Prometheus Books, 1983) 15–47; Sarah Ruddick, "On Sexual Morality," *Moral Problems: A Collection of Philosophical Essays*, 3rd ed., ed. James Rachels (New York: Harper and Row, 1971) 85.

[79] *See id.*; Walter Berns, "Pornography vs. Democracy: The Case for Censorship," *Public Interest* 22 (1971): 3–25; Catharine A. MacKinnon, "Pornography, Civil Rights, and Speech," *Harvard Civil Rights–Civil Liberties Law Review* 20 (1985): 1–70, 50; David A. J. Richards, "Free Speech and Obscenity Law: Toward a Moral Theory of the First Amendment," *University of Pennsylvania Law Review* 123 (1974) 45–90, 48.

[80] *See* Richards, "Free Speech and Obscenity Law" 75; Catharine A. MacKinnon, *Only Words* (Cambridge: Harvard University Press, 1996) 77; Ronald Dworkin, "Is There a Right to Pornography?" *Oxford Journal of Legal Studies* 1 (1981): 177–212, 195; Robin L. West, "The Feminist-Conservative Anti-Pornography Alliance and the 1986 Attorney General's Commission on Pornography Report," *American Bar Foundation Research Journal* 12 (1987): 681–711, 710.

basically indistinguishable from the claim that we have a constitutional right as a matter of law.[81] The right to sexual liberty – the moral right to engage in victimless sexual conduct – likewise became first entwined with, then indistinguishable from, and then simply drowned out by the constitutional claim that laws against sodomy violate various constitutional provisions. The right to be free of state-sponsored segregation has the same history: it became almost from the moment of its inception not just a moral right but a constitutional right to be free of de jure segregation, and a paradigmatic constitutional right at that. In all of these cases, the moral right and the argument that might support it – a claimed right to some conduct or mode of treatment that might be a basis for criticism of an existing law – becomes in short order a claimed constitutional right, and in all of these cases, the positivist argument – that a law is a bad law because it violates a moral right – becomes a quite different and decidedly nonpositivist argument altogether: precisely because the law violates a moral right, it therefore violates a constitutional norm, and is therefore not a law at all. The immoral law then is not a law at all, by virtue of the tour through the Constitution. Whatever claim that is, it is not a positivist one.

There are a few exceptions to this trend, but only a few. Judith Thomson authored a powerful libertarian deontological rights-based argument against the criminalization of some abortions, to take just one example, and she did not have the Constitution in mind when she did so.[82] More recently, Eileen McDonagh has broadened and deepened that claim, and although she has made nods toward the Constitution, and clearly believes that the argument has a constitutional correlate, she is not wedded to it; her argument for legal abortion and abortion funding does not turn on whether the right can be located in the Constitution or any of its parts.[83] Plenty of gay rights activists have argued for a right to marry without reliance on Constitutional claims.[84] Integrationists pushed against segregation on the basis of moral rights and as a matter of right and wrong before formulating a constitutional strategy, much less winning in court.[85] Nevertheless, both the logical and even the psychological

---

[81] *See* Chai Feldblum, "Gay Is Good: The Moral Case for Marriage Equality and More," *Yale Journal of Law and Feminisim* 17.1 (2005): 139–184, 143–5; Feldblum, "Sexual Orientation, Morality, and the Law: Devlin Revisited," *University of Pittsburgh Law Review* 57.2 (1996): 237–336. There is some evidence that marriage equality activists have begun to see the costs of rights rhetoric and are attempting to shift the ground. *See, e.g.,* "Talking Points about Marriage and Relationship Recognition," *aclu.org,* including in its "Things to Avoid" list for advocates the following advice: "DON'T talk about marriage as a "right," a "civil right" or a package of "benefits" (instead, talk about the security and legal protections of marriage that committed couples need to take care of each other)."

[82] *See* Judith Jarvis Thomson, "A Defense of Abortion," *Philosophy & Public Affairs* 1 (1971): 47–66.

[83] *See* Eileen L. McDonagh, *Breaking the Abortion Deadlock: From Choice to Consent* (Oxford: Oxford University Press, 1996) 115.

[84] *See, e.g.,* Mary E. Becker, "Family Law in the Secular State and Restrictions on Same-Sex Marriage: Two Are Better than One," *University of Illinois Law Review* 1 (2001): 1–56.

[85] *See* Mark Tushnet, "New Histories of the Private Law of Slavery," *Cardozo Law Review* 18 (1996): 301–8, 302; *see also* Gerald N. Rosenberg, *The Hollow Hope: Can Courts Bring About Social Change?* (Chicago: University of Chicago Press, 2008) 139 (arguing that Martin Luther King., Jr. urged African Americans not to rely on the courts and litigation to bring about social change).

compulsion, in this country, that a purely moral argument based on a moral right simply must imply a legal argument based on a constitutional right is powerful. It is hard to buck it. The Constitution is so morally pervasive in our legal culture, and its claims are so near-infinitely malleable, and its permanence so incontestable, that the Constitution simply sucks us all in. It is a two-step process. First, arguments against overly intrusive state regulations, as well as arguments for greater state regulation to correct for gross maldistributions of wealth or to promote social goods – health, education, and so on – tend to be framed in terms of individual rights, rather than, as Bentham would have preferred, in terms of utility. Gun control laws, some say, violate rights of self-sovereignty; antiabortion laws, according to others, violate rights of autonomy; segregatory laws violate rights to be treated as an equal; the lack of a legal regime that guarantees health care, say others, violate rights to health; the lack of high-quality education in much of the country violates rights to equality or rights that attend to privileges of citizenship. Rights-based arguments against existing laws are by no means in short supply. Those arguments, however, particularly in legal literature, quickly – often instantaneously – become arguments not about the moral right violated by the law, but about the content of the Constitution: gun laws violate the true meaning of the Second Amendment or the Fourteenth or First, abortion laws likewise, and so on. Once that occurs, the question has become a legal question rather than a political question, ripe, perhaps, for adjudication – a fact that by itself has far-reaching repercussions, which I have explored elsewhere.[86] My point here, however, is simply that once this occurs, the question has also become a question about our legal history, our case law, our traditions, and our precedent. Most grandly, it has become a question about what it means to be an American, as evidenced by the Constitution. Minimally, however, it has become a question of law. It is no longer a question about the *value* of a law, as measured against an independent nonlegal moral metric.

What is the consequence? The consequence of this is simply that one of the most powerful and in some ways distinctively American way of criticizing law on moral grounds – by reference to individual rights – has a pronounced tendency to become, in its representations in legal scholarship and advocacy both, not an exercise of moral deliberation but an exercise in legal deliberation – and therefore, eventually, an exercise for lawyers and judges, and one in which they relatively quickly claim expertise. When Americans complain on inchoate or articulated deontological grounds that a law violates rights, and then seek to ground the claim in something other than unadorned moral passion, we – meaning all of us, not just legal scholars, but also meaning legal scholars most emphatically – grope, almost instinctively, for the Constitution as the ground on which we want to make our stand. We do not reach for human rights, or Kantian rights, or universal rights, or

[86] *See* Robin West, "Unenumerated Duties," *University of Pennsylvania Journal of Constitutional Law* 9 (2006): 221–62.

cosmopolitan rights based on our bare "naked humanity." We reach, rather, for constitutional rights. This tilts our moral and political arguments toward the legal, obviously, but also, and only seemingly paradoxically, toward both the historical and the mythic: once the issue becomes *legalized* in a literal sense, and particularly once lawyers take the reins of the argument, it is about what the framers intended with respect to the Second or Fourteenth or Tenth Amendment, or what the court said or did not say in *Pierce*,[87] *Meyer*,[88] *Griswold*,[89] and so on, rather than what we, as a country, or as a state, or community should be doing about guns or segregated schools or the criminalization of abortion, or a federalist system of government. Inside the courtroom these arguments quickly become about precedent, and the meaning of various constitutional clauses. Outside the courtroom and the briefs – in what scholars are now calling popular constitutional space[90] – these constitutional arguments are also in a sense about a history, our constitutional history, that blurs with the mythic, and one toward which we take an almost religious or reverential attitude. Popular constitutional debate is indeed a debate about what the law is, but it is in a different register: it concludes with legal claims but is premised on claims about who we are, as Americans, given our mythic history, and what we are fated to be. Either on or off the court, constitutional argument is, at its hoary heights, a debate about our identity, as defined for us by our "founding" documents.[91] Yet whether we regard this debate – the debate about the Constitution's contents – as a debate about a matter of historical fact, or a matter of mythic fate, it is clear what it is *not*: it is not a debate about the value of the law by reference to an independent moral metric. It is not a debate about whether a contested law is a good law or a bad law by reference to a measure of goodness, or what we should do about it, if it is a bad law. It is a debate about who we are based on the path we have traveled, and who we are not, and what we must do, if we hold true to our sworn allegiance to both our ancestors and our Constitution. It is not a debate about what we should do, premised on a shared understanding that we even have a choice in the matter. Rather, it is a debate about who we are, and therefore what we must do to be true to ourselves. The popular constitutional debate seeks, and posits the existence of, a revelatory resolution to whatever question has been posed, not a political one and

---

[87] *See Pierce v. Society of Sisters of the Holy Names of Jesus and Mary*, 268 U.S. 510 (1925) (holding that Oregon's Compulsory Education Act, requiring attendance at public schools, violated the Fourteenth Amendment).

[88] *See Meyer v. Nebraska*, 262 U.S. 390 (1923) (holding that Nebraska's statute placing prohibitions on the teaching of and in non-English languages violated the Fourteenth Amendment).

[89] *See Griswold v. Connecticut*, 381 U.S. 479 (1965) (holding that a Connecticut law prohibiting the use of contraceptives violated the Fourteenth Amendment).

[90] Larry D. Kramer, "Popular Constitutionalism, Circa 2004," *California Law Review* 92 (2004): 959–1012; *see also* Robert Post and Reva B. Siegel, "Popular Constitutionalism, Departmentalism, and Judicial Supremacy," *California Law Review* 92 (2004) 1027–44.

[91] *See* Reva B. Siegel, "Constitutional Culture, Social Movement Conflict and Constitutional Change: The Case of the De Facto Era," *California Law Review* 94 (2006): 1323–1419, 1341; Robin L. West, "Constitutional Culture or Ordinary Politics: A Reply to Reva Siegel," *California Law Review* 94 (2006):1465–86, 1484.

certainly not a moral one. Censorial jurisprudence it is not, even of a deontological sort.

The Moral Costs and Benefits of Costs-Benefits Analysis

One familiar way that many of us – particularly those of us who are social scientists, economists, and public policy experts – criticize law, or a proposed law, both in legal scholarship and elsewhere – such as in think tanks and in administrative agencies – is by reference to the law's potential costs and benefits. What are the costs of a law, proposed law, regulation, or proposed change in regulations, what are its benefits, and do the former outweigh the latter? If so, then do not do it. This looks promising, and it certainly looks positivist: costs and benefits are "external" to law. Cost-benefit analysis, then, appears to be a counterexample to the general claim I have propounded in this chapter – to wit, that we lack a legal positivist, censorial jurisprudence. Is it? I think not.

As a large body of philosophical and economic literature can now attest, cost-benefit analysis is by no means as straightforward as it sounds: it is not obvious what a "cost" or "benefit" is – either in terms of definitions or simply in terms of what the phrase cost might or might not cover.[92] It is not clear, for example, in fact it is hotly contested, whether the costs of a proposed law or regulation protecting air quality should include, for example, the discounted value of the enjoyment of life someone who might live a hundred years from now might experience pursuant to a regulation that thereby constrains consumer choice as a cost, or the enjoyment of the enhanced air quality as a benefit, or whether a law passed to promote workplace safety should include as a cost of the law the forgone wages of the worker who would prefer the heftier paycheck to the safety rule passed for his benefit that depletes the amounts his employer might spend on wages, or whether a law that provides for compensation for injuries should include the emotional cost to a parent of losing a child to a miscarriage, or the economic cost of that would-be child's future income, or whether it should be offset by the cost the parents would have borne raising that child. Likewise, it is not obvious whether a "benefit" should include only tenuous benefits to only hypothetical people, or even quite real benefits to people in far-flung places around the globe, or benefits that cannot easily be quantified or monetized and so on. It is not clear whether the subjective and immeasurable feelings of satisfaction or satiation of desire should be measured as benefits by reference to foregone opportunities for market transactions that can be monetized, or whether

---

[92] *See* Lisa Heinzerling and Frank Ackerman, *Priceless: On Knowing the Price of Everything and the Value of Nothing* (New York: The New Press, 2005); Matthew D. Adler, "Incommensurability and Cost-Benefit Analysis," *University of Pennsylvania Law Review* 146.5 (1998): 1371–1418; Adler, "Fear Assessment: Cost-Benefit Analysis and the Pricing of Fear and Anxiety," *Chicago-Kent Law Review* 79.3 (2004): 977–1054; Adler and Eric A. Posner, *New Foundations of Cost-Benefit Analysis* (Cambridge: Harvard University Press, 2006); Madison Powers and Ruth Faden, *Social Justice: The Moral Foundation of Public Health and Health Policy* (Oxford: Oxford University Press, 2006); Mark Kelman, "Choice and Utility," *Wisconsin Law Review* 1979.3 (1979): 769–98.

costs and benefits that will be borne by affected but not yet born parties in future generations should be discounted, and if so by how much. It is not clear whether the subjective costs or benefits of a law or proposed law should be included if they have not been reflected in some kind of outwardly manifested behavior and therefore rendered themselves subject to objective appraisal or tabulation . . . and so on. All of these questions leave particular cost-benefit analyses open to considerable debate, and cumulatively they lead some skeptics to doubt the value of cost-benefit analysis across the board. Nevertheless, even with the debate over the particulars, and the uncertainty surrounding the entire "cost-benefit" enterprise, in many cases, the benefits of a law clearly outweigh the costs, or the costs clearly swamp the benefits, and it is clear that this rough appraisal can give us a way to criticize existing law, as well as proposed law, on the basis of a metric external to the law itself. It is all the more clear that an industry of scholars, as well as administrators and scientists within agencies engage in cost-benefit analysis, and then use the outcomes of those analyses to criticize, reform, or form both law and regulatory regimes. Whatever else it is that cost-benefit analysts are doing when they tally the costs and benefits of a law or a proposed law or regulation and then comment, criticize, or "censor" accordingly, they are not doing any of the variations on the theme delineated earlier: they are not criticizing law on the basis of other law.

Is cost-benefit analysis, therefore, an example of Benthamic "censorial jurisprudence"? To a limited extent, yes, and to that extent I want to endorse it and expand on its possibilities here, and then in considerably more detail in the following chapter. Nevertheless, cost-benefit analysis is not understood as a particularly salient example of positivist jurisprudence that saves positivism from its dour reputation as unduly complacent or as complicit with existing law. It is, rather, identified not with legal philosophy at all, and certainly not with moral or political philosophy. It is identified methodologically with economics and with law and economics. It is not perceived as a natural outgrowth of philosophical legal positivism, nor do legal positivists themselves show a particular interest in – much less pride of ownership over – this thriving form of legal analysis.

That alone is puzzling, and requires explanation: there is no question but that cost-benefit analysis is a cousin of Benthamic utilitarianism. Bentham, as do cost-benefit analysts today, sharply distinguished the content of law from its merit and sought to evaluate the latter by reference by an external metric – utility – which, he thought, could be subjected to fairly rigorous, and arithmetic, tabulation. Cost-benefit analysts do likewise – they sharply distinguish the content of a law or proposed law from its merit, and then seek to evaluate the law by reference to an external metric – the law's costs and benefits. Why, then, is cost-benefit analysis not the core of contemporary legal positivism? Why is it not understood as, and practiced as, the contemporary equivalent of Bentham's censorial jurisprudence?

There is one crucial difference, which I believe, in an inchoate and rarely articulated way, accounts for the discontinuity. For Bentham, censorial jurisprudence meant *moral* criticism *on moral grounds* of existing law. Bentham believed, as did many of his contemporaries, that the subjective "utility" that he thought law, like any willed act, should further, was a moral good, and that the subjective suffering, pain, or disutility that he thought law, or any willed act, should minimize was a moral harm. Utilitarianism, therefore, provided a *moral* metric of criticism of existing law. Mill, who modified virtually every aspect of Benthamic utilitarianism believed that happiness and suffering (rather than felt pleasure or pain), were better measures of moral worth, for reasons he put forward in his essay on utilitarianism, but otherwise, he quite famously followed Bentham to the letter on the more basic point: for *both* men, not just Bentham, utilitarianism was a moral account of what we should do with the power we have,[93] because of the moral measure of our well-being, as determined by a quantum of pleasure (for Bentham) and happiness (for Mill), or pain (for Bentham), and suffering (Mill). These qualities – pain, pleasure, suffering, happiness – were, the utilitarians believed, the central hedonic measures of the moral value of law, and of a law. The infliction of pain or suffering is immoral because suffering is a moral harm; likewise the provision of happiness or pleasure is morally good, because happiness and pleasure are themselves moral goods. Every agent with power in the world *should* aim to use his or her power to increase happiness and decrease pain and suffering, because this is what it means to be moral.

Bentham (not Mill) also believed, and again quite famously, and, perhaps, wrongly, that these moral harms and moral goods could be quantified – that they could be added, subtracted, and compared in an arithmetic way, thus rendering the moral criticism of law, as well as the moral criticism of any other act, rational and quasi-scientific. Add the utiles occasioned by a law, and subtract the disutiles. If the difference is positive, then you *should* enact the law if you have the power to do so, and if the difference is negative, then you should not. The moral decision that emerges is decidedly *calculating*.[94] Nevertheless, the subjective utility that for Bentham was the linchpin of censorial jurisprudence was a *moral* metric. A law that fails the test of utility is an immoral law; it is one that *ought not to be* enacted. The claim of "censure" built on the utilitarian-positivist calculus, then, was a moral censure, no matter how calculating its premise: it was a claim about the way law ought to be, based on a moral claim about what lawmakers and all other agents ought to do. And, it was a moral claim because of the nature of that which is to be minimized or maximized: pain, suffering, pleasure or human happiness. What the lawmaker ought to do is minimize the subjective suffering of all affected parties. The way to ascertain whether an act did so was in part through the application of pragmatic worldly knowledge. It was also, though, through the exercise of the moral sense: sympathy with the subjective well-being of others. Pain and pleasure yoke us to what we will do as well as what we ought to do, Bentham famously declared. It

93 Mill, *Utilitarianism*; Robin West, "The Other Utilitarians," *Analyzing Law: New Essays in Legal Theory*, ed. Brian Bix (Oxford: Clarendon Press, 1998) 197–222.
94 Bentham, *An Introduction to the Principles of Morals and Legislation*.

does not yoke us to the selfish or egotistic furtherance of our *own* pains and pleasures exclusively. That he never said, and did not believe. Through sympathetic engagement with the subjective lives of others, through the moral sense, these masters of all we do – pain and pleasure – yoke us to the moral demand that we act in the interest of all affected by our decisions, and not just ourselves.

Cost-benefit analysis is indeed a cousin of Benthamic utilitarianism, but it is a distant cousin, and the distance between them is both often overlooked and important. Let me start, though, with what they share, with the case for the consanguinity. Basically, the similarity is just this: cost-benefit analysis has famously, or infamously, held fast to the scientific ambitions of Bentham's utilitarianism. Like Bentham, cost-benefit analysts quantify and calculate, and like Bentham, they do so toward the end of rendering objective and mathematical what otherwise seems incalculable: the measure of a law's value to the affected community. Cost-benefit analysis in virtually all of its formulations aims for a way to understand the costs and benefits of a law, regulation, or act by reference to objective and observable criteria – such as a choice of a consumer or actor in an open market to spend money, to buy or sell a product at a particular price, or to take or offer a job at a certain wage – that can itself be quantified (whether or not commodified) so as to be tallied and compared arithmetically with competing costs or benefits.

The difference, however, too often overlooked in accounts of the continuities between Benthamic utilitarianism and cost-benefit analysis, is that the "cost" to be minimized, on modern cost-benefit analysis, is *not* subjective pain or suffering, and the benefit to be maximized is not subjective pleasure or happiness. Cost-benefit analysis, in other words, does not aim to maximize either the pleasures sought by Bentham or the happiness sought by Mill and does not aim to minimize either the pain feared by Bentham or the unhappiness or suffering described by Mill. Rather, a cost is understood as something that is manifested behaviorally and measured objectively. *Pain itself* is not understood as the cost of something that gets ascertained in cost-benefit analysis, although of course, pain may be reflected *in* a cost, such as in a lost wage, if pain prompts discontinuance of work; or in a purchased painkiller, if it prompts a pharmaceutical purchase; or in a forgone opportunity (that can itself be measured). The "benefit," likewise, is not pleasure or happiness but rather their objectively measurable manifestations.

The genesis of this divergence between the subjective, hedonic goals of the utilitarianism trumpeted by Bentham and Mill – the minimization of suffering and pain, and the maximization of pleasure and happiness – from the objective goal of cost-benefit analysis – maximization of benefits, minimization of costs – may be the discovery, in mid-twentieth-century economic thought, of purported insurmountable conceptual and epistemological barriers to the sensible comparison of interpersonal utilities. Those barriers render the subjective hedonic goals of the nineteenth-century utilitarians simply incoherent: if it is simply not possible to contrast coherently, and therefore balance, one person's subjective pain against another's subjective happiness, then it will not be possible to maximize subjective happiness or minimize subjective pain.[95] From that point (mid-twentieth century) on, the search was on, so to speak, for objective proxies for human well-being: market choices, preference curves, efficiency calculations, and so on. What was gained in this transition from Bentham, from hedonic utilitarianism to objective cost-benefit analysis, one might say, was some measure of quantification. That is the "benefit" I have referred to in the title of this subsection of cost-benefit analysis. Costs and benefits, by definition, can be quantified and measured, particularly if they are defined as that which can be quantified and measured and defined so as to exclude that which is immeasurable.

What has been lost, in this migration from the hedonic goals of the utilitarians, to the objective goals of the cost-benefit analysts? Well, once the focus shifts to objectively measurable costs and benefits, pain and pleasure are relegated to the immeasurable and nonquantifiable – that which cannot be reckoned. If bodies of regulatory and tort law aim to maximize benefits and minimize costs, then all those unmeasurable and therefore unreckoned bodily and emotional pains and pleasures of human beings – once *central* to utilitarianism – are *immediately* marginalized. They just do not exist if they cannot be measured. Second, with the shift to costs and benefits come distinctively political costs, which are almost entirely regressive, and for a simple reason: costs and benefits, unlike pains and pleasures, or suffering and happiness, are sustained by corporations as well as human beings. If the point of law is to minimize costs and maximize benefits, then corporations and the importance of their bottom line are conceptually on a par with human beings: law becomes centrally a humanly created institution, the point of which, however, is to maximize profit, including corporate profit. The focus is off of human beings who bleed, get sick, suffer, feel pain, and die and on to corporate entities that do none of that, as well as on those aspects of human life – egotistic profit maximization – that human beings share with corporate beings. Human biological life is marginalized. The additive result here is that cost-benefit analysis is bound to be more politically regressive than traditional utilitarian calculi that aim to increase happiness and pleasure, rather than "benefits," and to minimize pain and suffering, rather than "costs." Third, the shift blurs a powerful distinctively utilitarian argument for equality as a guiding norm for moderate redistributive principles: the marginal utility of a dollar is subjectively of less hedonic value to a wealthy person than a poor person. Without an appreciation of the basic coherence of this fundamental interpersonal comparison of these utilities, the moral case for redistribution is harder to sustain. For all of these reasons, the progressive political and moral potential of utilitarianism was lost or blurred, as it evolved into cost-benefit analysis.

Here, however, I want to stress a different point, to wit, that as utilitarianism gave way within consequentialist thought to cost-benefit analysis – and as moral philosophy gave way to economics as the discipline that might guide meta-thinking

---

[95] Lionel Robbins, "Interpersonal Comparisons of Utility: A Comment," *The Economic Journal* 48.192 (1938): 635–41.

about the criticism of law – it also lost its claim to being a moral baseline. Unlike pain, and unlike suffering, a "cost" is not something to which human beings have a moral aversion. A cost is not, that is, a *moral* harm. This simple difference between "costs" and "pain" or "suffering" is well reflected in ordinary usage. We do not tend to say to or of someone who we fear is about to inflict on a third party undue or unwarranted or unnecessary suffering: "Oh my God, do not do that – what you are about to do imposes more costs than benefits." If we want to stress the immorality of a proposed course of action, we just do not use cost-benefit analysis; we do not "talk that way," as Dworkin might say. We *do* tend to say "Oh my God, do not do that – you're hurting that person, and for no good reason." *Hurting someone* – causing pain or suffering – just *is* immoral, unless it is justified. A law that hurts people for no reason is immoral for just that reason: it hurts people for no good reason. Imposing costs, however, is just that. It is an imposition of costs. It might or might not be immoral, it all depends. A "cost" is the objective manifestation of some harm that *might be* a moral harm, and the imposition of a cost is an act that *might be* immoral if the cost it imposes is the objective manifestation of that moral harm. However, the imposition of a cost itself carries no particular moral punch one way or the other. A cost imposed on someone, something, or some profit center, unlike the pain felt by another human being, does not trigger a sympathetic, and hence distinctively moral, reaction. The imposition of unwarranted pain is an immoral act, unless justified, the imposition of a cost is something that might or might not occur.

The evolution, then, that happened over a period of several decades, from Benthamic utilitarianism to cost-benefit analysis, was a move from an account of the morality or immorality of action (whether flawed or not) to something very different, namely, a quasi-social scientific way of accounting monetary loss, or preferences, or market choices, or inefficiencies. Costs and benefits, after all, are sustained by artificial entities, no less than human beings: corporations, partnerships, institutions, nation-states. These entities do not suffer, feel pain, or experience happiness; they do not experience moral harms. It is natural human beings who do the latter, and although cost-benefit analysis may include the tabulation of some of those moral harms felt by human beings, it will include much else besides. Cost-benefit analysis, whatever else it is and whatever its usefulness, is *not* a moral critique of law. Perhaps unsurprisingly, then, legal positivists do not generally think of "cost-benefit" analysis as a distinctively positivist project. Its genesis, furthermore, is in public policy analysis and economics; it is not in legal philosophy, moral philosophy, or jurisprudence. It is not censorial jurisprudence.

A Missing Jurisprudence

Do we really lack a censorial jurisprudence? Obviously, as a culture, we have plenty of writing that criticizes existing or proposed law on the basis of nonlegal moral metrics. This is the stuff of politics. Citizens criticize law, proposed law, and the legislators and administrators that would create them on the basis of our felt desires, our freedoms, our needs, and our dreams; all of these criticisms can be and often are rights based, and all of them can be and often are moral critiques. In academic life, moral criticism of law on the basis of nonlegal moral metrics is the stuff of public policy schools, government programs such as the Kennedy School at Harvard, a good bit of applied ethics and applied political theory in the universities, and think tanks. Do we really lack for this stuff?

Yes, we do; in legal scholarship, applied censorial, positivist jurisprudence that criticizes existing law on the basis of moral ideals is peculiarly hard to find. Applied moral reasoning that is philosophically astute is generally understood to be either deontological or consequentialist: acts are evaluated morally either by reference to whether they are the "right thing to do" or by reference to whether they lead to morally good consequences. There are not clear correlates of either in legal scholarship, where the act assessed is the act that leads to a law or regulation. There is plenty of legal scholarship that assesses whether a law violates a constitutional right, and even an idealized constitutional right – a constitutional right that should be recognized by courts but is not. There is much less that assesses whether a law violates or fulfills a moral right, deontologically constructed, or an ideal constitutional right that would not be recognized under any judicial construction of constitutional law. There is some legal scholarship that assesses whether a law or proposed law will entail certain consequences: wealth, a diminution of wealth, efficiency, costs, or benefits. That literature is generally presented as economic rather than philosophical, and as measuring the propensity of the law to entail empirically verifiable, factual consequences, not moral harms or moral goods – pain, suffering, pleasure, or happiness – that might give us a moral reason to sympathetically engage. It assumes a factual rather than moral baseline of criticism. Thus, although there is plenty of scholarship critical of existing law on the basis of other law – constitutional jurisprudence – and plenty of scholarship critical of existing law on the basis of factual baselines – cost-benefit analysis – there is little scholarship that is critical of existing law on the basis of moral argument.

I know this sounds both counterintuitive and counterexperiential. After all, legal scholars criticize law all the time – it is the bread and butter of legal scholarship. Rarely, however, do they do so on the basis of developed moral conceptions of either the moral right or the moral good. As Matt Adler has recently noted, legal scholars – he thinks regrettably – tend not to follow developments in academic moral philosophy.[96] Most of us who might have paid attention earlier stopped with Rawl's *Theory of Justice*,[97] Nozick's *Anarchy, State, and Utopia*,[98] and Smart and

---

[96] Matthew Adler, "On (Moral) Philosophy and American Legal Scholarship," in *On Philosophy in American Law*, Francis J. Mootz, ed. (Cambridge: Cambridge University Press, 2009) 114–21.

[97] John Rawls, *A Theory of Justice* (Cambridge, MA: Belknap Press, 1971).

[98] Robert Nozick, *Anarchy, State, and Utopia* (New York: Basic Books, 1974).

Williams's *Utilitarianism: For and Against*.[99] As Adler shows, and as his own work on egalitarian welfare measures demonstrates, both rights-based and utilitarian moral philosophy have developed in ways that are of obvious relevance to arguments over the value of law and particular laws. There is an entire disciplinary field, then, if Adler is right, that legal scholars are neglecting that seemingly has at least as much relevance to our bread-and-butter work as economics or literature, both of which have been well ploughed. I suggested some reasons above this might be so: American arguments against positivism have directed legal scholars away from the sorts of moral arguments for which legal positivism, and perhaps only legal positivism, peculiarly sets the stage: critique of existing law on the basis of a nonlegal, moral metric. This cannot be the whole story, however: most legal scholars do not follow jurisprudential debates. Beyond arguments over positivism, are there other reasons to explain this? Why do legal scholars, whether or not philosophically inclined, and whether or not interested in positivism, Natural Law, and so on, just reflexively shy away from moral argumentation regarding law?

For some within both the "critical legal community" of the left and the economic libertarian movements on the right, the reason stems from a skepticism regarding not *positivism* but any purported moral metric that positivists might seek to deploy. Thus, many critical scholars – who tend to be positivists themselves – have embraced a moral relativism (or some other moral theory) that leaves only preferences and choices (on the libertarian right) or maldistributions of power (on the left) as a baseline of criticism. The criticisms that either of these baselines can generate is by necessity tepid. For others, particularly within the left-wing critical community, the reluctance to generate moral critiques of law stems from a global Nietzschean antipathy to all forms of moral argumentation, particularly as it pertains to law. For still others, it is because of a more specific skepticism regarding those forms of moral arguments that have had historical impacts on legal scholarship: both rights discourse and utilitarianism, in the twentieth century, have tended to become regressive as they have matured. For libertarians, it stems largely from a sort of residual antipaternalistic skepticism toward legalism based on any claimed moral compass, other than a moral commitment to individual liberty.

Yet what of traditional legal scholarship, where the neglect of moral theory, moral criticism, and the philosophical bases of it, is if anything broader and deeper than that on either the critical left or right? Adler posits simple ignorance as the reason for this – legal scholars are unaware of even the existence of the field of applied moral philosophy, or our taste for multidisciplinarity is on the wane. There's something to that, but again, it just cannot be the whole story – if there was a felt need for sophisticated moral argumentation that would ground legal critique, legal scholars

---

[99] J. J. C. Smart and Bernard Williams, *Utilitarianism: For and Against* (Cambridge: Cambridge University Press, 1973).

would search it out. The fuller explanation, I think, is that law itself is a normative discipline that simply overshadows, in both complexity and completeness, and certainly in its capacity to provide answers, the normative discipline of moral philosophy. The discipline of law provides its own baseline of critique for law. We can criticize some law on the basis of other law. Law in its entirety, in other words, is plenty normative enough: it is full, rich, supple, organic, detailed, and exhaustive. Law has built within it, so to speak, its own normative "pull" – like moral rules, legal rules seemingly provide reasons for acting, as both contemporary natural lawyers and legal positivists (for different reasons, in different ways) all argue. Legal scholars, who tend, like Bentham, not to be anarchic, and who tend, like Bentham and Fuller both, generally to approve of law, may be more inclined than most to find the normativity of law fully sufficient to meet any needs we may have for critical baselines.

Does this matter? Yes. It is a lost opportunity, in two directions. First, as Bentham, his contemporaries, and modern positivists have all claimed, moral argument gives a perspective from which to criticize law that is independent of law itself; as such, it is the basis of both radical and liberal criticism and hence reform. Adler is right to suggest that we should be quite routinely criticizing strict liability rules in tort, or duress and unconscionability conceptions in contract, or the lack thereof, on the basis of moral arguments about the extent of our responsibilities or duties toward each other, or on the basis of moral utilitarianism, or Kantian ethics, and so on, rather than on the basis of legal arguments about the deep underlying structure or commitments of tort and contract law themselves. This should be part of the "bread and butter" of legal scholarship, and if we are to do it well, it would behoove us to take more seriously than we do the recent (as well as classical) writings of ethicists and moral philosophers.

It is a lost opportunity in the other direction as well. We lose not only censorial jurisprudence but also the "legal critic" – the lawyer who criticizes law on the basis of nonlegal moral metrics, and does so toward the basis of reform, and does so, furthermore, as a recognized professional obligation. Just as moral philosophy might enlighten and clarify moral critique of extant law, so knowledge of law and legal process might enlighten moral critique. The lawyer, and legal scholar, should be engaged in processes of legal critique, beyond doctrinal critiques, as a "legal critic." The legal critic – by which I mean the lawyer criticizing law, so as to inform its reform – brings to that work values, knowledge, and discipline that the citizen-critic and the moral philosopher-critic lack.

That the legal critic would bring knowledge to these debates, I think, is self-evident, so let me conclude by saying something about legalist values. Much has been written over the past fifty years on the ways in which law schools strip law students of their preexisting moral values. This has become a cliché of legal-pedagogical reform. I am doubtful that it is the case, although I sympathize with the impulse behind the claim. Whether or not it is the case, however, that law schools rob students of the values or moral beliefs they brought to their education, law schools clearly *impart* values. The law graduate, by virtue of her education, has a pronounced appreciation, for example, of the importance of process to informed debate: the need to hear all sides, to protect and respect the dignity of all participants, the reasons to listen sympathetically to opposing viewpoints rather than combatively, and the importance of both fidelity to principle and common ground: all of this is the woof and weave of everyday classroom pedagogy and dialogue. She also has an understanding, and an appreciation, of the importance of those past "institutional settlements" – the rules given us by precedent, by habit, or by tradition. She should appreciate both the reasons for fidelity to past judgments – the wisdom in deference, the possibilities of reliance and the value of finality and certainty – and their limits: that these are man-made artifacts, the usefulness of which might expire as conditions change. She understands the value of law and the rule of law over chaos or anarchical violence, as well as the dangers of overly intrusive legalism. She has become accustomed to listening to arguments both by and on behalf of the "least of these," whether prisoners on death row or children in underfunded schools, as well as the most powerful. She has learned to balance present felt necessity with long-term interests, goals, and needs, as well as the role of both law and administration in mediating those tensions. She has a sense of the value of private settlement, private rule making, and private negotiation and contracting in social life, as well as their potential dangers. This list could be extended considerably. The point is simply that whatever else might be said of or for or against it, legal education is *not* as it is often claimed to be, "value neutral." It is intensely value laden. Those values, I believe, would well serve the public need for informed moral criticism of both law and its absence.

This, then, is the bottom line cost of the lack of a sustained tradition of censorial jurisprudence in contemporary positivism: the lawyer's professional role, on virtually any accounting, does not commit him to engage in sustained critique of extant law, with the goal of its eventual reform. Lawyers learn to reform law from "within" existing doctrine, so to speak, and learn plenty about the potential for legal reform through constitutional modes of adjudicative litigation. We do not, however, encourage or teach anything about the lawyer's role in the reform of law through more ordinary means of moral and political persuasion. That we do not is also, I believe, unfortunate: lawyers qua lawyers have much to add to reform, and there is no reason we could not systematize and teach what they have to add, as a part of our understanding of a lawyer's professional identity. One means to start building the foundation for doing so would be by recapturing the critical and reformist implications of English legal positivism – which was, after all, the philosophical root of not only massive amounts of English legal reform but of American legal realism – and hence New Deal lawyering – as well.

3

Critical Legal Studies – The Missing Years

The Anglo-American critical legal studies (CLS) movement came to maturity in the late 1970s, motivated, in part, from a sense of dissatisfaction with the state of doctrinal legal scholarship. Legal scholarship, the critical scholars argued, had become deadeningly, deeply conservative, and not in the ordinary sense. That is, it was not conservative because of a contested but defensible view that law-as-it-is is worthy of conservation, or even that law by definition is simply something that must be preserved and defended against all comers. Rather, legal scholarship had become unduly conservative – describing law in such a way as to render it resistant to change, reform, or criticism – for a host of transparently indefensible reasons: a lack of moral and political imagination among legal academics, a felt lack of responsibility for the moral or political consequences of existing law, a complacency bordering on complicity with law's injustices, an unwillingness to do the work or take the risks of arguing for change, more simply, a lazy satisfaction with the status quo, or at best a false belief in the necessity of things staying more or less as they are, with only modest changes in the doctrinal margins up for grabs, as it were.[1] With the possible exception of the American realists of the 1920s and 1930s, there has never before or since been an American academic legal movement so clearly, explicitly, and unapologetically driven by a critical, reformist, and for the most part genuinely radical and left-wing political impulse. The central point of the critical legal studies movement of the 1970s through the mid-1980s was to make the case for fundamental legal change: first, for its possibility, and second, for its moral necessity. The doctrinal law taught in American law schools, the critics claimed, was a substantial hindrance

---

[1] Three classic texts rehearsing the reasons for the moral outrage are Roberto Mangabeira Unger, "The Critical Legal Studies Movement," *Harvard Law Review* 93.6 (1983): 561–675, Duncan Kennedy, "Legal Education as Training for Hierarchy," in *The Politics of Law: A Progressive Critique*, 3rd ed., David Kairys, ed. (New York: Pantheon Books, 1998) 40–61, and Robert Gordon, "New Developments in Legal Theory," *The Politics of Law* 281–93, 289–90.

to that change. The attitude and methods surrounding it, however, were even greater obstacles. Law – particularly common law and constitutional law – is simply neither as necessary nor as justified as believed and taught by the mainstream of legal thought, doctrine, and pedagogy, or so the critics argued.

Virtually every major theoretical and jurisprudential innovation urged by the critical scholars in the 1970s and 1980s was accordingly aimed toward freeing critical thinking about law, by demonstrating either the possibility of or the ethical imperative to engage in radical legal critique and reform. Thus, "deviationist doctrine," and "deviationist lawyering," expressions coined by Roberto Unger, were meant to show the possible use of the master's tools – doctrinal argument and advocacy – as a means for promoting the radical end of furthering the empowerment of subordinated groups in directions and to degrees not contemplated by mainstream doctrinal discourse.[2] The point of deviationist doctrine and the deviationist lawyering needed to unearth it was to find a buried or marginalized egalitarian interpretation of staid legal doctrine and then to find a way to leverage that interpretation into a legal argument for political change that had been at most only dimly glimpsed, if that, by the original craftsmen of the doctrine itself. The promissory estoppel doctrine in contract law, for example, was first introduced into the common law as a means to hold individual promisors, such as grantors to nonprofit organizations, to their unbargained-for "donative" promises on which the promisee had relied in some way. In the hands of critical scholars, it became a possible tool to prevent massive corporate flight out of the country toward lower-wage laborers in Mexico or Asia, if used by radical lawyers with enough imagination: the workers whose jobs are displaced, the argument would proceed, rely to their detriment on an implied albeit unbargained-for promise made by employers that their hard work will be rewarded with economic security.[3] The corporate employers, then, might be estopped by the workers' reliance on their implied donative promise from closing the factory and relocating elsewhere to secure cheap labor. The "indeterminacy critique" likewise, according to the critics who fashioned it, was intended to demonstrate the possibility of finding latent but potentially liberatory meanings in only seemingly unambiguously regressive or oppressive legal declarations. Again using contract law as an example, the claim, ubiquitous in contract law, that the forms and the formalisms of contract increase both the liberty of individuals and their formal equality – all persons, after all, can be promisees or promisors, offerors or offerees, equally and formally, and all persons, not just some classes or statuses, can consent or withhold consent to the exchange of a commodity or labor for something of equal or greater value, at the promisor's discretion and according to his will – can be used to support

[2] Unger, "The Critical Legal Studies Movement" 576–83.
[3] Joseph Singer and Jack M. Beermann, "Baseline Questions in Legal Reasoning: The Example of Property in Jobs," *Georgia Law Review* 23.4 (1989): 911–96.

either free market or regulatory outcomes[4] and hence can be pointed as weapons or tools against the forces of the very capitalist interests that generate and typically profit from these formally equal and liberty-enhancing claims. To take a third example, the critics' multiple claims of "false necessity" were meant to cast an unflattering spotlight on the many ways in which the luminaries of the legal establishment – at least those within the legal academy – convinced themselves and their students that this is the only and hence the best possible world, both legal and otherwise, and that efforts at even imagining change much less implementing it are futile or irrelevant.[5] The critical idea that our doctrinal debates are "truncated" expressed the same insight: mainstream policy analysis, constitutional and common-law "balancing," and incremental or analogical reasoning do little but flatten the moral and political imagination, limiting ethical possibility to narrowly circumscribed and largely inconsequential changes at the margins of social organization.[6] Against the weight of false necessity and truncated thinking, the critics urged the academy and their students to consider the possibility they could use law in a genuinely progressive manner, although to do so, they had to first upend the complacent feeling that all is as it should be or the resigned sense that nothing can be changed, and then spur the confidence to imagine utopian alternatives.[7] The critical scholars' methodological innovations – the deployment of deconstructionist and deviationist lawyering, the arguments for the radical indeterminacy of legal doctrine, the claims of false necessity and truncated analysis – were all aimed toward effectuating this change in consciousness within the legal academy, and hence in the minds of generations of law students, and eventually in the practicing liberal and radical bar. I am going to call these the critics' "jurisprudential claims" – indeterminacy, false necessity, the truncated nature of traditional legal methods, the possibilities of deconstruction, and so on. They were all aimed at showing something important about the nature of doctrinal law and the possibility of achieving radical change: such law is not particularly principled or even lawlike, nor is it deeply embedded in much of anything. Rather, it is considerably less rational and far more plastic than commonly understood.

Virtually all of the remaining signature insights that defined the critical legal studies movement in those two decades were directed at making the moral case for the radical change that the jurisprudential claims showed were possible: for shorthand, a set of claims about the need for radical change that I call the critics' "moral brief." The moral brief in turn had two major dimensions: critical and aspirational. The

---

4 Robert W. Gordon, "Unfreezing Legal Reality: Critical Approaches to Law," *Florida State University Law Review* 15.2 (1987): 195–220, 212–13; Gordon, "New Developments in Legal Theory," *The Politics of Law* 281–93, 289–90.
5 Roberto Mangabeira Unger, *False Necessity: Antinecessitarian Social Theory in the Service of Radical Democracy* (Cambridge: Cambridge University Press, 1987).
6 Unger, "The Critical Legal Studies Movement"; Mark Kelman, *A Guide to Critical Legal Studies* (Cambridge: Harvard University Press, 1987).
7 Gordon, "New Developments" 289–92.

general target of the critical dimension of the moral brief was what was usually called by both the critics and some of their antagonists "liberal legalism": the (allegedly) settled consensus of the legal academic establishment, circa 1970 or so, on the basic wisdom, rationality, and generosity – the general okayedness – of virtually all Anglo-American liberal legal institutions, from the enforcement of contracts against later regretful contractors,[8] to the limits imposed by the negligence regime on tort recovery for accidents,[9] to the enforcement of individual rights against majoritarian will in constitutional law and adjudication.[10] The specific targets, more often than not, of the critics' attack on liberal legalism, were *not* the transparently conservative or free-market legal institutions that quite blatantly permeate wide swaths of our political order but rather, and only seemingly paradoxically, the purportedly "liberal" victories of contemporary legalism; the point being to show that even liberal legalism's most progressive sacred cows – the antidiscrimination norm in constitutional law and employment law, robust free speech doctrine in the First Amendment, and so forth – were complicit in the massive unjust subordination of entire peoples that is effectuated by liberal legal discourse. Thus, for example, the critics propounded a series of arguments intended to show that even our much-lauded (by the left) civil liberties – rights to free speech,[11] rights of arrestees and suspects to Miranda warnings, the protections of the exclusionary rule, and so on[12] – serve primarily to legitimate injustice. Just as the contractual liberty so loved by economic libertarians in fact serves to legitimate the orderings and subordinations effected by the private control of property, so the civil liberties accorded criminal defendants, and loved by civil libertarians, legitimate coercive interrogations,[13] whereas the liberties under the First Amendment legitimate, among much else, both hate speech and the control of information and knowledge by corporate media.[14] None of these "liberties," the critics argued, in fact liberate, or the degree to which they do, if they do, must be offset in a calculation of their overall progressive benefit, against the degree to which they further entrench unjust hierarchical distributions of wealth and social status.

More pervasively, the critics argued, in what will likely prove to be the most enduring contribution of the movement, that the entire panoply of liberal constitutional

---

[8] Duncan Kennedy, "Distributive and Paternalist Motives in Contract and Tort Law, with Special Reference to Compulsory Terms and Unequal Bargaining Power," *Maryland Law Review* 41.4 (1982): 563–658.

[9] Richard L. Abel, "Should Tort Protect Property against Accidental Loss?" *San Diego Law Review* 23 (1986): 79–124.

[10] Mark Tushnet, "An Essay on Rights," *Texas Law Review* 62.8 (1984): 1363–404.

[11] Tushnet, "An Essay on Rights" 1386–92.

[12] Louis Michael Seidman, "Brown and Miranda," *California Law Review* 80 (1992): 673–754; Seidman, "Rubashov's Question: Self-Incrimination and the Problem of Coerced Preferences," *Yale Journal of Law and the Humanities* 2.1 (1990): 149–80.

[13] Seidman, "Rubashov's Question" 164–65, 172.

[14] Mari J. Matsuda, "Public Response to Racist Speech: Considering the Victim's Story," *Michigan Law Review* 87 (1989): 2320–81.

rights – rights to equality, rights to nondiscrimination,[15] and rights to reproductive freedom, including access to abortion, rights to sexual liberty, and rights to privacy – also serve subordinating ends.[16] These judicially created antidiscrimination and privacy rights only seemingly equalize, or liberate. In fact, they alienate us from each other and ourselves, they legitimate massively unjust hierarchies that burden subordinated peoples with a false belief in the necessity as well as justice of their subordination, and they imprison all of us in various doctrinal and ideological straightjackets. The right secured in *Brown v. Board of Education*[17] to desegregated schooling, for example, widely viewed by mainstream legal scholars as the signature and unqualifiedly laudable achievement of the civil rights era, according to the critics, gives individual black children a right against schools segregated by state mandate, but, precisely by so doing, it also legitimates schools segregated by virtue of residential segregation and, more broadly, legitimates virtually all forms of racism other than narrowly defined, de jure, state-generated sorts.[18] More broadly still, it legitimates an only seemingly meritocratic system of reward and punishment across the board, and it does all of this by purging state-sponsored racism from the stew of economic life and then celebrating the pretty unpleasant stench that remains as quintessentially just, because nonracist. The consequence is a yet more effective perpetuation of private and institutional racism as well as continuing economic inequality across the board, insulated against critique by the appearance of fairness – an appearance hugely furthered by the antidiscrimination norm itself. The "right to privacy" likewise gives individuals a right against states that overreach on moralistic grounds – yielding rights to contraception,[19] abortion,[20] same-sex sex,[21] and likely, eventually, same-sex marriage – while at the same time massively and thoroughly legitimating injustice in the private sector, primarily by rhetorically valorizing that privacy within which private injustices occur, and hence state neglect of that injustice. Privacy rights, in effect, give the little people their sexual carnivals, all in the name of a much-celebrated right to privacy and limited government, which then insulates economic as well as sexual private markets from public or democratic

---

[15] Alan Freeman, "Antidiscrimination Law: A Critical Review," *The Politics of Law* 96–116.

[16] Tushnet, "An Essay on Rights"; Morton J. Horwitz, "Rights," *Harvard Civil Rights–Civil Liberties Law Review* 23 (1988): 393–406.

[17] 347 U.S. 483 (1954).

[18] Alan David Freeman, "Legitimizing Racial Discrimination through Antidiscrimination Law: A Critical Review of Supreme Court Doctrine," *Minnesota Law Review* 62.6 (1978): 1049–120. *Cf.* Derrick Bell, "Serving Two Masters: Integration Ideals and Client Interests in School Desegregation Litigation," *Yale Law Journal* 85.4 (1976): 470–517 (arguing that a commitment to integration per se shifted resources away from the fight for substantively adequate education for black students); Bell, "*Brown v. Board of Education* and the Interest-Convergence Dilemma," *Harvard Law Review* 93.3 (1980): 518–33 (arguing that blacks benefit from social and political change only when those changes also benefit whites); Bell, *Faces at the Bottom of the Well: The Permanence of Racism* (New York: Basic Books, 1992) (arguing that racism is constitutive of American culture, rather than anomalous).

[19] *Griswold v. Connecticut*, 381 U.S. 479 (1965).

[20] *Roe v. Wade*, 410 U.S. 113 (1973).

[21] *Lawrence v. Texas*, 539 U.S. 558 (2003).

control, thus perpetuating the economic inequalities those markets generate.[22] The critics' conclusion: the vision of social life that underlies these liberal legal settlements – the broad mural of individuals freely pursuing privately chosen ends, without interference from an overreaching or irrational state, while enjoying the protection of state law against both public authorities that would discriminate irrationally against them and private parties that would invade their rights – is both unjust and ungenerous. It guarantees us at most an alienated and spiritually impoverished world of withdrawn and isolated rights holders. It deprives us of our human entitlement to a nourishing community. At worst, it does so while simultaneously enforcing hierarchic social and legal regimes that routinely, and with only the slightest veneer of duplicitous justification, crush entire populations of subordinated peoples. Liberal legalism purportedly liberates and formally equalizes individuals to lead self-chosen lives of their own device. What it actually does is imprison or subordinate vulnerable people in various private and public markets that deprive life of authenticity, pleasure, and meaning.

Last, there was a now almost entirely forgotten dimension of the critical scholars' moral brief that was not so much critical as visionary, or aspirational. Some of the most original and the most prolific of the critical scholars – notably Roberto Unger and Peter Gabel – were also the most explicitly utopian. Unger and Gabel argued with considerable passion that there are other and *better* ways both to imagine and to organize our social worlds than the alienated forms of socialization represented by the "pact of the withdrawn selves" that we have come to call liberal legalism.[23] Life need not be so anxious, insecure, alienated, isolated, atomistic, and unhappy, as it apparently is under liberal legalist regimes. What liberal legalism gives us, through rights and liberties as well as much else, according to Unger and Gabel, is a life filled with fear of the Other and paranoid anxiety about that Other's desire to rip us off, viewed through the scrim of an illusion or a delusion that our brother will routinely and by nature stab us in the back rather than have our back, and all of that paranoia then drenched with a Lear-like dread of the ever-present possibility of exposure to the elements, should we lose our quest for a chunk of the shrinking pie in our invariably winner-take-all economic system and social life.[24] All of this, Unger and Gabel urged, could be otherwise. Our human nature, Roberto Unger argued in a series of books and articles in the late 1970s and early 1980s, is plastic, or at least

---

[22] Catharine MacKinnon, *Feminism Unmodified: Discourses on Life and Law* (Cambridge: Harvard University Press, 1987) 93–102.

[23] Roberto Mangabeira Unger, *Passion: An Essay on Personality* (New York: The Free Press, 1984); R. Mangabeira Unger, *False Necessity* (New York: Verso, 2004); R. Mangabeira Unger, *Knowledge and Politics* (New York: Free Press, 1975); Peter Gabel, "The Phenomenology of Rights-Consciousness and the Pact of the Withdrawn Selves," *Texas Law Review* 62.8 (1984): 1563–600; Gabel and Duncan Kennedy, "Roll Over Beethoven," *Stanford Law Review* 36.1 (1984): 1–56.

[24] Gordon, "Unfreezing Legal Reality" 207; Peter Gabel, "Book Review: Taking Rights Seriously," *Harvard Law Review* 91.1 (1977): 302–15, 315 ("[M]odern writers in the liberal tradition . . . defend a liberty that is only an anxious privatism and a legal equality that conceals practical domination.").

sufficiently malleable that we can reform and lift our expectations of each other and ourselves. We are not inherently egotistic, alienated, atomistic monsters. The depiction is false, Gabel argued: we do have a nature, but it is not that. With changed expectations of either who we are or who we can be, we can create a shared life that is more trusting, more communal, less hostile, less suspicious, and more welcoming toward strangers and intimates both, as well as a less alienated way of working with the natural world to create a shared and hospitable social home. History as well as moral imagination reveals other possibilities to us, and law can yield other outcomes.

To make these claims of contingency and indeterminacy – our social world is not necessarily what it must be and things could have come out otherwise – anything other than the most futile sort of straw grasping, it must also be the case that our natures *can*, in point of fact, yield a significantly better shared life. Indeed, our natures can – or so the critics argued. For Unger, our natures can yield any shape our imaginations can hypothesize;[25] our nature is a function of our moral imagination, not the other way around. For Peter Gabel, the most underappreciated of the utopian critical writers, we need not *imagine* a different nature, we need only reacquaint ourselves with our true desires, and hence our true selves: our natures are in fact at odds with the paranoid delusions of liberal legalism.[26] Accordingly, for Gabel, the problem with liberal legalism was not so much that it locks us in a box of false necessity (as was true for Unger[27]), and not just its disingenuous inegalitarianism: the problem was that it promised formal equality while yielding substantive inequality or that it promised liberty while yielding bad choices within hierarchically constrained markets (as argued in different ways by both Gordon[28] and Kennedy[29]). The problem, more fundamentally, is that liberal legalism shortchanges us; it holds up a false mirror of who we are.[30] We are capable of and we desire more meaningful connections with each other not because we are infinitely malleable but because of who and what we already are and because of possibilities we already possess: an unrealized potentiality, yes, but also unmet and repressed desires for lives with less road rage, less violence, greater happiness, and, essentially, more love. We have not only the possibility for but more simply the desire – from which we have been thoroughly alienated, to be sure – to refashion our law to render our lives more

---

[25] Unger, *Passion* viii.
[26] Gabel, "The Phenomenology of Rights-Consciousness" 1566–67.
[27] Unger, *False Necessity*.
[28] Gordon, "Unfreezing Legal Reality," 216, 220 ("Such isolating devices [like dividing contract cases into exceptional and ordinary ones] therefore becomes a means of legitimating, through normalizing them, the *routine* instances of exploitation and vulnerability in the market transactions – of denying the everyday realities of pain and coercion in business life. . . . The fetishism of "freedom of contract," for example, make it hard to see that a particular free-contract regime in force can be a means of facilitating as well as restraining domination and hierarchy in social life.").
[29] Duncan Kennedy, "The Structure of Blackstone's Commentaries," *Buffalo Law Review* 28.2 (1979): 205–382.
[30] Gabel, "The Phenomenology of Rights-Consciousness" 1566, 1570, 1573.

equal, to refashion community to render our lives less isolated.[31] We not only can but do desire to withdraw from the pact of withdrawal, and to create a community by doing so. Law should be a part of that struggle. Liberal legalism – the pact of the withdrawn selves, the compromised regard for the other represented by a liberal rights regime – is a massive hindrance, both in law and in imagination, to doing so.

Taken collectively, the alternatives to liberal legalism mounted by the utopian theorists – Gabel, Unger, and others – and the indictment of liberal legalism put forward in the writings of liberalism's critics – Morton Horwitz, Robert Gordon, Michael Seidman, and Mark Tushnet – were intended to show the moral case for massive, deep, nonincrementalist legal reform. They constituted critical legal studies' moral brief, as opposed to its jurisprudential agenda. The various jurisprudential demonstrations of indeterminacy and the arguments for the indeterminacy thesis showed the possibility of achieving the nonincrementalist reform called for by the moral brief. The moral indictment of liberal legalism and the jurisprudential commitment to deconstruction and indeterminacy thus, at least for a time, seemingly, went hand in hand: the latter showed the viability of the methods – deviationist lawyering and so on – that would render the former politically relevant. There were much remarked on fissures and differences within the entire apparatus from the start. Most notably, or at least most visibly, some of the deconstructionist writing – the trashing – had no political or moral ambition whatsoever, other than to demonstrate the irrationality of existing liberal legalist commitments. It was not intended to show the hidden but always-already-there progressive possibilities within extant doctrine; it was intended to show, more or less, the asininity of the entire enterprise. A sizeable number of critical writers quite explicitly rejected the Ungerian and Gabelian utopianism that suggested possibilities for an unalienated social life that went even an inch beyond the rough political brief for egalitarianism arguably implied by the political critiques of liberalism's subordinating rights and liberties regime. For the most part, however, for most of the participants in this movement – this is what made it a movement – the two strands, the moral brief and the jurisprudential claims, were mutually supporting. The utopian writing and the moral critique made common cause with the jurisprudential writing toward a common end: the alteration of social structures through deviationist doctrinal writing and practice, all of which could then tilt in a more progressive and more just direction. In brief, deconstruction and indeterminacy showed the possibility of radical legal reform; moral critique and moral vision showed its necessity.

It was these basic arguments, or sets of arguments – the utopian alternative social orderings, the moral and political arguments against liberal legalism, and the demonstration of the possibility of changing it through the exploitation of its indeterminate,

---

[31] Peter Gabel, "Building Power and Breaking Images: Critical Legal Theory and the Practice of Law," *NYU Review of Social* Change 11.3 (1982): 369–41, 374; Gabel, "Critical Legal Studies as a Spiritual Practice," *Pepperdine Law Review* 36 (2008): 515–33, 515, 519, 529, 530.

irrational, inchoate, or nonsensical doctrine, as expounded by a small army of decon-structionists – I assert, that defined the CLS movement. It is that movement – a moral argument and a jurisprudential argument, joined toward the end of progressive, left-leaning legal change – that is the subject of this chapter. Although it might never have been stated quite as crisply as it is here,[32] and although it had plenty of fissures from the start, there is no doubt that this movement, defined by these dual com-mitments to *both* the possibility and the moral imperative of politically motivated left-wing legal change, once existed. It was not a dream. It had a moment of birth, so to speak, growing pains, and enjoyed a young adulthood.

As its founders, countless commentators, and its most ferocious antagonists now routinely claim, however, somewhere toward the end of the 1980s or beginning of the 1990s, CLS so defined gave all appearances as having *died*, or at least, of going into a deep coma. By the mid-1990s, it had become commonplace to bemoan (or celebrate) the death of the CLS movement. Critical legal studies conferences ground to a halt (or ended in acrimony, at least the last one that I had a hand in organizing ended that way[33]). The flow of articles explaining or employing deconstructionist methodologies slowed to a trickle and then dried up completely. All talk of trashing as well as trashing itself disappeared, complaints about truncated thinking and the hidden harms of rights and civil liberties were muted. We quit hearing entirely about the "pact of the withdrawn selves" within which we are apparently living out our morally and socially stunted lives. Beethoven reversed course and rolled back over, quite comfortably. Articles and arguments explaining the reasons for the disappearance of the CLS movement began to appear in their stead.[34] Sadly enough, the bulk of this chapter – the first three parts that follow – participates in this new growth stock. I want to present a somewhat novel account – at least different from the standard accounts most often given in the literature – of why the critical legal studies movement, at least as defined here, died. My account also attempts to show what was in it that is worth resurrecting, and how to go about doing so.

[32] For other attempts to define Critical Legal Studies' essence, see Mark Tushnet, "Critical Legal Studies: An Introduction to Its Origins and Underpinnings," *Journal of Legal Education* 36 (1986): 505–17; Kelman, *A Guide to Critical Legal Studies*; Unger, "The Critical Legal Studies Movement." For seminal pieces on the indeterminacy thesis and deconstruction see, among others, Joseph William Singer, "The Player and the Cards: Nihilism and Legal Theory," *The Yale Law Journal* 94.1 (1984): 1–70; Clare Dalton, An Essay in the Deconstruction of Contract Doctrine," *Yale Law Journal* 94.5 (1985): 997–1114; Mark Kelman, "Trashing," *Stanford Law Review* 36 (1984): 293–348; Kelman, "Interpretive Construction in the Substantive Criminal Law," *Stanford Law Review* 33.4 (1981): 591–674; Gabel and Kennedy, "Roll Over Beethoven"; Alan Freeman, "Truth and Mystification in Legal Scholarship," *Yale Law Journal* 90.5 (1981): 1229–37.

[33] The 1995 conference on CLS and class at Georgetown (jointly sponsored by Georgetown and Ameri-can) ended with various walkouts, over disputes between CLS and Critical Race Theory.

[34] Gabel, "Critical Legal Studies as a Spiritual Practice"; Martha McCluskey, "Thinking with Wolves: Left Legal Theory after the Right's Rise," *Buffalo Law Review* 54 (2007): 1191–297; Richard A. Posner, "Legal Scholarship Today," *Harvard Law Review* 115.5 (2002): 1314–26; Mark Tushnet, "Renormalizing Bush v. Gore: An Anticipatory Intellectual History," *Georgetown Law Journal* 90.1 (2001): 113–26, 113 (relaying a remark from Duncan Kennedy, that CLS is "dead, dead, dead").

This is not, however, the entire story. There have also been, during the latter half of the aughts, the beginnings of what I call a "neo-critical" legal movement, owing largely to the groundbreaking and extraordinarily creative work of Janet Halley, the genesis of which I would date from the publication of the volume of essays she coedited titled *Left Legalism/Left Critique* in 2002.[35] The second purpose of this chapter is to put forward a partial but friendly critique of that movement, through critical readings of some of Halley's work and secondarily that of the other authors collected in *Left Legalism*. There is much about this neo-critical movement that is worthy of applause: its no-holds-barred examination of left-wing identitarian legal victories, its unflinching willingness to examine sacred cows, its unwillingness to be deterred from close looks at the false paths followed by large numbers of political fellow travelers since the 1990s. All of this is hugely admirable, and even heartening.

I urge, however, that neo-critical legal studies, to the degree it exists as a movement, should undergo a midcourse correction. First, however, let me broadly situate neo-critical scholarship in relation to its predecessor. Neo-critical scholars, and Halley in particular, are (as am I) quite self-consciously committed to the project of resurrecting both left and critical legal scholarship and indeed define their movement by that aspiration. Furthermore, there are unquestionably some commonalities (as well as common actors[36]) between neo-critical scholarship and the old critical legal scholarship, which I discuss subsequently. There are also, however, profound *dis*continuities between the two, which, I argue, swamp the common thread.[37] The most obvious difference between the two movements is in the content of what I have called here the "moral brief" that characterized the CLS movement, compared with that of the neo-movement. There is, first, in the neo-crits' moral brief, no sustained critique of liberal legalism along the lines put forward by the original critical legal scholars, and even more strikingly, there is virtually no reference in neo-critical writings to utopian possibilities of less alienated forms of human interaction.[38] What has

---

35	Wendy Brown and Janet Halley, eds., *Left Legalism/Left Critique* (Durham: Duke University Press, 2002).

36	Notably, Duncan Kennedy and Mark Kelman. *See* Duncan Kennedy, "The Critique of Rights in Critical Legal Studies," *Left Legalism/Left Critique* 178–228; Mark Kelman and Gillian Lester, "Ideology and Entitlement," *Left Legalism/Left Critique* 134–77.

37	There are virtually no deconstructionist pieces in *Left Legalism/Left Critique*. In contrast, the book consists mostly of pieces that carefully analyze and then criticize the reasons that the state privileges and recognizes the claims of some disadvantaged people – such as the learning disabled, or members of racially or ethnically defined cultures, or women or gay men claiming sexual harassment on the job – over the claims of other disadvantaged people – such as poor students, workers generally, or people enjoying sex at work. *See, e.g.*, Kelman and Lester, "Ideology and Entitlement," *Left Legalism/Left Critique* 134–77; Richard T. Ford, "Beyond "Difference": A Reluctant Critique of Legal Identity Politics," *Left Legalism/Left Critique* 38–79; Janet Halley, "Sexuality Harassment," *Left Legalism/Left Critique* 80–104.

38	Compare in this regard the essay on rights by Duncan Kennedy, "The Critique of Rights in Critical Legal Studies," in *Left Legalism/Left Critique* 178–228 (originally published, as noted in *Left Legalism* p. viii, in his book *A Critique of Adjudication: Fin de Siècle*, [Cambridge: Harvard University Press, 1997]), with the rights critiques of Mark Tushnet, Morton Horwitz, and Peter Gabel. *See* Tushnet,

supplanted both in neo-critical scholarship's moral brief are critiques of legal reforms generated by "identity-based" and "left-centrist" political movements and legal scholarship, including equality based struggles for gay marriage,[39] feminist interventions against sexual harassment of working women, reform of rape law,[40] the disability advocacy community's arguments for the recognition of disabilities generally and learning disabilities in particular as a "civil rights" issue,[41] and multicultural arguments for the protection of ethnic and racial diversity against the homogenizing interests of employers and state actors.[42] The problem with these left-legal struggles, generally, according to the neo-critics, is that they employ state authority and mechanisms to achieve their severely limited ends, further entrenching the purported victims in a crippling and unjust set of stifling identities and further underscoring the power, legitimacy and moral authority of the state in so doing. That's basically it, however.[43] Whereas the critical legal theorists targeted liberal legalism broadly understood – the set of principles enforced by courts that sustain liberal settlements in advanced capitalist societies – as unjust as well as incoherent, the neo-crits have a different target in mind: the expanded civil rights world, with its focus on the injuries sustained by various minorities, cultures, sexually harassed working women, disabled adults, and badly educated and learning-disabled children. Whereas the early critics were unabashed in their willingness to offer utopian alternatives of less alienated forms of existence, the neo-critics rigidly discipline against attempts to do so.

The more subtle, but more important, difference, however, as I argue in the last section, is jurisprudential. Basically, neo-critical legal scholarship has coalesced around a complex but largely Foucauldian understanding of power, including *both* an animating suspicion of state power and also a near-defining celebration of nonstate social, personal, and, above all, sexual power, that was unquestionably present in some strands of the old CLS movement, and indeed formed the basis of some (not all) of the claims for indeterminacy, but in nothing like the hegemonic and disciplining way that understanding defines the new. That unitary Foucauldian commitment to both the critique of state power and the examination, uncovering, and often the celebration of personal and particularly sexual power, and to the claim that critical scholarship should do nothing but that, in effect, precludes both the articulation of moral understandings of the harms or injuries occasioned by private

---

"An Essay on Rights," Horwitz, "Rights," *and* Gabel, "The Phenomenology of Rights-Consciousness." As discussed *infra*, at footnote 78 and the accompanying text, the more recent neo-critical essay on rights by Kennedy explicitly disavows the Marxist moral claims associated with earlier versions of the rights critiques.

39 Michael Warner, *The Trouble with Normal: Sex, Politics, and the Ethics of Queer Life* (New York: Free Press: 1999) *and* Warner, "Beyond Gay Marriage," *Left Legalism/Left Critique* 259–89.

40 Halley, "Sexuality Harassment," *Left Legalism/Left Critique* 80.

41 Kelman and Lester, "Ideology and Entitlement," *Left Legalism/Left Critique.*

42 Ford, "Beyond Difference," *Left Legalism/Left Critique.*

43 *See* Wendy Brown and Janet Halley, Introduction, *Left Legalism/Left Critique* 1–37.

actors employing the personal and social power they wield, as well as of any moral alternative to it that might be promoted by the use of state means. Rather, the target of Foucauldian criticism, in the neo-critical literature, is masked *state* power, or masked attempts to invoke state power, and the goal is its unmasking. The result is that the neo-critics have in effect retained, expanded, and deepened the focus on power that characterized some of the critical scholars' work, while dropping or aggressively disparaging the older critics' moral critique of liberalism's valorization of private power. The consequence, I suggest in the last part of this chapter, is not a movement that is non- and apolitical, but one that is increasingly libertarian. The neo-crits, I argue, have poured old wine into the new bottles, but they have seemingly kept the dregs and thrown out the best of the old brew.

What we should have kept from the critical legal studies movement, I argue in my conclusion, was not its then-nascent Foucauldian jurisprudence, but, rather, precisely the moral commitments, and the willingness to express them, that the neo-crits have gone to such lengths to disown: the utopian sensibility, the vulgar-Marxist quest for solidarity with working and poor people, the radical communitarianism, the unabashed humanism, the searing critique of liberalism, and the insistence on the moral case for radical reform of existing legal structures that protect capital, power, and privilege. What could and should have been discarded was the jurisprudence, both Foucauldian and otherwise: both the indeterminacy thesis itself and the crippling Foucauldian set of claims regarding the omnipresence of power by reference to which the indeterminacy critique is sometimes defended. The neo-critical theory movement over the past half decade has done precisely the opposite: it has almost entirely dropped the moral brief – "more theory, less politics" is the rallying cry – and it has turned aggressively against even remotely utopian or moral arguments for change. The result is a movement increasingly focused solely on the machinations of power, as reflected in law, that eschews moral critique. By so doing, it has become seamless with, not distinctive from, the mainstream legal scholarship that is its target. I argue that this is unfortunate and urge a U-turn.

So, my focus on this chapter, with apologies to John Prine,[44] is "the missing years" between the death of CLS and the rise of the neo-crits. More specifically, I want to try to account for the disaccreditation, within left-wing legal scholarship during that time, of the very idea of morally imperative legal change.

The Chapter has three major parts. In the first part, I try to show that the moral brief that was once definitive of CLS has indeed largely disappeared, although this comes with the burden of having to prove a negative. Nevertheless, it is possible to at least point to some signs that the moral brief that once defined the movement is now largely absent from both mainstream and neo-critical legal scholarship. In the second part, I quickly summarize the three main accounts generally given of its demise and put forward instead the argument that the disappearance of the critics'

[44] John Prine, "Jesus: The Missing Years." *The Missing Years.* Oh Boy Records, 1991.

moral brief is best explained by the inadequacies of its accompanying jurisprudence that defined the movement – including the claimed radical indeterminacy of legal texts, the omnipotence of the interpretive community, and the possibilities of textual deconstruction. A focus on existing legal texts, no matter how indeterminate, could not possibly ground a radical critique of liberal legalism then, nor can it now. Only a turn toward ordinary lived experience can show the limits of liberal legalism, and only a turn toward ordinary politics can seek to upend it. The CLS movement, far from espousing either turn, wound up in the peculiar position of resisting both: by insisting on the omnipresence of texts, they kept the scholar's focus on text rather than life, and by insisting on the collapse of law and politics *in law* – on the essentially political nature of legal settlements – it contributed to rather than challenged the belief, pervasive in the academy, that political change brought about through adjudicative law is the highest form of change attainable. This myopic fixation on existing legal text in the context of adjudication, even with the promise of vast interpretive freedom, I argue, is ultimately truncating; it dwarfs both moral imagination and political impact.

In the third part, I look at the neo-critical revival of critical legal studies, and the logic of their attempted revitalization of critical left-wing legal scholarship. In the conclusion, I argue for a quite different redirection and revival of critical legal studies that picks up on the discarded moral strands of what was once a vital if flawed intellectual movement.

THE DISAPPEARANCE OF THE CRITICAL LEGAL STUDIES MOVEMENT

It is hardly novel to note – in fact it has become a commonplace in the legal academy – that the CLS movement "died" sometime in the late 1980s, early 1990s, or thereabouts.[45] Both critical legal scholars themselves, in various retrospectives, autobiographies, and remembrances, and their critics, claim this routinely.[46] The claim is peculiar, however. The founders of CLS are still very much alive, active, teaching, and writing, some prolifically.[47] Many of the central methodological ideas,

---

[45] Gabel, "Critical Legal Studies as a Spiritual Practice"; Martha McCulskey, "Thinking with Wolves"; Posner, "Legal Scholarship Today"; Tushnet, "Renormalizing Bush v. Gore."

[46] Pierre Schlag, "Spam Jurisprudence, Air Law, and the Rank Anxiety of Nothing Happening (A Report on the State of the Art)," *Georgetown Law Journal* 97.3 (2009): 803–36.

[47] *See, e.g.*, Duncan Kennedy, *Sexy Dressing Etc.* (Cambridge: Harvard University Press, 1993); Kennedy, *A Critique of Adjudication: Fin de Siècle*; Kennedy, "A Semiotics of Critique," *Cardozo Law Review* 22 (2001): 1147–90; Mark Kelman, "Could Lawyers Stop Recession – Speculations on Law and Macroeconomics," *Stanford Law Review* 45.5 (1993): 1215–310; Kelman, Yuval Rottenstriech, and Amos Tversky, "Context-Dependence in Legal Decision Making," *Journal of Legal Studies* 25.2 (1996): 287–318; Kelman, "Market Discrimination and Groups," *Stanford Law Review* 53.4(2001); Robert W. Gordon, "Lawyers, Scholars, and the Middle Ground," *Michigan Law Review* 91.8 (1993): 2075–112; Gordon, "Imprudence and Partnership: Starr's OIC and the Clinton-Lewinsky Affair," *Fordham Law Review* 68.3 (1999): 639–722; Kairys, ed., *The Politics of Law*; Joseph William Singer, "A Pragmatic Guide to Conflicts," *Boston University Law Review* 70.5 (1990): 731–820; Singer, "No Right to Exclude:

furthermore, have not only not died but have been fully absorbed, albeit somewhat domesticated, by mainstream legal scholarship.[48] At least a couple of its basic
jurisprudential commitments have been retained, deepened, broadened, and ampli-
fied by the neo-crits, as I discuss in some detail in the last section. What, then, is it,
more precisely, that died?

In part what died was simply its institutional presence – the summer workshops,
the conferences, the networks of scholars, the directories, the loving bibliographic
compilations of all critical scholarship, the friendships, the intensity, the us against
them-ism, as some of its major voices were embraced by the upper echelons of the
legal academic brotherhood. What also died, I argue in this part of the chapter, was
what I have called the critics' moral brief, by which I mean both their moral criticism
of liberal legalism and their utopian imaginings of alternatives to it. The set of claims,
once central to and even defining of critical legal scholarship, that liberal legalism
legitimates unwarranted and unnecessary human suffering and does so largely by
valorizing and protecting a private realm of both oppression and alienation,[49] and

Public Accommodations and Private Property," *Northwestern University Law Review* 90.4 (1995–96):
1283–497; Singer, *Entitlement: The Paradoxes of Property* (New Haven: Yale University Press: 2000);
William E. Forbath, "Why This Rights Talk Is Different from All Other Rights Talk: Demoting
the Court and Reimagining the Constitution," *Stanford Law Review* 46.6 (1994): 1771–806; Forbath,
"Habermas's Constitution: A History, Guide, and Critique," *Law and Social Inquiry* 23.4 (1998):
969–1016; Forbath, "Caste, Class, and Equal Citizenship," *Michigan Law Review* 98:1 (1999): 1–91;
Pierre Schlag, "Normativity and the Politics of Form," *University of Pennsylvania Law Review* 139.4
(1991): 801–932; Schlag, "How to Do Things with the First Amendment," *University of Colorado Law
Review* 64.4 (1993): 1095–108; Schlag, "Law and Phrenology," *Harvard Law Review* 110.4 (1997): 877–
921; Mark V. Tushnet, "The Degradation of Constitutional Discourse," *Georgetown Law Journal* 81.2
(1992): 251–312; Tushnet, "Policy Distortion and Democratic Debilitation: Comparative Illumination
of the Countermajoritarian Difficulty," *Michigan Law Review* 94.2 (1995): 245–301; Tushnet, *Making
Civil Rights Law: Thurgood Marshall and the Supreme Court, 1956–1961* (Oxford: Oxford University
Press, 1996); Tushnet, *Taking the Constitution away from the Courts* (Princeton: Princeton University
Press: 2000); Gary Peller, "Race Consciousness," *Duke Law Journal* 1990.4 (1990): 758–847; Peller
and Kimberle Crenshaw, "The Contradictions of Mainstream Constitutional Theory," *UCLA Law
Review* 45.6 (1998): 1683–716.

[48] *See, e.g.,* Rachelle Y. Holmes, "Deconstructing the Rules of Corporate Tax," *Akron Tax Journal* 25.1
(2010): 1–54 *and* Peter T. Wendel, *Deconstructing Legal Analysis: A 1L Primer* (Frederick: Aspen
Publishers, 2009).

[49] For early direct critiques of liberal legalism that relied on the tally of suffering for which it was
responsible rather than its false claims of determinacy, see David Kairys, Introduction, *The Politics
of Law*; Edward Greer, "Antonio Gramsci and 'Legal Hegemony,'" *The Politics of Law* 304–9; Freeman, "Legitimizing Racism through Anti-Discrimination Law: A Critical Review of Supreme Court
Doctrine"; Gabel and Harris, "Building Power and Breaking Images: Critical Legal Theory and the
Practice of Law." Making a related point in a recent essay, Peter Gabel lists canonical CLS works
that in his view made use of a "higher law" defined "not as a metaphysical or religious abstraction,
but as an embodiment of the presence of social justice manifesting itself in the real world through
a spiritually elevating movement that provides a moral horizon for revealing what must be changed
about the world," and notes that none of the pieces listed "makes use of the indeterminacy critique,
and all of them are moral statements in which existing (or then existing) legal regimes obscured or
deflected the struggle for a more humane and just world." Peter Gabel, "Critical Legal Studies as a
Spiritual Practice" 526–28.

the utopian claims that human nature is either sufficiently plastic or sufficiently communitarian so as to ground radically different and more humane forms of social interaction, are nowhere near as prominent today as they were in the 1970s and 1980s critical literature.[50] We do not hear from either the neo-crits or from the critical legal scholars still writing, any longer, the claim that liberal legalism is an unnecessary and unwarranted legal regime, because it subordinates large numbers of people and contributes to massive suffering, or that those with the power to change it through ordinary legal methods should do so. The central, defining claims necessary to sustain this basic argument have virtually disappeared, as has the imperative that those with power should exercise it so as to effectuate meaningful legal change.

More specifically, what has been lost is an entire set of explicitly normative arguments about liberalism and legal regimes that support it that were once at the core of the critical legal studies movement, including prominently parts of the rights critique,[51] most of the more interesting legitimation claims,[52] and virtually all of the stab-in-the-dark utopian attempts to expose the relationships between liberalism and alienation or to envision the possibility of a social order undergirded by greater communion.[53] All of these arguments sought, collectively, to portray liberal legalism as a vehicle for the perpetuation of subordination, of misery, of alienation, of unwarranted harm, and unhappiness, and all of them sought to portray or at least to keep alive the possibility of a radically different social world than the one in which we now live. That is not because liberal legalism as it was then understood has withered away: liberal legalism was then and continues to be, in part, a set of premises, largely unargued, about the wisdom of legal orders in advanced capitalist countries, and particularly the United States, characterized by a somewhat checkered commitment to market freedoms, constitutional rights of individuals and increasingly of corporations, and an only highly circumscribed collectivization of social resources to achieve shared ends. The critique of that order was important then, but is more important now, because the need for greater cooperation on shared problems the solutions to which are illusive, given liberal legal premises – global climate change, corporate irresponsibility of an international scale, and wars over religious identity – looms ever larger. It is important to understand how, and why, the

---

[50] Unger, *Passion*; Unger, *False Necessity*. *But see* Gabel, "Critical Legal Studies as a Spiritual Practice."

[51] Tushnet, "An Essay on Rights"; Horwitz, "Rights"; Freeman, "Legitimizing Racial Discrimination"; Freeman, "Racism, Rights, and the Quest for Equality of Opportunity: A Critical Legal Essay," *Harvard Civil Rights–Civil Liberties Law Review* 23.2 (1988): 295–392; Seidman, "Rubashov's Question"; Bell, "Serving Two Masters."

[52] Gordon, "Unfreezing Legal Reality"; Kennedy, "Distributive and Paternalist Motives"; Kimberle Williams Crenshaw, "Race, Reform, and Retrenchment: Transformation and Legitimation in Antidiscrimination Law," *Harvard Law Review* 101.7 (1988): 1331–87; Mark Kelman, "Consumption Theory, Production Theory, and Ideology in the Coase Theorem," *Southern California Law Review* 52.3 (1979): 669–698; – , "Choice and Utility," *Wisconsin Law Review* 1979.3 (1979): 769–98.

[53] Gabel, "The Phenomenology of Rights-Consciousness"; – and Duncan Kennedy, "Roll Over Beethoven"; Unger, *Passion*.

critics' moral brief against liberal legalism disappeared from the scene of American legal scholarship and what might be done to recapture it.

We can see the disintegration of the critical scholars' moral brief most clearly, and understand its causes most clearly, by tracing the circuitous fate of each of its three core claims, or sets of claims, individually – the rights critique, legitimation arguments, and the role of utopian thinking – in both mainstream legal discourse and neo-critical thought. Through different routes, they each have either been distorted or have disappeared in toto across the board. I take them up in that order, first summarizing the arguments as originally put forward and then discussing their fate.

Wither the Rights Critique

Let me start with the rights critique, or critiques. The critics put forward not just one but at least three sorts of critiques of rights, which I call the political, phenomenological, and jurisprudential. The first two – the political and phenomenological – were part of the moral brief, the latter, distinctively, was part of the jurisprudential.

I start with the political. The basic political claim put forward by the rights critics was simply that the rights that have figured most prominently in liberal legal discourse, including privacy rights (such as the rights to same-sex sex, abortion, and contraception), the cluster of antidiscrimination rights, and rights to various liberties against the state, are regressive, rather than progressive, as they are widely believed to be. They have the effect of further hurting the interests of the already disempowered or relatively impoverished – and for three reasons.

The first is historical. Rights, in the United States and Great Britain, have historically overwhelmingly served to solidify the holdings, entitlements, wealth, and status of privileged property owners against the redistribution of wealth threatened by democratic change.[54] The right to keep one's property, and to keep it, specifically, against legalistic encroachments wrought through democratic lawmaking, in other words, just *is* the paradigmatic Anglo-American right: it is the prototype, so to speak, on which all rights are built.[55] There is nothing logically necessary about the structure of rights that dictates this result – positive rights do indeed proliferate in other parts of the world, as well as in international human rights law – but nevertheless, here, the identity of a right as a protective shield against state interference with private property is deep and secure. Therefore, other rights, including civil rights to equality, but all the more so our libertarian rights to privacy, speech, and so on, inevitably have a regressive legitimating tendency, even if that tendency is an unintended by-product of the party making the claim to right. When such rights are celebrated as being at the heart of our claim to justice – we live in a just society because we have and honor antidiscrimination rights, speech rights, and so forth, and we do so majoritarian will to the contrary notwithstanding – they further solidify

---

[54] Horwitz, "Rights."
[55] Horwitz, "Rights" 396–7.

the exalted standing, so to speak, of property rights, and therefore the inequalities, including the material, that property rights protect. Rights basically protect privilege and wealth, so as we honor the right to desegregation, speech, and sexual privacy, we further entrench the equation of rights with justice, and particularly of minoritarian rights with justice. By so doing, we also further entrench the identification of justice with the extremely minoritarian right of property owners to compilations of wealth held by the most privileged, and to hold it against majoritarian and democratic attempts at redistribution. Even the most progressive-sounding rights therefore, and only on first blush paradoxically, have this regressive by-product.

Second, rights are regressive, the rights critics argued, because they legitimate privilege, simply by leaving untouched – and eventually valorized – that which is not covered by the right's definition of injustice. A right to be free of one form of injustice lends a touch of legitimacy and moral right to the injustices against which one has no rights. For example, African Americans and others now have a "right" to a state that does not intentionally discriminate on the basis of race – a right to a color-blind state. That right leaves untouched private, institutional, and social discrimination and by so doing legitimates the greater wrong than that which it prohibits: if it is *state* discrimination that is evil, then the private kind must be not only OK, but deserving of protection, because to end it would require the kind of state race consciousness both forbidden and declared unjust or evil by the right itself.[56] To take another, a "right" of criminal defendants to be read Miranda rights, to a lawyer, to the benefits of the exclusionary rule, and to habeas corpus relief legitimates an incarceration system of penal control that houses more prisoners per capita than any other country in the world, and in facilities that are cruel and serve no even conceivable end – deterrence, retribution, or rehabilitative. That injustice is all the more insulated against criticism, by the legitimating rights of suspects and defendants at the preincarceration phases of the criminal justice system.[57] More generally, rights legitimate injustice by overstating their own force: by equating justice with the content of the right, greater injustices not only go untouched, but are rendered either legitimate, or simply less visible.

Third, rights are regressive because at least in this country, they are almost uniformly negative, by which is meant that they give us protection against overreaching state action, and no entitlement at all to state action that might counter pernicious

---

[56] This claim was at the heart of the Critical Legal Studies' analysis of race law, and eventually became central to the critical race scholarship movement, although in a considerably modified form. For early articulations, see Bell, "Serving Two Masters"; Freeman, "Legitimating Racial Discrimination"; Peller, "Race Consciousness"; Kimberle Crenshaw et al., eds., Introduction, *Critical Race Theory: Key Writings That Formed the Movement* (New York: The New Press, 1995). For critical responses to this claim from critical race scholars, *see* Crenshaw, "Race, Reform, and Retrenchment"; Williams, "Alchemical Notes"; Richard Delgado, "The Ethereal Scholar: Does Critical Legal Studies Have What Minorities Want?" *Harvard Civil Rights–Civil Liberties Law Review* 22.2 (1987): 301–322; – , "Critical Legal Studies and the Realities of Race – Does the Fundamental Contradiction Have a Corollary?" *Harvard Civil Rights–Civil Liberties Law Review* 23.2 (1988): 407–14.

[57] *Cf.* Seidman, "Brown and Miranda": Seidman, "Rubashov's Question."

private oppression.[58] By identifying our "rights" with justice, we embed the idea that justice requires a minimalist government, rather than an interventionist government that can right private wrongful subordination. Our "rights" not only do not give us rights against that private subordination but perversely protect us, within the private sphere, *against* just the intervention that might correct it. Thus, we not only have no right to be protected by the state against exploitative labor contracts, domestic violence, private racist speech acts, and so on, we have a right to be protected against states that would try to do so through ordinary legislative interventions. Likewise we not only have no right to state assistance against the harms of deprivation – rights to shelter, health, food, or clothing – but we have a right against a state that would try to do so. The idea of a "right" in other words not only does not "extend" to positive rights to governmental assistance against private wrongs, but the negative rights we enjoy actually protect those spheres of private inequality, and the interests of the stronger within them, against such ordinary state-sponsored or democratically driven assistance. The "right to privacy," from the perspective of this critique, not only is not peripheral, it is the quintessential right: when we have a right of any sort, it is typically a right to keep the state out of our private affairs, including our private oppression, subordination, or abuse of each other.[59] Rights almost uniformly insulate the private sphere, and valorize that sphere when they do so. The result is that whatever forms of private subordination that occur within it – privatized domestic violence, private racism, private economic exploitation, and so on – are rendered not just invisible to state, and hence democratic, reordering but more profoundly are perversely celebrated as a part of the private sphere, to which individuals, including those on the receiving end of the violence, racism, and exploitation have a right to be kept free of all state interference. Both the exploited and the exploiter have rights to keep that exploitation untouched by state interference. Rights are positively bad, they are harmful. They are harmful to the party of humanity, as Mark Tushnet once inartfully claimed.[60] We would be better off without them.

Let me turn now to the phenomenological. The phenomenological critique of rights, generally associated with Peter Gabel, was related but by no means redundant to the political. Gabel argued that rights are experienced phenomenologically by rights holders as a defense against the alienation from the other that the state requires as a precondition of its legitimacy, and hence are experienced as a part of the massive psychic denial of the falsity of that "fabric of appearances through which we make each other hostage to the illusion that it is distance rather than

---

[58] *See* Horwitz, "Rights" 399–400; Tushnet, "An Essay on Rights" 1393–94.

[59] Thus, Catharine MacKinnon's early critique of *Roe v. Wade* explored the ways in which the privacy right it created to be free of moralistic interference with the decision to have an abortion legitimated the sexual subordination of women by men in the private sphere effectuated by private acts of violence. MacKinnon, *Feminism Unmodified* 93–102.

[60] Tushnet, "An Essay on Rights" 1364.

a good heart turned outward that the law in us requires."[61] The state's worldview into which both legal rights and constitutional rights victories are assimilated falsely posit the other as a fearful source of unwarranted and unwanted invasion, against which law and its insulating aura of protective rights are a second-best solution, our best defense. Rights – both constitutional and civil – basically regulate the inter-action of persons who have internalized a false belief that ordinary human close-ness between nonintimates, civil intercourse, is at heart assaultive. Sometimes, of course, against this baseline false belief of false selves, each in denial of their need for connection, social intercourse is regretfully necessary – to create contracts for mutual benefit, to create families for the tightly constrained emotional nurturance necessary to the reproduction of the species, or to man the bowling teams and the like that might strengthen the necessary bonds of involvement that keep civil society functioning. Where closeness is necessary, rights and law are the vehicle by which we navigate this treacherous terrain: thus, the pact of the withdrawn selves. Rights both sanction – as in allow – the permitted interaction; thus, we have rights to con-tract, to commerce, to marry, to bowl together, and so on – and protect us from the unwarranted interactions – assaults on the bus, in back alleys, in shopping malls, and in our homes – as we seek the benefits of the right-defined closeness with the others permitted us. However, the baseline, rock-bottom, and thoroughly false assumption is that social closeness is generally unwarranted and unwanted and undesired: if we do not consent to it, and within pretty tightly constrained definitions of consent, it is presumptively assaultive, and we therefore have rights to be free of it. We come together in a social pact to guarantee our mutual right to withdraw and our mutual power to reconnect, where necessary, for mutual benefit.[62] Interaction outside the zone of rights, by contrast, is constructed by the false self in a state of denial of desire as posing nothing but threat – threat by a competitor for private goods and services in a panoply of markets, and at worst an assailant with a Hobbesian instinct for possession, power, and dominance who will seek honor and glory, as well as material gains, at our expense. Rights then both facilitate the interaction with others where prompted by necessity and protect us against the horror of our fellow citizens, not a one of whom is to be trusted for nary a second.

Now, if our nature is as malleable as Unger claimed,[63] or as unalienated as Gabel argued, and if the baseline created by the state to maintain its legitimacy is as alienating as Gabel asserted, this regime of only-permitted-by-right intimacy is both unnecessary and deeply wounding. We could have a vastly more spontaneous, more enlivening, and simply more hospitable interactive world than we have. Rights protect us, but what they mainly protect us against are the demons of our paranoiac

---

[61] Gabel, "Phenomenology of Rights-Consciousness" 1599.

[62] *Id.* at 1566–70.

[63] Unger, *Passion* 15–23 (describing the ideal personality, which is stable yet always open to transfor-mation).

imaginings.[64] By so doing, they impoverish us both materially and spiritually; they implicate us in a regime that protects capital against human interest, but they also alienate us against our own humanity, including our human quest for genuine closeness with our fellow social beings.

The third critique of rights put forward by the critics, was jurisprudential rather than any part of the moral brief: rights purport to stabilize legal, constitutional, and moral arguments by grounding them in something uncontestable, and incontestably good, but they in fact do no such thing. Rights are as unstable and as indeterminate as the rules they inadequately embody.[65] Accordingly, purely legal rights – a right, say, to a contract remedy for breach of contract or a tort remedy for defamation and so on – no more guarantees certainty in a legal dispute than do the rules from which the rights are derived. A legal right is in part an expectation that an interest is and will be protected by the application of legal rules by impartial courts. That expectation, however, is no more justified than the certainty of the rules that give rise to it. Furthermore, the rules are themselves indeterminate. The same can be said, although the argument is more complex, of constitutional rights: they have no more of a grounding in the Constitution than legal rights have in doctrinal law. Political and moral rights likewise have no claim to certitude. A claimed right, in political discourse – to health care, to ownership of guns, to free speech, to an abortion, and the like – can be checked by a counterright – to be free to spend one's hard-earned money on something other than health insurance, to a state that protects one, through gun control laws, against private violence, to live in a public world that is free of hateful utterances that defame or subordinate, or, of course, to a right to live, a right to participate in the decision to have a child, and so on. A "right" in political and constitutional disputation serves at best as an exclamation point – it rhetorically shows that the speaker cares deeply. It does nothing, however, to render the various interests or positions to which all that passion gives voice more embedded in law, politics, or morality. The articulation of an interest as a "right" by no means creates an unmoveable bulwark against change, interference, or recalibration of the protection of the various interests – interests in health, guns, abortion, and so on, to which a right might be claimed – toward which it so desperately strives.

That, in essence, was the rights critique. It was all over the place, when I entered the legal academy in 1980. The rights critiques included some of the classic CLS articles – notably Tushnet's "Critique of Rights" in the *Texas Law Review*,[66] Gabel's "Pact of the Withdrawn Selves,"[67] and Horwitz's reply to the race scholars' response

---

[64] Gabel, "Phenomenology of Rights-Consciousness" 1576–80.

[65] *See* Tushnet, "An Essay on Rights" *and* Kennedy, A *Critique of Adjudication: Fin de Siècle* 315–38 (later republished, as noted earlier, as "The Critique of Rights in Critical Legal Studies," *Left Legalism/ Left Critique* 178–228).

[66] Tushnet, "An Essay on Rights."

[67] Gabel, "The Phenomenology of Rights-Consciousness."

to the rights critique in the *Harvard Civil Rights–Civil Liberties Law Review*.[68] These articles, and the arguments they made, as I argue in a moment, are still relevant, exciting, convincing, infuriating, somewhat thrilling, and bristling with possibility. They were also prescient, and they also did not go far enough. We can see now with considerably greater clarity what the rights critics only glimpsed then: that the rights revolutions of the 1960s and 1970s would indeed turn out to have a bite to them that would swamp their goodness. We can now see quite clearly, rather than simply speculate, that the logic of those rights to desegregation and privacy from the 1950s, 1960s, and 1970s would turn out to imply a panoply of not-so-friendly-to-the-party-of-humanity rights in the nineties and aughts – rights to guns,[69] rights to corporate speech,[70] rights of religious parents to homeschool,[71] rights not to purchase health insurance[72] – that would be argued by a right-wing empowered by the Warren Court's indirect resuscitation of the *Lochner* era and that at least some of those rights would come to be embedded in law, by a court perfectly capable of using rights rhetoric toward the end of regressive rather than progressive redistribution. Liberal rights, once harmful to the party of humanity, now look downright lethal. The time for the rights critique, in other words, to have its full day in court, so to speak, is *now*, when we can fairly assess the damage done as well as the gains made, rather than during their heyday. Where is it now? Whither the rights critique?

The short answer: it is almost, but not quite, nowhere. More specifically, the jurisprudential rights critique – that rights are indeterminate and embody nothing but interests – has survived, whereas the prongs of the critique that constituted a part of the moral brief – that rights valorize and protect private-sphere subordination, and construct a false and alienating individualism – has died. Duncan Kennedy has reprised his earlier mid-1990s rights critique in a chapter of the Halley-Brown volume, intending, apparently, to re-present it to a new generation of readers.[73] The contrast, however, between Horwitz, Gabel, and Tushnet's 1980s pieces, and Kennedy's original critique, now republished in the 2004 volume, is telling, and sobering. The early rights critics typically joined the rights critique based on the moral or political grounds rehearsed earlier in this chapter – that rights are positively harmful for some set of reasons – with the jurisprudential claim: to wit, that rights discourse is unstable and that rights themselves are indeterminate. Thus, the moral claims against rights – that rights perpetuate private-sphere subordination, valorize property rights and hence exacerbate wealth inequalities, degrade democracy while insulating the private sphere, and are for all of these reasons harmful to the party of

---

[68] Horwitz, "Rights" 6.
[69] *District of Columbia v. Heller*, 128 S.Ct. 2783 (2008).
[70] *Citizens United v. Federal Election Commission*, 558 U.S. 50 (2010).
[71] In re Jonathan v. Superior Court, 165 Cal. App. 4th 1074 (Ct. App. 2008).
[72] Randy Barnett, Nathanial Stewart, and Todd Gaziano, *Why the Personal Mandate to Buy Health Insurance Is Unprecedented and Unconstitutional* (The Heritage Foundation, 2009).
[73] Duncan Kennedy, "The Critique of Rights," *Left Legalism/Left Critique* 178–228.

humanity – were typically "paired" with the jurisprudential claim that rights, like the rest of law, are indeterminate, grounded only in state action rather than human nature or even human aspirations. If we take Kennedy's revamped rights critique as emblematic of the rights critics of the aughts, the differences between the "then" of rights criticism and the "now" is stark. Basically, the moral brief is gone – excised – leaving only the jurisprudential claim. Rights are unstable. As such, they are no more harmful than helpful. There is no moral valence to this claim one way or the other.

Let me be more specific. As noted earlier, Morton Horwitz, the eminent Harvard legal historian, in his reply to the minority scholars' response to the rights scholars, had stressed the historical role of rights and rights rhetoric in the eighteenth and nineteenth century's protection of property, capital, and contract rights against both democratic and judicial attempts at redistributing the nation's wealth.[74] Any rights movement, he worried, is a double-edged sword: rights movements tend to revalidate the protection of property that is at the core of rights consciousness, and contemporary claims for civil and liberal rights are no exception.[75] They create a limited right against the state against irrational discrimination, but precisely by so doing, they posit the state as the usurper, the presumptively illegitimate thief who wrongly – discriminately – robs the citizen of natural entitlements.[76] The racist state is targeted by antidiscrimination rights, and rightly so, but precisely by so doing, the state is again vilified, strengthening rather than challenging the presumptive rightness and goodness of private over public power.[77] There is none of this in Kennedy's 2000s rights critique (or the original piece from which the latter is taken).[78] Rather, Kennedy makes occasional reference to "Marxist" and "neo-Marxist" critiques of rights, but only to distance himself from them. In so doing, he jettisons the fundamental pillar of the moral brief, to wit, the claim that even benign or progressive-sounding rights are harmful, because of the degree to which they bolster property against the democratic redistributive instincts of relatively less properties peoples:

> But there is no more a legal logic to Liberal rights than there is an economic logic to capitalism. For this reason, Marx's presentation of the selfishness and exploitation of civil society as necessary consequences of abstract property and contract rights seems seriously wrong. But his psychological analysis of the public/private distinction and of rights consciousness retains its power, at least for me. His notion was that the belief in universal political rights functioned, together with the belief in universal private rights, as a fantasy resolution of our contradictory experience of being, at once, altruistic collective and selfish individual selves. At the same time, the fantasy

[74] Horwitz, "Rights" 396.
[75] *Id.* at 397, 400–2.
[76] *Id.* at 400.
[77] *Id.* at 402–4.
[78] Kennedy, *A Critique of Adjudication: Fin de Siècle* 315–38 (later republished, as noted earlier, as "The Critique of Rights in Critical Legal Studies," *Left Legalism/Left Critique* 178–228).

performed, for the beneficiaries of capitalism, the apologetic function of explaining why they were entitled to the profits they derived from exploiting the propertyless.

I don't think it plausible that rights consciousness, in and of itself, plays either an intrinsically progressive or an intrinsically conservative role in our current politics. But, from my postrights perspective, and with deference to believers, I do think the view of rights as universal and factoid, and so outside or above politics, involves denial of the kind Marx analyzed. As with the denial of the ideological in adjudication, there are many ways to theorize the conflicts that give rise to this particular form of (what seems to me) wishful thinking. And, as with adjudication, psychologizing denial involves suspending dialogue with those for whom the reality of rights is close to tangible.[79]

Second, Peter Gabel, in his 1984 article, coined the expression the "pact of the withdrawn selves" and argued, partly through narrative, that the effect on consciousness of a rights regime that posits others as sources of danger rather than as co-humans is deleterious. It fosters an atomism that is isolating: needlessly withdrawn selves. Alienation, he argued, is not a natural condition, it is a constructed condition, and it is rights, as co-opted and transformed by the state, that do the constructing.[80] Again, Kennedy's rights critique contrasts. There is no mention of the alienating effect on consciousness of rights, beyond the claim that rights ossify our understanding of human relations.[81] Whether it does so for better or worse, however, is not even asserted much less argued. Lastly, in his 1980s seminal article, "The Critique of Rights," Mark Tushnet offered multiple critiques – he numbered them for ease of reference – but gave prominent pride of place to his signature contribution: that rights "do positive harm to the party of humanity."[82] Rights reify relations, and they falsely promise a permanence they cannot deliver (and somehow they manage to do both, although the tension between these claims was not addressed). What they primarily do, however, is sanctify a private sphere of entitlement within which those with power exercise it in a protected and even valorized fashion against those who lack it. The right not only insulates that private inequality, it celebrates it, and by so doing, it harms people. Again, Kennedy's article contrasts. Rights, Kennedy argues, can be either positive or negative; there is no reason to assume the latter.[83] Therefore, their negativity, here and now, at least in the United States, is not the reason to lose faith.

Horwitz's, Gabel's, and Tushnet's moral critiques all contrast more than they converge with the jurisprudential rights critique offered by Duncan Kennedy in the 1990s, and now in *Left Legalism*. Kennedy professes in his essay to explain

---

[79] Kennedy, "The Critique of Rights," *Left Legalism/Left Critique* 216 (emphasis added).
[80] Gabel, "The Phenomenology of Rights-Consciousness" 1576–80.
[81] Kennedy, "The Critique of Rights," *Left Legalism/Left Critique* 215–16.
[82] Tushnet, "An Essay on Rights" 1384.
[83] Kennedy, "The Critique of Rights," *Left Legalism/Left Critique* 215–16.

the story of his own progressive "loss of faith" in rights,[84] by which is meant his own realization, gained over years of study, that liberal rights – rights to equality, rights against discrimination, rights to privacy, rights to abortion, rights to same-sex marriage, and so on – cannot deliver the goods they promise; thus, the loss of faith. What they promise, he argues, is an extralegal moral point or ground on which to base or criticize legal entitlements, legal rights, legal interpretations of texts, or at least legal arguments.[85] In fact, however, rights simply give voice to interests, and to those interests held by the political victors in an ordinary process of rhetorical contestation.[86] They do not *prove* anything, we might say, about the actual ontology of our moral universe. They give political arguments in various fora – legal, political, or rhetorical – an exclamation point: the rights claimant really means whatever it is he feels we have a right to, he feels strongly about it. However, this is all that rights claims register – the intensity of the feeling of those who assert them. They do not register the existence of anything other than the interests the rights protect, asserted vigorously. So, to whatever extent the underlying interests of a rights claim conflicts with other underlying interests that might someday be ascendant, to that degree, the right, even if embedded in law – higher law, or constitutional law – will be insecure. The right to own a gun might someday give way to the right to gun control – the right to be free of gun violence – if those who have the latter interest someday gain more political power than those who wish to arm themselves and assert the right to gun control as fiercely as gun owners these days assert the right to gun ownership. The right to purchase an abortion might someday give way to the fetus's right to life or the public's interest in protecting potential life, should that interest someday prove of greater political weight. Rights might give us a way to record where we now stand. They do not, however, preexist political or legal discourse "outside" the realms in which that discourse occurs, whether legal or political. Access to legal abortion, then, to take an example, cannot be explained or justified by reference to a constitutional "right to privacy," itself justified by reference to a right to bodily integrity, or equality or liberty, that exists outside of the constitutional discourse and that the latter strives to mirror. Access to legal abortion might be expressed in these terms, but it cannot be explained or justified by them. We might feel that it can, but that is only because our interest in access to abortion now outweighs in various political realms the interests that others assert in limiting that access. Obviously this could change, and when and if it does, the right will give way likewise. The right – whether it is a right to liberty, equality, dignity, or so forth – does no independent "moral" work.

Thus, Kennedy's rights critique does more than give short shrift to the moral brief against rights, it undermines it. Rights, in Kennedy's account, do little but delineate the strength and fact of felt interest. They "come from" nowhere but felt interest, and

[84] *Id.* at 191–97.
[85] *Id.* at 209–13.
[86] *Id.* at 209.

they suffer the same fate as interests that decline in intensity across time; they are part of the political landscape so long as is the felt interest and as vulnerable to decline or replacement by conflicting rights as are the interests themselves. To "lose faith" in rights is apparently simply to recognize this fact.[87] Rights that do nothing, however, other than to give a delineation to the interests valued by those who assert them cannot possibly do any harm – at least any harm independent of those done by the interests for which they speak. Rights cannot, then, harm the party of humanity; they cannot wrongly insulate the private sphere against democratic or political or moral critique; they cannot further embed economic entitlement and privilege in political consciousness; they cannot alienate persons from felt needs, desires, or each other; they cannot contribute to an alienated culture or the further impoverishment of persons; and they cannot legitimate greater injustices than the injustice they purport to rectify. They might, of course, and often do, give a delineation to interests that seek to do all or some of these things, but then again, they might give delineation to interests that seek to do the opposite. To *worry* over rights, then, is as fetishizing as to have "faith" in them: if one is displeased with the dominance of the interests that our current menu of rights seemingly protects, the thing to do is to seek to displace the interest. To lose faith in the security of rights in a moral reality that transcends political structure, is, accordingly, to lose as well any reason to worry about what rights do. Rights do nothing but, for better or worse, represent interests, strongly felt.

This is consequentially wrong, however. One can accept the premise – indeed one should accept the premise – that rights have no "outer" origin that gives the claims made on their behalf some extralegal, political, constitutional, or moral significance beyond the legal, political, constitutional, or moral significance of the interests that motivate them and also realize that both rights and rights consciousness nevertheless have force, power, and consequence. Rights consciousness itself does things: it exists, it causes things to happen, it harms some people, it benefits others. An interest felt by gun owners in wanting weaker gun control laws is one thing; the existence of a right to own a gun – both a moral right and a constitutional right and the change in consciousness that right effectuates – is quite another. That the latter is an expression of the former does not mean it is nothing but the former, dressed up. Rather, the right changes our political landscape, in ways that the interest does not. Obviously, when constitutionalized, it constrains legislators; some laws that would control guns and gun violence are struck. Gun violence goes up. There are other consequences as well, less obvious but more serious, that attend whether the right is constitutionalized. The gun owner, by virtue of the right, and by virtue of rights consciousness, is *valorized* not just ossified: he becomes, as do all rights owners, a particular type of quintessential American hero. When the interest some have in gun control laws bows to a "right" to own a gun, the rhetoric surrounding the debate changes, and profoundly: as we acknowledge and eventually celebrate the right to

---

[87] *Id.* at 212–13.

speech, and worship, and so on, and hence celebrate our eccentrics, dissidents, loners, geniuses, and mavericks as in some way quintessentially American, so we now acknowledge, and may eventually celebrate, our Second Amendment right to own a gun, and hence tolerate, and eventually celebrate, those walking in our parks, streets, homes, and political rallies openly carrying armed weapons as American prototypes. That is a powerful rhetorical shift. Last, political power likewise shifts as a result of the articulation of an interest in the form of a constitutional right. Local governments are disempowered while gun owners are empowered, less armed citizens are disempowered *vis-à-vis* more armed citizens, armed residents of domestic homes and neighborhoods are empowered compared with the less armed residents of those same domestic homes. All of this becomes harder to change through ordinary democratic process, harder to criticize through ordinary means of persuasion, and harder to challenge through constitutional forms of litigation, precisely by virtue of the existence of the right.

Later, I discuss in more detail these and other harms occasioned by rights discourse, when engaged both by the political left and the political right, that have still gone relatively unnoticed, even after the rights critiques of the 1980s.[88] The problem with the critical legal studies' moral brief against rights that I want to highlight is that it did not go far enough; it was bare bones at the time and remains undeveloped. It was also relatively ineffective. It was, however, remarkably *prescient*: we are now awash in new and regressive rights that have all of the effects noted by the rights critiques of the 1980s but that carry harms that go beyond those effects as well. Yet we still do not have a developed understanding – or several competing understandings – of the ways in which "faith in rights" by liberals in the '60s and '70s legitimated and strengthened the movement toward these ascendant right-wing rights of the '90s and aughts: rights to guns, rights to homeschooling, rights to opt out of mandatory health insurance, rights to corporate speech, and so on. Below, I draw out some of those continuities and discontinuities.

What I want to note here, is a more limited point. The difference between the '80s rights critique of the critical legal studies movement, and the rights critiques of the 2000s, as exemplified by Kennedy's updated piece, is that whereas the former rested on both moral and jurisprudential grounds – rights harm the party of humanity *and* are indeterminate, as are all other forms of law – the latter has retained the indeterminacy critique and basically jettisoned the moral brief. Rights, Kennedy argues, then and now, are grounded in interests, and as interests change, so do the rights that reflect them. They have no necessary moral valence one way or the other. The "rights critique" that emerges from this observation is not only paltry, although it is that, but it is also peculiarly morally denuded. Rights are neither good nor bad. They do not liberate, as liberals contend, but they do not oppress either. They do not

---

[88] *Infra* 63–66.

express our humanity or alienate us from each other. They merely reflect interests. To believe otherwise is simply a category mistake. We should neither have faith in their goodness nor worry over the harms they might do. We should regard them, at most, with a sense of irony.

So, whither the rights critique? Why did the argument that rights are indeed harmful to the party of humanity fall by the wayside? What happened to the moral critique against rights in liberal legalist regimes?

One possible answer to that question, which is to date largely unexplored in the literature that chronicles the death of critical legal studies, is that the moral brief urged by the rights critics of the 1980s was in effect *undermined* by the indeterminacy critique, and between the two, the indeterminacy critique is what survived. The denuding and truncation of the rights critique, I believe, was a direct consequence of the survival of the indeterminacy critique, with which it was always in tension, although the tension was largely unnoticed early on. The indeterminacy of rights renders the harms they do, and therefore any reason to worry over them, as well as any good they do, and therefore any reason to have irrational "faith" in them, insignificant, just as a matter of logic. Rights are transient, according to the indeterminacy claim, particularly as evidenced by Kennedy's critique, and the interests they reflect equally so. It is as naïve to worry over rights as to have faith in them, and for the same reason; they have no outside origin in anything other than interest, which in turn has no salience without power.[89] Rights, in Kennedy's retelling, are no part of the solution to our political situation, thus the lack of faith.[90] We should stop relying on rights arguments to achieve political gains as though rights have some existence outside of the political argument we aim to make. Rights are no part of the solution. They are, however, by the same token, no part of the political problem.[91] They mirror interests, and more specifically, they mirror the interests of those who have ascended to a position of power. Far from being an articulation of truth asserted in the face of power, as claimed by rights romantics, they are basically a recordation of powerful interests, and we can better understand them if we begin by acknowledging that fact.

The "right critique," however, stops there. We need not and should not *worry* over what they do: we need not worry that they alienate us from ourselves and each other, insulate the private sphere, further embed privilege, and so on. They do these things, after all, only contingently. They'll do other things, perhaps more congenial, perhaps not, when other interests come to the fore. It all depends on the congeniality of the interests.

What follows from rights' indeterminacy is *not* that it is unwise to pursue progressive political goals through a strategy of rights articulation. Just as rights have no

---

[89] Kennedy, "The Critique of Rights," *Left Legalism/Left Critique* 209–14.

[90] *Id.* at 212–14.

[91] *Id.* at 215–16.

outside origin, they have no necessary strategic valence; they are no more necessarily regressive than progressive. All that follows is that when making a rights-based argument for a progressive political end, one ought to do so with a tone of ironic detachment from the enterprise; that one do so, in other words, knowing that the right is of one's own creation; that it does not originate in "human nature," "God's will," or universal reason. However, this implication from indeterminacy does not simply represent a departure from the broader defining worries over the efficacy, humaneness, and wisdom of our liberal rights. Rather, it jettisons and undermines those arguments. Rights, according to the moral brief, including liberal rights, have unintended consequences that favor regressive political forces. They are harmful to the party of humanity. They are so, because of what rights are and have been in this culture, not because they are wrongly believed to come from a secure moral Archimedean point outside politics. If this is true, then there is a good reason – several in fact – to be wary of rights arguments, with or without the requisite ironic detachment: they promise short-term gains with longer-term costs that are substantially weightier. With a right to an end to de jure segregation came the valorization of de facto racism. With a right to privacy came the valorization of the private sphere, and the subordination that occurs within it. With a right to speech came suspicion of the state and of democracy, and hence a suspicion of state action taken against corporations, and hence, eventually, the valorization of corporate speech, and so on. Worry over the unintended consequences of liberal rights' tendency to strengthen the hand of the political right need not be premised on a naïve view of rights' origins. It is, rather, premised on a claim – contestable to be sure – that rights, in this culture, in this country, given our history, have a structure that is at heart regressive and inhumane.

Thus, Kennedy's indeterminacy critique renders the moral critique – that rights are harmful – incoherent. Rights cannot harm the party of humanity if they have no consequence; they are not regressive if they have no content; they do not consistently favor wealth even when they appear not to, if they have no necessary valence. They can, apparently, be used for good or ill. This is not a rights critique. It is, rather, a plea for irony: a plea that we discard a misguided faith in rights' certainty, their permanence, or their origination outside politics. For those who never had such a faith, the limited claim that rights reflect and record interests is redundant. For those who recognize that rights, contingent to be sure, have an origin firmly in politics, and in culture, and in legalism, and who worry that that very contingent but firmly etched point of origin is regressive, individualistic, and conservative at its core, the neo-critical critique of rights is worse than redundant. It has simply become yet another voice arguing a false promise: litigated rights, no less than interests, indeed no differently than interests, pursued through courts, albeit with irony this time rather than moral fervor, can change culture, law, and politics all, in any direction one sees fit to pursue. The rights critique is now indistinguishable from the liberal legal regime that originally was its target.

Wither Legitimation

The Gramscian idea of hegemonic legitimation played an outsized role in the critics' moral brief against liberal legalism.[92] The idea of "legitimation" generally has a complex history, but as the critics used it, it was simple enough: even a fully realized ethical principle, moral ideal, or laudable political innovation might render a larger injustice or wrong acceptable in the minds of those who suffer it as well as those who inflict it, by legitimating the regime that occasions the wrong, and, more specifically, it might legitimate wrongs caused by the particular relationships within the scope of the moral advance, if those relationships are also the source of the wrong.[93] Some legitimating effects are clear and widely understood and simply understood as worth the cost, although rarely understood in that language. For example, it is commonly understood that a robust right to free speech legitimates the harms such speech often causes, such as harms caused by hate speech, the defamation of public officials, pornography, and the like – and, at least according to civil libertarians, we assume that it is better to absorb those harms than seek to prevent or redress them through state action. Sometimes, however, if the "legitimating cost" of a legal right or innovation is sufficiently high, and sufficiently hidden, the legitimating cost might outweigh whatever benefit the right confers. Often, the legitimating cost of a legal right or moral principle is hard to unearth; it becomes a cultural presupposition, rather than a contestable harm that we can readily identify, seek to minimize, or otherwise confront.

The critics were perhaps the first radical legal academics to notice that American law, and particularly our constitutional scheme of rights and liberties, carries high legitimating costs indeed. They made two broad legitimation-cost arguments. The first I have already noted, because it became an integral part of the rights critiques: rights that protect the exercise of private power against state intervention legitimate the harms caused by exercise of the right protected and thereby insulate those harms against even moral examination, much less political change.[94] Even if the existence of the right is warranted, it has a tendency to render the harms inflicted through exercise of the right not only nonremediable by law – because of the

---

[92] Greer, "Antonio Gramsci and 'Legal Hegemony,'" *The Politics of Law*; Gordon, "New Developments in Legal Theory," *The Politics of Law*; Crenshaw, "Race, Reform, and Retrenchment" 1350–66.

[93] Gordon, "New Developments in Legal Theory," *The Politics of Law* 286–87 ("Law . . . is one of these clusters of belief – and it ties in with a lot of other nonlegal but similar clusters – that convince people that all the many hierarchies in which they live and work are natural and necessary.").

[94] *See, e.g.*, Tushnet, "An Essay on Rights" 1393–94; Gordon, "New Developments in Legal Theory," *The Politics of Law* 287–88; MacKinnon, *Feminism Unmodified* 152, 93–102; Kelman, "Consumption Theory"; Kelman, "Choice and Utility" 797 ("[Neo-classical economics] is a method that could only be invented and adhered to by apologists, those whose interest was in reassuring us all of the beneficence of whatever order happens to emerge from the interplay of market forces, regardless of the nature of the society in which that market functions."); Kelman, *A Guide to Critical Legal Studies* 263 ("legitimation" as "law creates and reinforces ideology that makes it difficult, in a cognitive sense, to perceive both its injustices and its mutability").

existence of the right – but also, eventually, invisible to both law and culture. The "right" to commodify and then freely buy and sell labor, for example, as Marx in the nineteenth[95] and Hale in the early twentieth century[96] both pointed out, legitimates the harms caused by the buyer's exploitation of the weaker position of the seller, where the penalty of not participating in these free contracts might be severe deprivation. Likewise, rights to buy and sell consumer goods cast a legitimating blanket over the terms of those contracts of sale that might be onerous to purchasers rendered dependent on the goods bought and sold. Thus, markets themselves, both for goods and labor, legitimate both inequalities they create and protect, as well as specific harms caused by the rights to freely engage in them.

More specifically, even the palliative doctrines in contract law – such as unconscionability, duress, implied warranties, and the like – by forgiving weaker contractors of some onerous contractual obligations, legitimates larger patterns of alienation and exploitation in contracts.[97] Likewise, rights against state-sponsored discrimination as described earlier, when combined with rights to contractual liberty, seemingly legitimate private discrimination in various ways.[98] Rights to privacy legitimate the various subordinations – economic, cultural, sexual, private, and intimate – that occur within those protected private spheres.[99] In each case, the right to engage in conduct, even if the right has been constructed for a good reason, insulates the harms caused within the sphere of private behavior protected by the right – harm that is often sustained by the very people for whom the right was ostensibly created – and it is insulated not just from legal redress but even from public scrutiny or moral censure. The harms caused workers by exploitative working conditions, consumers by credit terms for credit cards or purchase terms for products, racial minorities by sanctified private patterns of discrimination, or weaker members of families by the privacy of patterns of intrafamily abuse and domination are all rendered invisible – they are legitimated – by the insulating and privatizing right to sell labor, buy products, be free of state discrimination, or enjoy the privacy of the family against state moralism – rights that increase the liberty, ostensibly, of workers, consumers, people of color, and women. The cumulative effect of all of this legitimation, according to this first of the two legitimation arguments put forward by various critical scholars, is that we are rights-rich, and well-being-poor. We have a wealth of rights, each of which protects us against some specified harm occasioned by or threatened by pernicious state action: the harm of moralistic legislation, intrusions on our liberty, irrational state-sponsored discriminatory behavior, invasions of privacy, and so on.

---

95 *See* Robin West, "Law's Nobility," *Yale Journal of Law and Feminism* 17.2 (2005): 385–458, 396–7.

96 Robert L. Hale, "Bargaining, Duress, and Economic Liberty," *Columbia Law Review* 43.5 (1943): 603–28; – , "Coercion and Distribution in a Supposedly Non-Coercive State," *Political Science Quarterly* 38.3 (1923): 470–94.

97 Peter Gabel and Jay M. Feinman, "Contract Law as Ideology," *The Politics of Law* 172–84.

98 Freeman, "Antidiscrimination Law: A Critical Review," *The Politics of Law*.

99 MacKinnon, *Feminism Unmodified* 93–102.

In each case, the right protects us against state intrusion but, by virtue of so doing, legitimates the private conduct within the sphere of conduct created by the right. The right to familial privacy thus legitimates the domestic violence and the subordination that occurs within the closed doors, the right to speech legitimates the harms occasioned by hate speech and pornography, the right to a lawyer legitimates the abuses of the penal system, and so on.

The second argument, which also borrowed heavily from Marx, concerned the legitimating function not of rights per se, as of the individual act of consent, in liberal legal systems.[100] Consent, in liberal legal regimes, is widely viewed as legitimating that to which consent was given, just as rights legitimate the behavior that the right protects. If I consent to a transaction, a change, a contract, a regime, a rule, a law, or a judgment, then for various reasons I will be presumptively viewed as benefitting from the change, contract, regime, rule of law, and so on. Because I benefitted from the change, that change is not only protected against legal intervention but against moral or political critique as well. The consensual change, in other words, is fully legitimated: protected against both legal and moral challenge. We have a laundry list of reasons, reflected in ordinary speech, moral theory, liberal theory, and normative economics, for *why* consensual changes should be so protected against even criticism, much less legal challenge. From common sense: "If I didn't want it, I wouldn't have agreed to it." "I might not know much, but I know what I like." "Nobody knows me better than me; I'm not a child, who is somebody else to decide what's good for me?" From liberal theory: "To presume otherwise would be unduly paternalistic." From economics, and normative law and economics: "If no one else is hurt and both parties consent to the transaction, it is a Pareto optimal change." "It's wealth maximizing." From libertarianism: "A regime that respects our consent, expands our liberty." The collective effect of these maxims, clichés, presumptions, and circular definitions – consent increases wealth, for example, because wealth is what is created when both parties consent to a change[101] – is to reinforce, and mightily, the sanctifying, purifying, cleansing power of individual consent. If an individual consents to something, in a culture that protects autonomy and views autonomy as exercised with every act of consent, two (quite different) things follow from the giving of consent: whatever was consented to is therefore (most likely) *legal*, and second, whatever was consented to is, by virtue of its consensuality, therefore *good*. Whatever new world is created by the act of consent is equally legal as but also morally better than the one that preceded it, solely by virtue of the act of consent. Barring adverse affects on nonconsenting third parties, the postconsent world is, by

---

[100] Kelman, "Choice and Utility"; – , *A Guide to Critical Legal Studies*; Gabel and Feinman, "Contract Law as Ideology," *The Politics of Law*; Kennedy, "Distributive and Paternalist Motives"; Robin West, "Authority, Autonomy, and Choice: The Role of Consent in the Moral and Political Visions of Franz Kafka and Richard Posner," *Harvard Law Review* 99.2 (1985): 384–428; West, "Submission, Choice, and Ethics: A Rejoinder to Judge Posner," *Harvard Law Review* 99.7 (1986): 1449–56.

[101] Richard A. Posner, *The Economics of Justice* (Cambridge: Harvard University Press, 1981) 61, 68.

definition, better than the world that existed before the act of consent. Consensual transactions, in short, improve our world.

This is false, however. As a number of critical theorists argued, but as ordinary reflection should reveal, a postconsensual world is not necessarily good or morally superior to the preconsensual world by virtue of its consensuality, for any number of reasons. Choices, of course, might be limited. Working for minimum wage might beat working for no wage at all or not working, but it might nevertheless not be a living wage. Working conditions might be noxious, obnoxious, or poisonous; the workplace might be saturated with asbestos, harassment both sexual and otherwise, mind-numbing repetitive labor, and eardrum-shattering noise. The fact that the only alternative to all of this – unemployment – is worse for those who consent to it all, hardly makes the harms caused by all that consensual labor disappear.[102] If the belief that the consensual world is inevitably better than the preconsensual world contributes to a world in which the harms done by the consensual transaction are minimized, then the postconsensual world might well be worse than the preconsensual world. That someone chose to have a baby rather than an abortion means that her motherhood was indeed consensual; it does not mean, however, that saddling a poor mother with the task of raising a child in a social world that provides only negligible help is not a real harm suffered both by the mother and her child.[103] A post–*Roe v. Wade* world in which the "right to choose" legitimates the poverty of motherhood is not necessarily better even for the chooser than the world that preceded it. Second, our perception of our choices might be colored by sour grapes: we might feel our choices to be better than they are because they are all we can reasonably expect to have.[104] We might indeed "cling to" our guns, whiskey, and carnivals, as candidate Obama famously and near-disastrously opined, if we have no realistic option of having meaningful work, transformative education, and fulfilling relationships.[105] We might desperately want to have a child, even if

---

[102] Hale, "Bargaining, Duress, and Economic Liberty"; Hale, "Coercion and Distribution"; Kelman, "Consumption Theory"; Kelman, "Choice and Utility" 797 ("[Neo-classical economics] is a method that could only be invented and adhered to by apologists, those whose interest was in reassuring us all of the beneficence of whatever order happens to emerge from the interplay of market forces, regardless of the nature of the society in which that market functions.").

[103] Robin West, "From Choice to Reproductive Justice," *Yale Law Journal* 118.7 (2009): 1394–433; West, "Authority, Autonomy, and Choice."

[104] Jon Elster, *Sour Grapes: Studies in the Subversion of Rationality* (Cambridge: Cambridge University Press, 1983).

[105] Then-candidate Obama was quoted as saying:

> You go into these small towns in Pennsylvania and, like a lot of small towns in the Midwest, the jobs have been gone now for 25 years and nothing's replaced them. And they fell through the Clinton administration, and the Bush administration, and each successive administration has said that somehow these communities are gonna regenerate and they have not. And it's not surprising then they get bitter, they cling to guns or religion or antipathy to people who aren't like them or anti-immigrant sentiment or antitrade sentiment as a way to explain their frustrations.

we cannot responsibly raise one, if that is the only way we can envision finding love in the world. We might want to have a relationship with one man, and agree to sex we do not want with him, if we think the relationship will protect us against more threatening violence from others. We might consent to a change because we have come to falsely believe that the change is in our interest when it in fact is not: we may have a limited view of our own interests, we may mistake our interests for that of someone else on whom we have become dependent, or believe ourselves to be dependent.

Of course, it does not follow from any of this that intervention by the state into these consensual relationships or transactions is therefore warranted. It does not follow from someone's lack of self-knowledge that anyone else knows the person's interest better, that other available options would be an improvement, that the person should be incapacitated from making self-regarding decisions, or that the individual is in any way incompetent. It does not follow that the state is all knowing or should be more powerful. It does not follow that individuals do not more often than not know what is best for them. It does not follow that communities should engage in moralistic or perfectionist legislative acts. All that follows from the claim that consent does not ensure that the postconsensual world is a good one for the person rendering consent is that the postconsent world should not be immunized from critique – and that the consensual transaction that led to it should not be immunized from moral censure. Sex that is consensual is not rape, but that consensual sex is not rape does not imply that all acts of consensual sex are therefore good – consensual sex might not be good at all for any number of reasons consistent with the presence of consent.[106] It might not be pleasurable, it might not have been wanted, it might transmit disease, it might impregnate against the desires of either or both parties, and so on. All that follows from the consensuality of consensual sex is that *if* it is bad, it is bad for reasons other than coercion; it is bad for reasons other than whatever it is that makes rape bad. Likewise, that an exchange of goods is consensual means that it is not theft, but the consensuality of an exchange does not imply that the exchange was fair or good for both parties; it might not be, for any number of reasons. That a labor contract is consensual means it is not slavery, but that it is not enslavement does not imply that it is not exploitative or harmful. Consent to a sale, to sex, or to work does not imply that any of these transactions create value, where value is defined as anything other than wealth, even if the consent does imply that the sale, the sex, and the work are not rape, slavery and theft. What does follow is the need for critique.

Katharine Seelye and Jeff Zeleny, "On the Defensive, Obama Calls His Words Ill-Chosen," *NYTimes.com*, April 13, 2008. Available at http://www.nytimes.com/2008/04/13/us/politics/13campaign .html.

[106] West, "Authority, Autonomy, and Choice"; West, "Submission, Choice, and Ethics"; West, "Harms of Consensual Sex," *The Philosophy of Sex: Contemporary Readings*, 5th ed., Alan Soble and Nicholas Power, eds. (New York: Rowman and Littlefield, 2008) 317–25.

The "legitimating" function of consent is that it masks the force and sometimes even the logic of moral criticism of postconsensual states of the world. The consensual transaction becomes the good transaction, by force of the legitimating power of consent, and likewise, the bad transaction becomes the coerced transaction, in the minds and rhetoric of anyone sensing the transaction's immorality. This is illogical, and politically disastrous, in liberal regimes that valorize consent and autonomy. "Consensual" implies freedom from force or coercion – a consensual transaction is one that is the product of consent rather than force – but consensual does not imply good, and the false belief that it does both makes critique of consensual transactions all the harder and funnels critique into the confusing and often counterexperiential claim that the consensual transaction is for some deep reason in fact coerced. Consensual sex, labor, or consumer purchases can be good, bad, or neither. Consensual sex might be harmless or wondrous, if desired and enjoyed by all parties, or it might be harmful, if it is harassing, unwanted, intrusive, or alienating for one or both parties. Consensual labor might be joyful or monotonous, it might be rewarding or stifling; consumer purchases might increase or decrease well-being whatever the case for whether they increase or decrease wealth. These straightforward enough lived truths are precisely what are obfuscated in our commonsensical utterings, our liberal presuppositions about the dangers of paternalism, and our definitions of wealth and efficiency. We assume, commonsensically, that adults are always right about what they consent to; that the very suggestion that consensual transactions might be worth investigating or criticizing is an open invitation to state invasion, moralistic intrusion, and unwarranted paternalism; and that consensual transactions by definition increase the well-being of consenting parties, no less than their wealth. Consent thus "legitimates" the world to which consent is given: it renders it insulated from critique as well as legal regulation.

Why this happens, and how this happens, are hard questions. That it happens, however, and routinely, in liberal legal discourse, is itself an important claim and one that motivated broad swaths of the critics' brief against liberal legalism.[107] Consent shields from critique that to which consent is given, and that should count as a cost of consensual ethics broadly, across the board. Sometimes, that cost might be outweighed by the increase in self-regarding freedom that consensual regimes confer. Sometimes, however, that increase in liberty might be negligible and the legitimation cost quite high. When it is, the contract for sale, the work contract, or the sexual transaction might be sensibly targeted for sustained criticism, whether or not legal regulation. Critical scholarship was largely aimed at opening up to criticism that which might not otherwise be, by virtue of its apparent consensuality, from consensual sexual transactions, to consensual sales of goods, consensual labor contracts, and so on.

---

[107] Elisabeth Mensch, "The History of Mainstream Legal Thought," *The Politics of Law* 18–39; Kelman, *Critical Legal Studies* 269–95; Unger, "Critical Legal Studies" 655–56.

So, that was the skeletal outline of the legitimation argument. It differed, of course, depending on context – on what harm was being legitimated and by what route, by what right, or by what act of consent. Nonetheless, the core of it was clear, and shared across doctrinal context: real harms suffered by real people are legitimated by abstract rights and nominal acts of individual consent. As rights and the ethics of consent both constitute the moral essence of liberalism, and particularly of liberal legalism – they are liberalism's key moral inventions – these legitimation arguments about their hidden costs were hugely important. Rights and consent – rights and liberty – the critics argued, are rhetorical tools that occasionally deliver the goods but also routinely legitimate harms. They do so duplicitously. A gain in rights or in the consensuality of our world might be on occasion worth the legitimating cost, to secure a rights-based gain. However, it is always worth knowing what the costs might be. A wide swath of critical scholarship was simply an accounting of liberalism's legitimating harms.

Arguments regarding the legitimating force of rights and consent, however – once the bread and butter of critical scholarship – are now muted, both within and outside critical scholarship. Unlike the indeterminacy critique or deconstructionist methodology, they have not been absorbed in mainstream writing in those areas of law that are heavily influenced by the liberal valorization of consent, such as constitutional law, contract law, or contract-related fields. This is most striking in the context of rights, if only because during the Clinton, Bush, and now the Obama administrations – all of which came to power after the articulation of the rights and legitimation critiques – there has been an expansion, not a diminution, of rights and their role within liberal legalism. Thus, we now recognize, whether originating in courts, in advocacy, or simply in scholarship, rights that were not on the horizon when the rights critique and legitimation critiques were first penned: rights to gun ownership originally pushed by fringe militias but now embraced by the Supreme Court and mainstream scholarship both,[108] a right to same-sex sex and same-sex marriage once pushed only by various sex radicals and now accepted by a number of states and a broad cross-section of the public,[109] a right to sexual privacy

---

[108] *District of Columbia v. Heller*, 128 S.Ct. 2783 (2008); Randy E. Barnett and Don B. Kates, "Under Fire: The New Consensus on the Second Amendment," *Emory Law Journal* 45.4 (1996): 1139–260; Sanford Levinson, "Assessing *Heller*," *International Journal of Constitution Law* 7.2 (2009): 316–28; Levinson, "Why Didn't the Supreme Court Take My Advice in the Heller Case – Some Speculative Responses to an Egocentric Question," *Hastings Law Journal* 60.0 (2008–9): 1491–506.

[109] *Goodridge v. Dept. of Public Health*, 798 N.E.2d 941 (Mass. 2003) (holding that the state of Massachusetts could not deny marriage recognition to same-sex couples); *Perry v. Schwarzenegger*, 704 F.Supp.2d 921 (N.D. Cal. 2010) (holding that California's Proposition 8 banning gay marriage violated equal protection and due process guarantees; note that the challenge to Prop 8 was argued in federal court by Theodore Olsen, former Solicitor General under President George W. Bush, and David Boies, who represented presidential candidate Al Gore, against Olsen, in *Bush v. Gore*, 531 U.S. 98 (2000)); *Answers to Questions about Marriage Equality* (Washington, DC: Human Rights Campaign, 2009); William N. Eskridge Jr. and Darren R. Spedale, *Gay Marriage: For Better or Worse? What We've Learned from the Evidence* (New York: Oxford University Press, 2006); William N. Eskridge

recently expanded by Supreme Court doctrine so as to include same-sex sexuality,[110] corporate rights to speech also accepted by the Court,[111] a right aggressively pushed by Christian conservative advocacy groups to "homeschool" one's children to avoid the secular curriculum of the public schools[112] that is accepted by a few courts and more notably by almost all cash-strapped state legislators and education administrators,[113] a "right to die" and to assisted suicide pushed by liberal advocacy groups,[114] and a right argued by libertarian advocacy groups and scholars to avoid a mandate to purchase health insurance.[115] All of these new rights have severe legitimation costs or run legitimation risks: they legitimate, in order, the shrinking of dollars for police protection of citizens against the violence of private perpetrators; the shrinking of dollars for public education and a weakening of the felt duty of states to provide it; the shrinking of public dollars for palliative care and a weakening of the duty to ensure it; the expanding powers of corporations to oversee and dictate the terms and limits of public discourse, the presence, and felt legitimacy – the natural okayedness – of coercive, blanket mandates of sexual participation in various private and intimate spheres, including the workplace and school; and, most recently and obviously, the lack of public health care for all citizens. If ever there was a need for a healthy robust body of scholarship challenging the legitimating logic of rights, that time would seem to be now. We are awash in new rights, virtually all of them are regressive, and virtually all of them legitimate real harms suffered by real people: victims of gun violence, victims of sexual coercion, uninsured sick people, uneducated and undereducated homeschooled children, and citizens mal- and misinformed relentlessly through a media saturated with the corporate interests of their corporate owners. All of this proceeds uninterrupted by left-wing legal critique. Yet there has been precious little – almost no – writing from critical theorists that challenges the legitimating function of the new rights that have been articulated in and outside of courts since 1990 or so.

Jr., *The Case for Same Sex Marriage: From Sexual Liberty to Civilized Commitment* (New York: Free Press, 1996); Robin West, *Marriage, Sexuality, and Gender* (Boulder: Paradigm Publishers, 2007).

[110] *Lawrence v. Texas*, 539 U.S. 558 (2003). For critical reviews of *Lawrence*, see Catharine MacKinnon, "The Road Not Taken: Sex Equality in *Lawrence v. Texas*," *Ohio State Law Journal* 65.5 (2004): 1081–96 and Cass Sunstein, "Liberty After Lawrence," *Ohio State Law Journal* 65.5 (2004): 1059–80.

[111] *Citizens United v. Federal Election Commission*, 130 S. Ct. 876 (2010). For discussion of corporate speech, *see, e.g.*, Daniel J. H. Greenwood, "Essential Speech: Why Corporate Speech Is Not Free," *Iowa Law Journal* 83.5 (1989): 995–1070.

[112] Kimberly A. Yuracko, "Education Off the Grid," *California Law Review* 96.1 (2008): 123–84; Robert Reich, "Testing the Boundaries of Parental Authority over Education: The Case of Homeschooling," *Moral and Political Education*, eds. Stephen Macedo and Yael Tamir (New York: New York University Press, 2002) 275–313.

[113] *In re Jonathan*, 165 Cal. App. 4th 1074 (Ct. App. 2008).

[114] *See* Robert Nozick, Thomas Nagel, Ronald Dworkin, T. M. Scanlon, and John Rawls, "Assisted Suicide: The Philosophers' Brief," *The New York Review of Books* 44.5 (March 27, 1997).

[115] Barnett, Stewart, and Gaziano, *Why the Personal Mandate to Buy Health Insurance Is Unprecedented and Unconstitutional*.

Likewise, the role of consensual ethics in masking or legitimating harms caused by those consensual transactions has grown, not shrunk, since the articulation in the 1980s of the legitimation critique. The actual consent of consumers is now routinely invoked to legitimate the imposition of usurious interest rates by credit card companies, the consent of landowners is invoked to legitimate the sufferance of a wide range of environmental harms, the consent of workers invoked to legitimate workplace dangers, and so on. More insidiously the consent of citizens to risks is inferred from behavior in the calculation of various costs of regulations and then used to justify deregulatory actions. Yet there has been little from critics on the legitimation costs of these consensual transactions or the use of implied consent to justify deregulatory regimes. Consent to sex is taken as full justification for a collective blindness to both societal and individual pressures to engage in unwanted sex, so long as the sex is short of rape; the consensual purchase of services or goods or the consensual decision not to purchase such services or goods, such as insurance, is taken as consent to the sufferance of various risk; the consent to marriage is justification for the privacy of the relations thereby created and the relative invisibility of harms that may occur with them; consent to purchase an abortion is taken as justification for the full privatization of the costs of child rearing; consent to purchase, or not, a gun for use in one's home is taken as justifying the privatization of police protection against private violence; the consent to purchase, or not, private education for one's children, or the decision to homeschool, or not, is increasingly invoked as justification for the inadequacies of the public schools, and so on. One would think that the expansion of the use of consent by right-wing and conservative commentators and some scholars to justify what seems to be harmful state neglect of real harms would have led to an increase in the analysis of legitimation as a force in liberal legal regimes, but it has not. Nor have these arguments been absorbed in mainstream legal discourse, at least if measured by law review scholarship. The legitimating force of both the idea of rights and of the act of consent seems to have survived the critics' skeptical attacks.

And what of neo-critical thought? With one exception that I discuss later, neo-critical thought has simply abandoned legitimation arguments – they do not appear. In at least one arena, however – namely, the sexual – neo-critical literature is marked not simply by an abandonment of legitimation arguments but by an aggressive rejection of the *logic* of legitimation critiques. This is perhaps most clearly exemplified by Janet Halley's influential brief against radical feminism and, specifically, her arguments against feminist analyses of sexual harassment. It warrants a more detailed look.

As is well known, radical feminists have argued for decades that women consent to sex or tolerate sexual advances both at work and elsewhere that they do not welcome and that are harmful to them. In some circumstances, according to both radical feminists and now the law, the sufferance of that sex, or sexual advance, is and should be actionable sexual harassment, if it interferes with work or school performance.[116] Much more broadly, however, some feminists have argued that the consensual sex that women and some men routinely tolerate, enjoy, suffer, or impose on each other can cause harms that are wrongly *legitimated* by the real or apparent consent participants render. Sex for pay; sex for a grade or a promotion; sex in exchange for financial security; sex in exchange for protection from potentially violent men; sex in exchange for feelings of self-worth or acceptance by peers; sex motivated by a conception of value overly influenced by fashion magazines, music videos, or pornography; sex in exchange for the approval of one's community or religious authorities; or sex given from a sense of duty all might be *consensual*,[117] and therefore not rape, but all of that sex might also be nevertheless *harmful*: unwanted sex, even if consensual, might interfere with a girl's or a woman's sense of autonomy, self-possession, physical and moral integrity, her own pleasures, and her sense of her own power in the world – her ability to act on the basis of her own hedonic desires. The woman or girl's consent to sex she does not want in any of these circumstances legitimates these harms and insulates the sex from the political or moral criticism that it might otherwise garner.[118]

In a number of articles[119] and then an important book, Janet Halley has defended all of this consensual sex – sex at work, sex on battlefields, sex by prostitutes, sex with trafficked women and girls, sex under the bleachers, unpleasurable or unwanted sex – against these and related feminist critiques and on two grounds. First, sexuality is a realm within which power is exercised, enjoyed, and celebrated.[120] Power, and particularly sexual power, seems to operate as a sort of proxy for individual and human well-being. The exercise of power is not only all there is that is worth studying, as Foucault famously opined,[121] but it is also all there is that is struggled for in life, perhaps by definition. All else is subterfuge, dishonesty, slave morality, or false consciousness. The exercise of power in the realm of sexual relations is therefore a

---

[116] *See* Reva B. Seigel, "A Short History of Sexual Harassment," in *Directions in Sexual Harassment Law*, Reva B. Seigel and Catharine MacKinnon, eds. (New Haven: Yale University Press, 2003) 1–39. Major cases in sexual harassment law include *Meritor Savings Bank v. Vinson*, 477 U.S. 57 (1986) (holding that harassment resulting in a "hostile environment," even without economic quid pro quo, was prohibited by Title VII); *Oncale v. Sundowner Offshore Services*, 523 U.S. 75 (1998) (holding that same-sex harassment is prohibited by Title VII); *Burlington Industries, Inc. v. Ellerth*, 524 U.S. 742 (1998) (holding that employers can be vicariously liable for harassment between employees).

[117] West, "Harms of Consensual Sex."

[118] Robin West, "Sex, Law, and Consent," in *The Ethics of Consent: Theory and Practice*, Franklin G. Miller and Alan Wertheimer, eds. (New York: Oxford University Press, 2010) 221–50.

[119] Janet Halley, "Sexuality Harassment," *Left Legalism/Left Critique* 80–104; –, "The Politics of Injury: A Review of Robin West's Caring for Justice," *Unbound: Harvard Journal of the Legal Left* 7.1 (2005): 65–92; – , *Split Decisions: Taking a Break from Feminism* (Princeton: Princeton University Press, 2006).

[120] Halley, *Split Decisions* 11, 13, 15, 348–63; Ian Halley, "Queer Theory by Men," *Duke Journal of Gender Law and Policy* 11 (2004): 7–54, 46–48 ("Ian Halley" also publishes as Janet Halley).

[121] Michel Foucault, "Confinement, Psychiatry, Prison," *Politics, Philosophy, Culture: Interviews and Other Writings, 1977–84*, ed. Lawrence D. Kristman, trans. Alan Sheridan et al. (New York: Routledge, 1988) 178–210, 200–05.

virtually unqualified good – a good that might be alchemized in all sorts of forms but one that should never be questioned, moralized over, or regulated.[122]

In the most extreme forms of this argument within the contours of queer theory's response to feminism, harms caused by sex even in the absence of consent – rape – are accordingly downplayed or minimized. Either consensual or nonconsensual sex with children, for example, Foucault famously argued, should be criminalized only if there is both objective evidence of injury and a well-articulated "no" from the child. The injury of nonconsensual intercourse alone is illusory, and the desires of children are sufficiently sexualized that it would be unduly Victorian to presume lack of consent in the face of ambiguous denials.[123] Radical feminism, David Kennedy argues in his libertine response to the Clinton impeachment, unduly fetishizes consent.[124] Halley, too, expresses skepticism: women's claims of sexual violation across the board, including claims of rape, Halley argues, are often the result of a "sex panic"[125] and warrant skepticism. Women claim rape, she avers, to disclaim responsibility for their own desires, and even if the sex is truly nonconsensual, the harms of rape are often relatively trivial and just overblown.[126] Against nonexistent or trivial harms, sex is so overwhelmingly good – because so overwhelmingly an exercise of power and so overwhelmingly conducive to pleasure – that the withholding of consent to its offer is just not particularly believable.[127]

More important, however – because more plausibly – she has argued that *consensual* sex in all its forms – including the kind that is harassing – should be drastically deregulated.[128] Consent to sex completes the circle, so to speak, of sex's purity: sex is almost always innocent, and when consensual, there can be no "legitimate" basis for criticism. Consensual sex is just too good to be circumscribed, or bound, by claims of its unwelcomeness or unwantedness. The claims that consensual sex is in fact unwelcome or unwanted are likely false in any event.[129] The harms sustained, even if the claims are true, are trivial.

Halley's critique of sexual harassment law thus rests squarely on a near-total rejection of the logic of the critique of legitimation, at least in the realm of sexual power. Consent to sex, it turns out, truly *does* legitimate the sex that follows. To do otherwise, Halley argues, in an echo of both the liberal and libertarian valorization of consent, particularly in the realm of sex, is to presuppose women's lack of agency

---

[122] Halley, "Queer Theory" 36–38.

[123] Foucault, "Confinement," *Politics, Philosophy, Culture* 200–5.

[124] David Kennedy, "The Spectacle and the Libertine," in *Aftermath: The Clinton Impeachment and the Presidency in the Age of Political Spectacle*, Leonard V. Kaplan and Beverly I. Moran, eds. (New York: New York University Press, 2001) 279–96.

[125] Halley, "Sexuality Harassment," *Left Legalism/Left Critique* 99–101.

[126] Halley, "The Politics of Injury" 83.

[127] Halley, "Sexuality Harassment," *Left Legalism/Left Critique* 98.

[128] Halley, "Queer Theory by Men" 36; Halley, "Sexuality Harassment," *Left Legalism/Left Critique* 98.

[129] Halley, "Sexuality Harassment," *Left Legalism/Left Critique* 98.

and victimization and to deny the meaningfulness of their own deliberations.[130] The very possibility that a woman or a man might consent to sex they do not welcome, and that that sex to which they consent might be harmful to them, is near oxymoronic. That she consented means she welcomed it, and that she did not resist means she consented. Sex is then unbound, and the censorial, repressive hand of the sex regulator, in this case, under the guise of enforcing sexual harassment law, is stayed. Consent to sex thus insulates that to which consent is rendered – sex – from critique. The result, from Halley, is a libertarian defense of sexuality against feminist criticism – not different, in outcome from libertarian defenses of market transactions – including market transactions in sex – against Marxist critique.[131]

The difference, and it is a striking one, between libertarian arguments premised on the purifying function of consent and neo-critical arguments such as this one that have the effect of likewise insulating consensual sexual transactions from criticism, is that the neo-critical arguments are premised *not* solely on the purifying power of consent but also on the intrinsic goodness or innocence of sex itself – and thus extends at least somewhat to nonconsensual as well as consensual sex. The consensual transaction, for libertarians, is good, by definition – whether that to which consent is given is sex or anything other. Consent purifies, for both libertarians and neo-critics, but for queer theorists and neo-critics, sex, and sexual power, does so all the more. Nonconsensual sex, then, for neo-critics, is, possibly overregulated: we have "fetishized" sexual consent, as David Kennedy complains;[132] we refuse to see it when children render it, according to Foucault;[133] we are far too likely to believe women who claim that they did not consent to sex they secretly very much wanted, Halley argues,[134] following a line of argument popularized by Freud. Radical feminists are right to blur the line between consensual and nonconsensual sex, but they draw the wrong judgment, according to Bersani's classic defense of lethal sex, "Is the Rectum a Grave?": what should be inferred from the blurring, is not that what passes as consensual sex is in fact nonconsensual, as feminists argued but, rather, that what is claimed as nonconsensual is often in fact consensual, and of value.[135] Both consensual sexual harassment and nonconsensual rape might well be sites for the enjoyment of power. Consensual sex, however, is doubly legitimated in neo-critical writing: first, because the sex is consensual, and second, because the consent is sexual. Consensual sex should be untouched by noxious regulations,

[130] Halley, "Sexuality Harassment," *Left Legalism/Left Critique* 101; Halley, "The Politics of Injury" 83.
[131] I spell this out in more detail in my response to Halley. West, "Desperately Seeking a Moralist" 19–23, 35.
[132] Kennedy, "The Spectacle and the Libertine."
[133] Foucault, "Confinement," *Politics, Philosophy, Culture* 204–05.
[134] Halley, "Sexuality Harassment."
[135] Leo Bersani, "Is the Rectum a Grave?" *October* 43 (1987): 197–222. For a critique of Bersani's argument, see Marc Spindelman, "Sexuality's Law," *Columbia Journal of Gender and the Law* 20.2 (forthcoming 2011).

such as sexual harassment laws. At least in the context of consent-to-sex, the neo-critics are the legitimators, not the critics of the legitimating power of consent: far from criticizing the legitimating effects of consent to sex, neo-critics, following Foucault, participate in the legitimation of harms that consent legitimates. It is the sex that needs defending, apparently, and it needs defending against those who would criticize the legitimating function of our consent to it, rather than those who might be harmed by all that legitimated sex needing defense against sexuality's law.[136]

What of the second prong of the critical scholars' legitimation argument: that liberal rights largely legitimate more suffering than they curb? Here, there is a surface similarity between neo and critical scholarship – identitarian civil rights are the target of neo-critical legal scholarship, just as they were the target of much critical scholarship. Nevertheless, the neo-crits have rejected rather than embraced, expanded, or elaborated on the older arguments concerning the legitimating effects of those rights. This marks a sharp difference between neo-critical and critical scholarship on civil rights obscured by surface resemblances, but the story is a complicated one.

Let me start with the similarities. Both the critical legal studies movement of the past and the neo-critical theorists today worried, and worry, that identity-based legal reforms, and particularly those reflected in legal rights, are in some way perniciously regressive.[137] They also both share the large worry – echoed in nonlegal left scholarship for decades now –that identity-group scholarship and legal advances come at the expense of a hypothesized, vigorous, more class sensitive, and presumably more radical scholarly agenda and theoretical program.[138] Thus, the critique of formal antidiscrimination rights played a major role in the development of the critical legal scholars' critique of rights,[139] and the critique of radical and cultural feminism, as well as gay rights advocacy, has played a comparably major role in the development of neo-critical legal theory.[140] There is, then, an important shared point of contact between the two movements: they both view liberal gains on behalf of identity groups as more regressive than progressive, as mired in an essentially conservative legal liberal ideology, and as diserving the groups that they purportedly serve. Both movements downplay the distinctive harms directly identified by the rights under challenge: the harm of racial discrimination occasioned by state actors, the harm

---

[136] With thanks to Marc Spindelman for the phrase, "sexuality's law." *Id.*

[137] *Compare* Richard Ford, "Beyond 'Difference,'" *Left Legalism/Left Critique* 60–68 *with* Alan Freeman, "Antidiscrimination Law: A Critical Review," *The Politics of Law* 96–116 *and* Horwitz, "Rights" 405–6.

[138] *Compare* Horwitz, "Rights" 405–6 *with* Ford, "Beyond 'Difference,'" *Left Legalism/Left Critique* 74–75 *and* Brown and Halley, Introduction, *Left Legalism/Left Critique* 16–17 (discussion of affirmative action).

[139] Freeman, "Legitimizing Racial Discrimination through Antidiscrimination Law"; Derrick Bell, "The Dialectics of School Desegregation," *Alabama Law Review* 32.2 (1981): 281–98; Freeman, "Foreword: The Civil Rights Chronicles," *Harvard Law Review* 99.1 (1985): 4–83; Freeman, "The Republican Revival and Racial Politics," *Yale Law Journal* 97.8 (1988): 1609–22.

[140] *See, e.g.*, Halley, *Split Decisions*; – , "The Politics of Injury"; – , "Queer Theory by Men."

of domestic and sexual harassment and violence, or the harm suffered by gay and lesbian citizens by virtue of being deprived of the opportunities to partake of marital privileges or participate in military service.

The arguments, however, put forward by critical legal scholars on the one hand and neo-critical scholars on the other against these identity-protective rights are tellingly different. The older critical scholars' rights arguments ran the gamut of subject matter, but they shared a common logic: the right in question, the critics argued, legitimates greater harms, and hence greater suffering, borne both by those for whom the right was crafted and others. Thus, a right against state discrimination legitimates the larger problem and harms of private racism;[141] the right to familial privacy legitimates and insulates the larger problem of private intimate violence;[142] the right to contractual liberty and property rights legitimates the problem of economic exploitation.[143] In each case, the right purportedly expands liberty, equality, or both against the imagined or real dangers of state intervention, while in fact protecting the private sphere within which subordination proceeds unimpeded. By providing rights against state power, in effect, the law legitimates and insulates the private power into which the state cannot intrude and that is in fact more destructive. The consequence is that the needs of relatively weak people are both unaddressed and obfuscated. Rights provide a wall of insularity within which people's suffering goes unaddressed. Accordingly, Mark Tushnet, the author of perhaps the definitive rights critique of the era, called for a progressive discourse that would focus not on rights, but on needs, suffering, and human welfare.[144] Rights might sometimes serve as proxies for need – they obviously do, in the hypothetical case of social welfare rights. However, social welfare rights are not the paradigm – the paradigm rights, in United States liberal legalism, are property rights and speech rights. Both underserve the needs of poor and disempowered people, and both employ the language of rights to legitimate rather than ameliorate the suffering they endure and the harms they sustain.

By contrast, the neo-critics' brief against identity rights – women's rights, gay rights, civil rights on behalf of disabled persons, and antidiscrimination rights, at least when used to protect ethnic and racial difference – rests *not* on a worry that these rights or others legitimate suffering through protecting private power but, rather, on a worry that in the guise of addressing private hierarchies they further empower the state. Concern for human suffering, or concern for harms, or a commitment to an antiharm project, in Halley's damning language, is emblematic of a "slave morality"[145] and

[141] Freeman, "Legitimizing Racial Discrimination" 97, 113–14.
[142] MacKinnon, *Feminism Unmodified* 93–102.
[143] Hale, "Bargaining" 606; Horwitz, "Rights" 402–3.
[144] Tushnet, "An Essay on Rights" 1394.
[145] Halley, *Split Decisions* 357–59. *See also* Lauren Berlant, "The Subject of True Feeling: Pain, Privacy, and Politics," *Left Legalism/Left Critique* 105–33, 107 ("The central concern of this essay is to address that place of painful feeling in the making of political worlds. In particular, I mean to challenge a powerful popular belief in the positive workings of something I call national sentimentality, a rhetoric

not properly the subject of critique or the goal of truly radical politics.[146] Rather what identity-based rights legitimate is not suffering but the enhanced power of the state, and particularly the power of the state to solidify and regulate, rather than liquefy the "identities" of the groups so regulated. Rights intended to protect the distinctive ethnic culture of African Americans, Richard Ford argues, do little but trap them in state-mandated identities.[147] Gay rights ostensibly meant to strengthen the position of gay and lesbian citizens by, for example, extending the "right to marry," simply perpetuate the power of the state to identify citizens as gay and lesbian, and then to stratify, assimilate some and marginalize others.[148] Rights won through the Violence against Women Act (VAWA) or rape reform laws further identify women as potential victims in need of protection by the state, thus strengthening the state and furthering the stereotype of women as weak and vulnerable.[149]

State power to protect the rights of protected groups, also, according to the new critics, further enhances the state's power at the expense of private power. Thus, rights against, for example, domestic violence and rape, when they become a part of "state feminism" or "governance feminism" have the effect of protecting women against sexual violence, but they do so at the cost of the sexual power of would be sexual actors – a.k.a. perpetrators – who might have otherwise exercised that power in a way that would be both good-in-itself but also disruptive of dominant patterns of empowerment.[150] Civil rights and gay rights likewise empower the state, primarily, and at the cost of both further imprinting the differentness of those whose rights are being protected, and more directly by restricting the freedom of those who would otherwise exercise individual, private, or intimate sexual power.[151] The root anxiety motivating this set of arguments is *not* that rights will lead to a net increase of suffering by subordinated parties – an anxiety dismissed as emblematic of slave morality – but rather, that rights, once embraced by the state, will result in a net decrease in nonstate power.

---

of promise that a nation can be built across fields of social difference through channels of affective identification and empathy.").

[146] Halley, *Split Decisions* 345–46. The review of my *Caring for Justice* is entirely turned over to critiquing the idea that harm or injury should be relevant to political critique. Halley, "The Politics of Injury."

[147] Halley and Brown, Introduction, *Left Legalism/Left Critique* 13–16; Ford, "Beyond 'Difference,'" *Left Legalism/Left Critique* 63–68.

[148] Halley and Brown, Introduction, *Left Legalism/Left Critique* 14–16; Michael Warner, "Beyond Gay Marriage," *Left Legalism/Left Critique* 267 ("As long as people marry, the state will continue to regulate the sexual lives of those who do not marry. It will continue to refuse to recognize our intimate relations, including cohabiting partnerships, as having the same rights or validity as a married couple. It will criminalize our consensual sex."); Warner, *The Trouble with Normal*.

[149] Janet Halley, "From the International to the Local in Feminist Legal Responses to Rape, Prostitution/Sex Work, and Sex Trafficking: Four Studies in Contemporary Governance Feminism," *Harvard Journal of Law and Gender* 29.2 (2006): 335–424, 377–85 (arguing that "sovereigntist" laws presuming non-consent to sex with armed combatants during war diminishes the personhood of women prisoners who may in fact want to consent).

[150] Halley, "From the International to the Local" 377–85.

[151] *See* Warner, "Beyond Gay Marriage," *Left Legalism/Left Critique*, and – , *The Trouble with Normal*.

Let me sum this up and make a few observations. The neo-critics have embraced the target of the earlier critical legal theorists' legitimation critiques – identity-based legal rights – and a part of the logic of those earlier critiques – that those identity-based rights legitimate greater injustices. However, they have transformed the content of the legitimation argument completely. The legitimation arguments against identity-based rights propounded by the neo-critics are not moral arguments against a status quo that increases suffering through disingenuously trumpeting rights of subordinated groups and the individual freedom of the downtrodden. Rather, the neo-critical attack on identity-based legal reform is based on a political worry, not particularly different in kind from the liberal legal ideologies that CLS once sought to problematize, that identity rights limit the power of individuals to exercise power to fashion their own rules and their own identities free of state interference. The former was explicitly grounded in a moral commitment to reduce human suffering – again, the worry was that rights legitimate unwarranted human suffering, and do so *sub silentio*. The latter is explicitly grounded first in a denunciation of moral commitments of all forms, progressive or otherwise, and second in a twinned political commitment in favor of individual power and against state empowerment. As a consequence, the neo-critical claims against identity-based rights have considerably more in common with liberal and libertarian political goals – they both seek to maximize individual power – and conservative political goals – they both seek to minimize state power – than the neo-critics sometimes care to acknowledge, and certainly have more in common with those political impulses than with any progressive impulse grounded in a concern for human suffering.

In only one example, that I can discern, have neo-critics picked up on and expanded rather than so vigorously rejected the logic of old legitimation claims. Echoing earlier critical arguments against the legitimating effects of rights discourse on hidden harms, Mark Kelman has argued against the entire rights-generated industry of individualized, targeted, educational programs for children with learning disabilities, largely on the grounds that the newly minted right to such an education for children with special needs legitimates the larger harm of unequal educational opportunity for poor children.[152] The article argues convincingly, in my view, that the proponents of the right of a child with a learning disability to an individualized learning program have failed to show that the benefits of such a right are greater than the legitimating costs it confers – it reinforces our sense of the overall fairness of the distribution of educational resources, reducing the political will and capital to address the much larger deprivation of poor children from high-quality education and the resources that would be required to provide it.

The contrast between the logic of Kelman's argument against civil rights for children with learning disabilities and the arguments of other neo-critics against sexual harassment laws, gay marriage, and the like, however, is vivid. Kelman's argument is

---

[152] Kelman and Lester, "Ideology and Entitlement," *Left Legalism/Left Critique*.

retro. It depends explicitly and repeatedly on a tallying of costs, benefits, harms, and suffering and depends rhetorically on a concern for human suffering – the suffering of poor children deprived of education (many of whom, of course, are learning disabled) in part by virtue of the unwarranted commitment of educational resources to individualized educational plans for children with learning disabilities.[153] The right is thus both regressive in outcome – it benefits primarily the well-off learning-disabled population, who get enhanced and individualized educational products – and misguided, to the degree that it is progressive in intent – more children would be served, including, likely more children with learning disabilities – by directly addressing the maldistribution of educational resources to poor children.[154] Note what it is not. It is not an argument that the newly won rights of children with learning disabilities to individualized assessments wrongly deprives them or the learning-abled children of opportunities to exercise power in such a way as to redraw or problematize the line between learning disabled and learning abled. It is not an argument that the problem with the newly minted right is that it further enhances state power. There is no talk about "governance disabilitism." There is no worry about squelched individual or private power, wrongly overregulated by nanny-ish states. The argument, rather, rests on the straightforward (and thoroughly falsifiable) utilitarian claim that the right created here has serious legitimation costs – as measured in harms suffered by poor children – that swamp whatever benefits it might win for children with learning disabilities.

Whither Alienation

We can be far more brief regarding the third leg of the critical theorists' moral brief against liberal legalism – that liberal legalism perpetuates an alienated form of life that limits our moral and social lives to paranoically distanced interactions, drenches us in an unwarranted suspicion that the other is by nature egotistically and relentlessly seeking our exploitation, and presents all of these as necessary truths about our nature, rather than a function of the way we have constructed liberal social organization.[155] This "alienation critique" has disappeared from contemporary legal scholarship, both in neo-critical discourse and mainstream discourse. It is nowhere. Its disappearance from mainstream discourse perhaps requires no comment; it never had a presence in any event. In neo-critical scholarship, the absence of the alienation critique is overdetermined. The alienation critique rested unequivocally on a normative commitment to the felt, hedonic value of communitarian forms of solidarity[156] and against the isolating and atomistic modes of alienated life prompted

---

[153] *Id.* at 135–37, 160–64.
[154] *Id.*
[155] *Supra*, footnotes 23 to 31 and accompanying text.
[156] Gabel, "The Phenomenology of Rights-Consciousness" 1566–7; – , "Review of Taking Rights Seriously," *Harvard Law Review* 91.1 (1977): 302–15; – , "Critical Legal Studies as a Spiritual Practice."

by, presupposed by, and arguably created by liberal legal institutions in advanced market societies. Those institutions, the critics argued, leave human needs unmet – the needs of people for health care, housing, nutrition, and so on – but also leave what Gabel consistently called (and still calls) the "spiritual" needs of the well-fed and housed unmet; needs, in short, for social solidarity.[157] Liberalism presupposes a stunted conception of what it means to be a human being, and what it leaves out is our capacity for and our natural inclination toward human solidarity, or commitment – with one another, with communities, with neighbors, with those whom we encounter on the street, at grocery stores, on the metro, on the assembly line, and in the next workspace cubicle. The vision of human nature that liberal rights presupposes, and in which our own conception of ourselves is pickled, assumes a state of mutually assured destruction between each of us: I will not interfere with your sphere of selfhood and privacy on the mutual promise that you will not interfere with mine, and then beyond these walls of noninterference, we can, when we atomistically discover a need for each other, reach out – not with a hand but with a contract, filled with clauses that protect us against the self-serving community-undermining breaches of the other. Tellingly, the core image used to capture the conception of interaction here is one of prisoners trying to achieve mutual gains through a gauze of ignorance of the others' motives. We are all prisoners in our own false understanding of our own and each others' relentless egotism. From that basis of knowledge of our nature, we proceed to make contracts to further mutual goals. Our interactions stop there; all else leads to our own destruction or exploitation.

The falsity of this depiction of life in liberal market society, Gabel argued, is fully knowable, but only through a frank assessment of our hedonic selves. We can know it is wrong by owning, so to speak, our true desires. The craving for solidarity is no less real, although far more buried, than a craving for food, and the evidence for it lies in our own selves. We know it when we surprisingly and spontaneously achieve a real connection with a stranger on a bus, a neighbor at a meeting, or a teller in a bank.[158] We know it when we feel the desire for a more immediate and simpler connection with a landlord, tenant, employer, or employee than one based on mutual fear of exploitation as represented in a "standard form" contract.[159] All of these frustrated connections – the yearning for them, the denial of the yearning, and the construction of a conception of our nature that presupposes their nonexistence – are harms; they contribute to felt suffering. They make our lives less pleasurable, they make our selves less fully human. They are a denial not only of our potential – as Unger argued[160] – but of our nature.

---

[157] Gabel, "Critical Legal Studies as a Spiritual Practice" ("spiritual" feature, p. 519; commitments, p. 519; practice, p. 520; awareness, p. 525; foundation, p. 528; dimension, p. 529; and outcomes, p. 530).

[158] Gabel, "The Phenomenology of Rights-Consciousness" 1568.

[159] See the exchange between Peter Gabel and Patricia Williams in Patricia J. Williams, "Alchemical Notes: Reconstructing Ideals from Deconstructed Rights," *Harvard Civil Rights-Civil Liberties Law Review* 22.2 (1987): 401–34.

[160] Unger, Introduction *Passion*; – , *False Necessity* 41–44.

Neo-critical discourse is explicitly premised on a dismissal of even the coherence, much less the plausibility, of all such claims regarding human nature, human need and human suffering, as well as the desire to minimize that suffering. Echoing a now long-standing consensus in postmodern writing, claims of "nature," whether of the human kind or any other, are not just false, they are disingenuously essentialist. In Halley's slightly newer consolidation of Freudian, Nietzschean, and Foucauldian premises, claims of human suffering, and the desire to minimize it, are dismissed as sentimental, slavish, and priggish or feminine.[161] They are unseemly and smothering; they reek of the maternal.[162] In Lauren Berlant's more extensive treatment of this claim (and her critique of my invocation of it), the argument that we should or could respond to the pains of others is declaimed as somewhat infantile, apolitical or antipolitical, and undertheorized.[163] Unmet human needs and suffering should not be the target of left critique or the subject of decent scholarship, legal or otherwise.[164] A smothering maternalism overly concerned with the suffering of others thwarts the agency and possibilities of the sufferer.[165]

Power, Foucault declared, is all that should be of interest.[166] Echoing Thames's ancient claims for water, for the neo-critics, basically all there is, is power. Local and interstitial no less than state-generated power determines the categories of knowledge that in turn create the entities – cats that break things, homosexuals, sexual perversions, criminals, Chinese pottery, and so on – that populate the shared space in which we live out our lives. Our felt suffering is a construction of power no less than any other entity, and our sympathetic engagement with the suffering of others likewise. Both might then be objects of study, but they cannot possibly be motives for action. Concern for suffering, harm, or need – whether our own or others – is slavish (Nietzsche), smotheringly maternal (Freud), and disingenuous (Foucault). The focus must be relentlessly on power, not the needs of ourselves or others, whether for greater human connections in our lives or otherwise.

The root difference, then, between critical legal studies and neo-critical theory is this: whereas critical legal scholars at least at times acknowledged sympathy for human suffering as the motivation for purportedly left-wing theoretical legal work,[167] and the causes of it as the subject,[168] the neo-crits have aggressively disavowed both.

---

[161] Halley, "The Politics of Injury" 82, 87, 88.

[162] Halley, "The Politics of Injury" 74; Halley, *Split Decisions* 64, 67.

[163] Berlant, "The Subject of True Feeling," *Left Legalism/Left Critique.*

[164] *Id.* at 123–28.

[165] Halley, "The Politics of Injury" 83–84.

[166] Foucault, "On Power," *Politics, Philosophy, Culture* 96–124, 104.

[167] *See, e.g.,* Kennedy, "Paternalist and Redistributive Motives" 563 ("[T]he basis of paternalism is empathy or love, and its legitimate operation cannot be constricted to situations in which its object lacks 'free will.'").

[168] Gabel, "Phenomenology of Rights-Consciousness" 1563 ("[O]ne of my goals . . . is to clarify the relationship between the effort to overcome our alienation, which I see as a fundamental aim of all progressive social movements, and the struggle over the meaning of law that this effort inevitably entails."); Unger, *Passion* viii ("there is fire yet in some of the old and implausible commitments of our civilization – the project of ethics that sees love rather than altruism as its crowning ideal").

Concern for suffering or need is misplaced sentimentality. We need more theory and less politics and absolutely no moralizing; claims of suffering and need are squarely of the latter not the former. There is no talk of the party of humanity, or any case for a discourse based on needs rather than rights, much less of the pact of withdrawn selves or the sufferance of alienation. There is contempt for all of that and a good bit of psychologizing regarding the roots of any expression of concern for it. Hard-headed neo-critical scholarship has not simply disowned legal scholarship motivated by a concern for human suffering and unmet need. Rather, concern for suffering is squarely in its crosshairs. The alienation critique was its first casualty.

The disappearance of the alienation critique from mainstream discourse is as total, but differently motivated. Liberal legal theory is not Foucauldian; there is no commitment to the idea that "power is everywhere" or all that is worth studying. Nor is it Freudian; there is no suspicion of sympathetic moral engagements as maternalistic and smothering. Nor is it Nietzschean; there is no worry that slave morality permeates concerns about human suffering or injustice. It is, however, committed to a denial of the coherence or relevance of phenomenological criticism, or even observation: the more subjective the harm, the deeper in the human psyche the wound, the less susceptible to quantification, calculation, comparison, or compensation. What counts as harms, in cost-benefit calculations, are those that are observable, quantifiable, and rankable: lost wealth is the paradigm; lost opportunity costs and profits, as measured by market data, come next; and lost surplus value comes third. Purely subjective harms not manifested in market transactions or behavior that is easily determined through empirical means will not rank. The complaint that liberal legalism alienates us from each other, and does so by alienating us as well from our own desires, is not about a claim that demonstrably exists; it is more or less on a par with a complaint that it frustrates our powers for extrasensory perceptions.

Let me summarize. Critical legal studies is not dead, as often claimed by both its founders and its harshest critics. Its members are alive, thriving, and writing, and some of the core jurisprudential ideas – particularly the indeterminacy claim, as I discuss subsequently – are still circulating. Some of its central methodological tenets have been embraced and expanded by neo-critical writing that explicitly aims to reinvigorate left-wing legal critique, and particularly left-wing legal critique against identity-based progressive norms that have in some way been accepted by the legal establishment: the antidiscrimination norm, antisexual harassment law, multiculturalism, and so forth.

What *has* died is the critics' moral brief against liberal legalism and, more specifically, the rights, legitimation, and alienation arguments that were at its core. Thus, the "rights critique" has not developed beyond its initial articulation in the early 1980s; in fact, it has reappeared in recent years in only a severely truncated and denuded form. Likewise, the various "legitimation" claims that swirled around critical theories of civil liberties during the late 1970s and 1980s have been muted; we simply do not hear of them. The utopian claims against the alienation, atomism, excessive individualism, anomie, isolationism, and existential barrenness of life within liberal society have been aggressively disowned by those who today claim the mantle of critical scholars. The neo-Marxist articulation of the contours of a radically different and more humanitarian social order that does not sacrifice either spontaneity or equality is gone. We do not hear, any longer, at least from critical legal scholars, about the "pact of the withdrawn selves" perpetuated by rights discourse, of the potential for solidarity or love pointed to by the unconscionability and duress doctrines in contract law, of the hidden communitarian or anti-subordinationist meanings in seemingly illiberal or liberal swaths of the common law of tort, contract, or property. Nor do we hear much of the rage against the complicity, smugness, arrogance, or unwarranted conservatism of the legal academy in the face of the global scale of massive human suffering that in any reasonable reckoning ought to belie their assurance that our basic institutions are just. These moral claims were central, not peripheral – they were defining – of the old critical legal studies movement. Yet they are neither expanded on nor targeted for criticism by legal scholars that write in the areas that generated them. Furthermore, they have been either ignored or contemptuously disowned by neo-critical scholars.

Their disappearance has left a mark. It is deeply regrettable. We are, arguably, in the age of Obama, more rights-rich and welfare-poor than we were twenty or thirty years ago when the rights critiques were first penned: rights are now, if anything, more regressive, more legitimating, and more alienating than they were then. There are also simply more of them. We are now not only living out a pact of the withdrawn selves but a pact of heavily armed withdrawn selves, insecurely protecting our property and families against the threatening other, and the even more threatening state, with the aid of newly minted First, Second, and Fourteenth Amendment rights to guns, privacy, sex, and corporate speech. Many contemplate the addition of a Parents Rights Amendment and a Rights of the Unborn Amendment to the Constitution, and others foresee the day when we can add to our list of unenumerated Constitutional rights the right not to buy health insurance, the right to die, the right to marry members of the same sex, and the right to homeschool our children. "Constitutional rights," through amendment, interpretation, or judicial enumeration, is now a growth stock, surely as robust as during the 1960s, yet we have no critical sensibility seeking an understanding of the legal consciousness that undergirds it. Our legally protected contractual right to consensually obligate ourselves to usurious rates on credit cards, to marriages and intimate relationships that are then protected by privacy rights against inquiry into their potential harms, to workplace contracts that are exploitative and lacking in union support, and to a host of other conditions legitimates all sorts of harms, and the ideology of consent continues to further embed itself in our legal and social consciousness. Our right to consensually opt out of health insurance, if the Court will only so grant it, legitimates the lack of large swaths of the public to access to health care, our right to purchase a gun legitimates the inadequacy of the protection many of us receive from the state against private violence, particularly in the home, and our "right to die," were it ever to be sanctified in legal discourse by Supreme Court authority, might give us some peace of mind at the end of life, but it would also legitimate the lack of public support for the costs of palliative care. Our alienation from ourselves and others has not abated in the past twenty years since we have stopped talking about it; between private ownership of guns – one gun for every two citizens – and the supplanting of face-to-face communication with the Internet, the desires and frustrated needs for real human contact in liberal societies could only have deepened, not lessened. If ever there was a time or place for a moral critique of liberal legalism, it is here and now; if ever there was a set of ideas more thoroughly abandoned without ever having had a thorough hearing, it is that. It is our loss.

WHO DID THIS, AND WHY?

Why did we lose the critics' moral brief? A number of explanations have been put forward since the beginning of the century for the death of the critical legal studies movement: that CLS suffered a mortal blow by the departure and disaffection of feminists,[169] that CLS could not survive the disagreements of a group of critical race scholars,[170] that the ascendancy of conservative legal scholars in the academy made indeterminacy critiques and deconstructionist methodology distinctly unpalatable. In retrospect, however, it is clear that critical legal studies did not die. Its jurisprudence in fact has fared quite well: the indeterminacy critique has been absorbed and generally embraced in mainstream legal discourse, and its Foucauldian insistence that only power is worthy of study, to the exclusion of other subjects, has been embraced and deepened in neo-critical theory. Substantively, critiques of the civil rights settlements that the critical legal scholars authored – critiques of the antidiscrimination norm and, to a lesser degree, liberal feminist gains likewise – have been taken up with gusto by neo-critical thought, flowering into a thoroughgoing attack on radical and identitarian as well as liberal identity-based legal movements. That critique now targets not just antidiscrimination norms but also multiculturalist ideals and affirmative action ideology, not just liberal feminism but also antirape initiatives and antisexual harassment laws identified with radical feminism, and not just gay rights to equal treatment but also more fundamental and arguably more radical gay and lesbian initiatives, such as those for marriage rights and inclusion in military life. These are important continuities. Critical legal thought has not died.

What has died is *not* critical legal studies in toto, but rather the critical legal studies movement's once defining moral brief against liberal legalism: the rights, legitimation, and alienation critiques, as well as the utopian theorizing of ways to

---

[169] Duncan Kennedy, "Psycho-Social CLS: A Comment on the Cardozo Symposium," *Cardozo Law Review* 6.4 (1985): 1013–32; *but see* Robin West, "Deconstructing the CLS-Fem Split," *Wisconsin Women's Law Journal* 2 (1986): 85–94.

[170] Crenshaw et al., Introduction, *Critical Race Theory*.

be that are truer to our nature. Accordingly, the critical legal studies movement that was identified with both indeterminacy *and* the moral brief against liberal legalism has indeed disappeared. Thus, what needs explaining is not the death of critical legal studies but, rather, the disappearance of its moral brief. Why did that die?

The most straightforward, and the most unexplored, explanation, I believe, for the disappearance of the critics' brief against liberalism from our current scholarly scene is that the moral claims at its heart were incompatible with the jurisprudential, or more simply the methodological, claims that captured the imagination of so many of the critical legal scholars. That jurisprudence, as noted earlier, has survived, albeit in a transformed way, in both mainstream and neo-critical legal theory. My claim, then, is that there was a tug-of-war in effect between the jurisprudence and the moral brief that jointly defined critical legal studies in the 1970s and 1980s and that the jurisprudence, in effect, won. The indeterminacy thesis in particular, but more broadly the cluster of ideas that surround it, in fact undermine, rather than bolster, the moral brief that was once at the heart of critical legal studies. What happened in the "missing years" then – the years between the critical legal studies origination, when it was committed to both the moral brief and the jurisprudence and the present, when only the jurisprudence survives – is that the moral brief gave way to the indeterminacy critique with which it had been fatally pinned from birth. The indeterminacy claim survived, and the moral brief did not.

Let me try to trace this evolution. It is a complicated story. In the early 1980s, the jurisprudential claims with which critical legal studies was identified – including the indeterminacy of law, deconstructionist criticism, and the Foucauldian focus on power as generative of all known reality – and the moral brief with which it was also identified – the rights, legitimation, and alienation critiques of liberal legalism – were widely regarded as mutually supportive.[171] The indeterminacy thesis was intended to displace the feeling of complacency, or resigned necessity to an unpalatably conservative legal regime with a sense of possibility. It did so by asserting, repeatedly, that the apparent meanings of existing legal doctrine were not the only possible interpretations of that legal doctrine but that they were the product of the political dispositions of the interpreter. Other and better possible interpretations were available. Indeterminacy underscored, then, the possibility of achieving legal change through doctrinal interpretation. At the same time, Foucauldian analyses of power were intended to show, and largely did show, that power emanates from any number of sources, not just the state. The idea of the state as exercising power over relatively powerless subjects, therefore, is a misunderstanding. Foucauldian understandings of power highlighted the presence of power in the private and intimate spheres and thereby underscored the need for moral critique of the use of that power – the use of power, in other words, by private contractors, family members, intimate partners, white people, straight people, men, husbands, employers, women, law professors,

---

[171] Gordon, "New Developments in Legal Theory," *The Politics of Law*; Unger, *False Necessity* 3.

students, shopping-mall owners, multinational corporations, unions, neighborhood associations, and so on. It is not just states that have and wield power. Power courses through the social circulatory system. The use of that power might be for good or for ill. A jurisprudence that focuses only on the power of states to create laws will be willfully or unwillingly blind to it. A jurisprudence that centers power as the object of inquiry, by contrast, will be constantly attuned to it.

Foucauldian premises, then, uncovered or unmasked what was a *subject* of the moral brief's critique – private power – from the obfuscating gauze of a liberal discourse that relentlessly identified state power as the problem to be solved by the rule of law. This was neatly complemented by the jurisprudential project of the original critical movement and the moral brief: whereas the indeterminacy claim revealed the possibility of changing law in radical directions, the Foucauldian jurisprudential understanding of power in social and intimate life reinforced the moral claim that private power was often harmful – harms obscured by liberal legalism's insistence on the private-versus-public distinction and its focus on the state as the source of oppression. Foucauldian premises complemented the critique of liberalism – it highlighted the contours of the public–private divide, made visible the powers obscured by rights held by individuals against the state, and alleviated collective blindness to private-sphere subordination, all of which are necessary to an understanding of the ways in which liberalism promotes and protects capital from moral critique. At the same time, the indeterminacy critique complemented the critique of the complacency that accompanied that complicity.

What became clear in the missing years is that this mutually supportive relationship, between the jurisprudential claims – the claimed indeterminacy of texts, borrowed from literary theory, and the claimed omnipresence of power, taken from Foucauldian political theory – and the critical legal scholars' moral brief against liberalism – the rights, legitimation, and alienation critiques– was strategic rather than lasting. The alliance between the indeterminacy thesis on one hand and the moral brief against liberalism on the other was useful only so long as two conditions held. First, the received interpretations of existing law had to be as staid and unimaginatively regressive as the critical scholars claimed – thus requiring the unshackling of the bonds of false necessity. Second, there had to be a real possibility within actual law for the radical reimagining the critics advocated; perhaps most important, the perceived object of power – the state – had to in fact be pervasively but falsely believed to be the sole source of power, either for good or ill, in a social world. Foucauldian analyses of power is useful to a theorist holding a moral brief against liberalism, in other words, as long as the power wielded by private parties is in fact truly hidden and worth unveiling and the project of doing so dominates, in importance, all other use of intellectual progressive capital. When any of these premises *do not* hold, the seemingly natural alliance between the jurisprudential and moral claims – between Foucauldian political theory and textual indeterminacy on one hand and a moral brief against liberalism on the other is lost.

The premises do not hold anymore. I am not sure they ever did, but they clearly do not hold now. One or the other had to go, and what went was the moral brief.

Let me expand on this just a bit, starting with the indeterminacy critique, and then turning to Foucauldian political theory. Again, my claim is that the indeterminacy of texts so central to early critical legal studies scholarship is a friend to the moral brief against liberalism only if certain conditions hold. When they do not, as they do not now, the indeterminacy critique undermines rather than strengthens the moral brief, and for several reasons. First, the indeterminacy critique (i.e., the meaning of texts is indeterminate; it is the social conditions of the reader that account for both interpretation and the felt certainty of meaning) keeps the attention and the ambitions of would-be radical legal actors focused on legal *texts* and therefore on the most conservative and incrementalist mode of political change available. This is the drip-drip process of change through adjudicative decision making.[172] The indeterminacy thesis, no less than liberal legalism, holds out the promise that change – whether radical or liberal – can occur through deviationist adjudicative *lawyering* rather than through politics. If this is a false promise – and I think it is – then the indeterminacy thesis contributes to the same "brain drain" first occasioned by liberal legal claims of the generation prior: politics deferred, deflected, redirected toward the realms in which it has been repeatedly shown to fail – namely, the federal courts.[173] If the interpreting judges rather than the originating lawmakers are responsible for the legal regime, as the indeterminacy thesis holds, then change must come through the exertion of influence on the actor whose interpretation actually controls, and that would be the judge rather than the lawmaker. Both responsibility for law and the ability to change it, then, according to the most straightforward understanding of the indeterminacy thesis, in fact rests with the *judge* rather than the legislator. One real-world consequence of any judicially centered worldview, whether liberal or radical, is a massive diversion to the courts, and away from politics, of progressive capital, labor, and imagination. The political problem with the indeterminacy thesis – and the political basis for its tension with the moral brief – lies just here, in the falsity of the basic premise of its liberatory promise: its promise that through radical reinterpretation of preexisting law, radical change is an eminent possibility, and the premise of that promise that judges, not legislatures, can change our law so drastically as to change our social world radically. The promise is based on a premise that is underdefended in radical legal thought, likely untrue, and widely believed to be absolutely essential for the moral brief to even be of relevance.

[172] Robin West, "Are There Nothing but Texts in This Class? Interpreting the Interpretive Turns in Legal Thought," *Chicago-Kent Law Review* 76.2 (2000): 1125–68.

[173] For arguments to this effect, see Gerald N. Rosenberg, *The Hollow Hope: Can Courts Bring about Social Change?* (Chicago: University of Chicago Press, 1991), and West, "From Choice to Reproductive Justice."

There are, however, conceptual problems as well. The fundamental problem is that the indeterminacy thesis suggests both the possibility of change and, perversely, the lack of need for it. The indeterminacy thesis undercuts the case not just for the *necessity* of received interpretations – the truncated discourse, the oppressive feeling of false necessity and so forth – but also for the viability of the claimed harms done by liberal legal settlements. It thereby undercuts the critical basis of the moral brief. The moral claims are in tension with even the most mundane versions of the jurisprudential claims with which it was always twinned, and for two reasons.

First, a law that can mean either this or that is not doing any harm, because it is not really doing anything. It cannot be, then, that the liberal legal law targeted by the critical legal studies movement – the panoply of civil rights and liberties, the array of contract and tort rights and duties – harm us, by falsely depicting us as more atomistic than we are or by creating and then insulating a private sphere within which private subordination can proceed unimpeded. Rather, if the indeterminacy critique is right, then it is the *interpretation* of all of that law that is doing the harm. It is the interpreter of law, then, not law's creator, and not law itself, that does these harmful things. This assignation of power, choice, and hence moral responsibility on the interpreter of the law makes some positive and progressive difference as long as the impediment to change is an unduly conservative judiciary. It goes some distance toward exploding the suffocating pretense that legal interpreters (i.e., judges) have no power and hence no existential responsibility for the decisions they make, when in fact they do have some degree of freedom, some power, and therefore some responsibility for the consequences of their decisions. It also, however, relieves both the law itself and the law's originator, from the citizen who voted the legislature into office to the drafter – rather than the law's interpreter – of all agency, responsibility, or blame. It is not *the law* that does these harms, and therefore not the legislator who voted for it, the drafter who wrote it, or the citizens who empowered those people to do those things. It is, rather, the law's interpreter, who is the judge. Thus, the harms done by "law" are illusory, because the causal chain is wrong. The harms are done by the interpreter of the law, not by the law itself.

Yet look at how this assignation of responsibility for law's meaning and impact affects the claims central to the moral brief, if it is the law itself, rather than its interpretation, that causes the harm, starting with the rights critique. Rights, Tushnet argued, harm the party of humanity; they are, he argued, distinctively *harmful* to people and their quite real interests. A discourse of needs, he insisted, rather than of rights, would be preferable. Rights, Horwitz argued, create walls of privilege that ordinary law cannot penetrate, and by so doing, they further enhance the hand of the powerful private actor, thereby magnifying the harms sustained by the weaker party within the rights-protected relationship. Rights, Gabel added, further our alienation from ourselves and each other. Rights obviously in fact do none of this, however, if the claim of indeterminacy is correct. Rights cannot do these things because rights are paper tigers; rights do not do anything. It is difficult to have this both ways. Perhaps rights, themselves a species of law, itself a textual expression, do nothing. Perhaps rights are harmful to the party of humanity. Either claim might be true. It is hard to see how both can be.

Thus, in the neo-critical version of the rights critique, the complaint that rights actually harm people is simply dropped. Rights, Kennedy argues, contra Marx, Tushnet, Gabel, and Horwitz, are not any more "negative" than they are "positive"; they are not unduly tied to property interests or inherently regressive. They do not harm or help the party of humanity. They can be either positive or negative. They can be regressive or progressive. There is no reason to think that they will be either this way or that. There is no reason to worry about the harm rights do to the party of humanity, to people's unmet needs, or to the withdrawn selves caught in the pact they define. The "unmasking" of rights, then, according to the rights critique of the aughts and teens, has just dropped the harms-focused part of the bill of particulars. Marx, the early Tushnet, Gabel, the party of humanity, and all of those withdrawn selves are effectively tossed under the bus. The rights critique that remains is decidedly not an unmasking of a purportedly liberal and humane doctrine that carries with it real potential for harming people. What is revealed is rights' impotence, not their destructivity: rights do not do anything. The unmasking of rights is simply a matter of unmasking their origin in human will and power, rather than in some ontological realm external to law and politics. To lose one's "faith in rights" is not to lose faith in the proposition that the possible benefits of good, liberal, humanistic rights – maybe the human rights movements, maybe the positive rights of the South African Constitution, maybe a right to be free of racism – might outweigh the possible harms done by the deeper meaning and content of the idea of rights, worldwide – rights to property, contract, guns, and so forth. It is, rather, to lose faith in the proposition that rights have some origin other than in human interest and will.

Finally, it is worth recalling that the indeterminacy thesis was a strikingly minimalist claim: it holds only that legal texts can be the subject of multiple and often conflicting interpretations. In an extreme form – all legal texts are always indeterminate – the claim might be regarded as radically disabling of the rule of law. In moderate versions, however – some law is somewhat indeterminate some of the time, depending on context – the indeterminacy thesis is blandness personified; hence, the incorporation of moderate versions of the indeterminacy thesis in traditional legal scholarship. Given the indeterminacy of the indeterminacy thesis itself, what made the indeterminacy thesis noteworthy, when it was first put forward, was not so much the thesis itself – there was just too much there that most law professors could agree with. Rather, it was the arguments for it that were propounded by various wings of the critical legal studies movement. Some of those arguments were more plausible than others, and some were undoubtedly more radical. They were always more interesting than the indeterminacy thesis itself. More to the point here, some, but not all of them, implied the incoherence of the critics' moral brief. It was those interpretations of the indeterminacy thesis that prevailed. It is worth disentangling all of this.

Over the course of about a decade, the critics generally put forward not just one but at least five arguments for the pervasive indeterminacy of law. First, borrowing Derridian insights from developments in literary criticism and anthropology, some of the critics argued that textual interpretation in general – not just legal interpretation, and not just interpretation of legal texts but interpretation of *all* texts, from Coke commercials to canonical or noncanonical literature to Supreme Court decisions to Model Codes – simply *is* the sort of process that can yield readings very different from those conventionally viewed as apparent. Law is conveyed through language, and language *itself* contains the key to the question why law is seemingly so pervasively indeterminate: whatever texts we build from, language will have multiple and contradictory meanings because language is the sort of thing that yields contradiction.[174] Law is indeterminate, then, because it is composed of words and texts, and words and texts are indeterminate. Call that the *linguistic claim*. The second argument for indeterminacy rested not on the nature of human *language* but on the content of human *longing* and was put forward in Duncan Kennedy's early writings. Our human nature, Kennedy then argued, although now only fitfully believes, might just be such that the law we create contains contradictory meanings. If we feel contradictory impulses, for example, toward individuation and community, if we are naturally both drawn to and threatened by the other, and if those impulses run deep, then the law we create perhaps unsurprisingly will reflect those felt and natural contradictions. Our law is indeterminate and contradictory because we have contradictory passions, and it is those passions that drive us.[175] Law is indeterminate, then, because of the nature of the human beings that create it. Call that the *psychological claim*. Third, others – notably Bob Gordon – argued that the doctrinal project of liberal legalism might generate contradiction because of legalism's deeply conflicted political goals: law, perhaps distinctively of all forms of social control, attempts to coordinate, order, oppress, rank, and subordinate *by claiming* liberatory and egalitarian ideals. If this Chomskian sort of claim is right, then the expressed, aspirational ideals of law – maximize individual liberty, provide a modicum of substantive equality and a heavy dollop for formal equality, treat likes alike, and so on – are in rank opposition to its realpolitik purposes, which are roughly to maintain order through preserving and embedding social hierarchies of wealth, rank, status, strength, and privilege.[176] Tension between actual purpose and stated ideal unsurprisingly is revealed in self-contradictory texts. Call that the *political claim*. Other critics – notably Mark Tushnet – claimed that the contradiction in law

---

[174] Clare Dalton made famous use of this interpretation of the indeterminacy thesis in her piece on contract law. Dalton, "An Essay in the Deconstruction of Contract Doctrine," *The Politics of Law*.

[175] Kennedy, "The Structure of Blackstone's Commentaries."

[176] Gordon, "Unfreezing Legal Reality."

might be a function of the quite specific historical context in which it arises. The contradictions in the U.S. Constitution, for example, between an ideal of a rule of law and the reality of rule by Supreme Court justices, or the more blatant contradictions between a stated ideal of general welfare and a thoroughgoing commitment to the protection of the propertied class, is a function of events and of the fate of various ideas in American history.[177] Call that the *historical claim*.

Once we see the sheer number of claims put forward by the critics for indeterminacy, it is easier to see why the claim caught on like wildfire: it meant different things to different people. My point here, however, is that some of these arguments, but not all, are in tension with the moral brief against liberalism. The last two – the political and historical – are *not* in tension with the critics' moral brief, and in fact they lend it indirect support. Liberal legal rules might be indeterminate because of inconsistencies between the realpolitik goals of liberalism or because of contradictions in the U.S. Constitution; those rules might nevertheless harm human interests in the way claimed by the critics' moral brief. The moral brief is, however, in tension with the first two arguments. If all of our texts, not just legal, are indeterminate, then everything we do with language will be subject to the same indeterminacy as law, including claims of protest or complaint about the harms we suffer. It is hard to sustain the claim that legal texts – the texts (whether written or not, whether codified or cultural) that contain our "rights" or our contract duties and so forth – harm our interests, or our needs, if our interests and needs *themselves* are embodied in "texts" that are likewise indeterminate and have the same powers and limitations of all indeterminate texts. If harms and needs – not only laws and judicial decisions – are themselves textual products, then those textually inscribed harms are as indeterminate as our textually inscribed laws. There's no "there there" for the indeterminate laws to chaotically harm. Our purported harms are expressed in texts that are themselves as indeterminate, as meaningless as well as meaningfully overloaded, as the legal text that might attempt to address them.

The indeterminacy thesis, particularly if coupled with a claim about the omnipresence of text – coupled with the claim, that is, that there are *nothing but* texts in this class – destabilizes the concept of harm no less than it destabilizes the concept of law, if our harms, interests, pains, and so forth are, like law, embodied in texts that are themselves as contradictory as the texts that purport to regulate them. Of course, our harms, interests, and so forth might not be embedded in texts; it might be that our texts are indeterminate, whereas our psychological states, such as harms and interests, are pretty firmly rooted in our bodies, nontextual and relatively stable, subject to the processes of biological growth and decay rather than the processes of textual interpretation. Yet this is not so, if all we know of harm, like all we know of law, is given us through texts we interpret, and those texts are likewise the product

---

[177] Mark Tushnet, *Red, White, and Blue: A Critical Analysis of Constitutional Law* (Cambridge: Harvard University Press, 1988) 1–69.

of the power of interpretive communities. Lastly, the psychological claim likewise unsettles the moral brief. The psychological claim puts forward a yin-yang explanation of our internal contradictions as the reason for law's indeterminacy: law reflects contradictory goals of solidarity and atomism, basically, because we harbor contradictory urges toward communion with our fellows and lethally hostile aggression against them. This is a far cry from the heart of the moral brief: that liberal legalism imposes on us a false (Gabel) or unduly constricted (Unger) vision of human nature as atomistically isolated, thus alienating ourselves not only from our fellow global inhabitants but from our true desires.

There was one last and most thoroughgoing argument for the indeterminacy thesis, however, eventually put forward by critical legal scholars that depended not on Derrida, the inherent contradictions of the Constitution, or of our desires, but on Foucault and a set of Foucauldian claims about power and texts both. Everything we see and everything we know, Foucault famously argued, from the most ordinary to the most extraordinary categories of thought and speech, we see and know because of the power of someone or some group that has so defined our categories of thought, knowledge, and speech, such that we know what we know, see what we see, and think what we think.[178] Knowledge, then, masks power and, more specifically, masks its origins in power. Power is both everywhere and most often hidden, thus the necessity for unmasking it. It is hidden in the furniture of the world, in the language we use to describe it, in what we think we know about it, and in our ways of being, acting, seeing, and feeling. What is not obviously and blatantly power – such as the power at the end of a gun – is power disguised. Legal texts are indeterminate, then, if Foucault is right not because of the nature of our longings, our Constitution, or the nature of language, but simply because the received meaning of all texts – what we know that they mean – like our knowledge of the meaning of all concepts, are a function of some constellation of political power. Our knowledge of the meaning of *any* text, on this view, is a function of power: either of the interpreter or the interpretive community, but in neither case of the text itself. A Foucauldian orientation toward power is thus one way to account for the phenomenon of textual meaning in the face of textual indeterminacy. We understand a text to have a meaning because of a constellation of power that has produced that understanding. To unmask power, then, in the context of liberal legalism, is in part to effectuate a Foucauldian analysis of the power of legal interpreters to ascribe meaning to the empty vessel of legal verbiage.

More broadly, over the last two decades of the twentieth century, Foucault's worldview came to play an outsized role in critical legal theory as it had in critical theory more generally. If Foucault's large claims about power are right, then they provide a thorough basis not only for the indeterminacy thesis but, more generally, for the basic realist and critical claim that both law and our knowledge of it are the

---

[178] Michel Foucault, *The Order of Things* (Routledge, 2002) xvi–ix.

product of contingent exercises of power: the former may be a product of sovereign power, but the latter – what we know when we know the law – is a product of social power, cultural power, or individual power, as is all knowledge. If "all that we know" is a product of various constellations of power, then obviously all that we know about law is likewise. So, a doctrinal claim that the law of contract or tort *is* thus and so – that the doctrine of consideration requires a bargain or that a promise not backed by consideration is not enforceable – is not "about" anything in the sociolegal world, its grammatical form notwithstanding. It is not a declaration that refers to promises, bargains, or consideration in the world. Rather, it is a declaration of knowledge by someone with some measure of power that, if influential, remakes the world in such a way: this promise but not that one *will be* enforced, this rather than that *will constitute* a bargain, and so forth. A statement of doctrinal law is thus a creative remaking of the world, not a description of the world. If power is everywhere, then of course it lies behind the forms of law. Yet that looks obvious; at least it is obvious to legal positivists. It is also true, however, of every claim we make regarding legal doctrine; it is as true of the scholar as of the judge that the interpreter exercises power when making a statement about the legal world. Now of course, if this is true of every statement we make on any topic whatsoever, the claim that it is also true of claims we make about legal doctrine look trivial. Nevertheless, whether or not it trivializes them, Foucault's fanciful reveries on power, and the claims he made on the basis of them, render the critical claim that the legal is the political, that law is importantly contingent, that law is invariably made and not discovered, not only by judges but by all its participants, including lawyers and scholars both, seamless with at least one compelling worldview.

Although it provided a foundation for the indeterminacy critique and eventually for the contingency of law and legal claims, Foucault's broad claim regarding the omnipresence of power is what eventually emasculated the moral critique. What we know, according to Foucault and now legions of Foucauldian devotees, is a function of power, and this includes what we may know about our withdrawn selves; about the suffering or harms sustained within private realms insulated by liberal rights; and about the affairs, deals, contracts, or work environments to which we may have tendered our consent. Our knowledge of these matters, too, is a function of interests and power, whether of the sufferers themselves or of others who have a stake in promoting them. The role of critical theory, then, in a world saturated by Foucauldian insight, is to expose the dynamics of power behind claims of injury, no less than behind claims of right. Claims of injury, like claims of right, are put forward by those with sufficient power to have those claims read as true, and claims of injury are received by those either with a stake in such claims of power or whose knowledge has been so shaped as to render the claims familiar and congenial. A moral brief premised, as was the critical legal scholars' brief of the harms of liberal legalism, on the suffering of persons, has no traction in such a world. Either the critics' moral brief or the Foucauldian premises of the claims of contingency had to go, and so, the moral brief was jettisoned. Without an anchor in knowable suffering, the moral brief has no referent; it is a set of claims about the suffering wrought by liberal legalism, the claims of which are as doubtful as the liberal rights that purportedly cause the suffering claimed.

Neo-Critical Theory and Critical Legal Scholarship: Some Contrasts

Finally, why has the moral brief against liberalism disappeared from contemporary neo-critical theory? The indeterminacy thesis itself plays only a negligible role in neo-critical theory. One would think, then, that if the reason for the demise of the moral brief was its incompatibility with the political premises of the indeterminacy thesis with which it was originally twinned, the brief would play some role in neo-critical writing, even if not in mainstream discourse.

The appearance is misleading, however. The indeterminacy thesis has not been abandoned or denounced. Rather, the indeterminacy thesis plays a negligible role in neo-critical theory, today, simply because it has been swamped by the more sweeping implications of its underlying Foucauldian justification. If the meaning of texts is a function of conflicting interest and power, and their meaning accordingly is as indeterminate as those fluctuating constellations of power and interest that produce their dominant interpretation, then this is obviously just as true of claims of suffering, harm, and injury put forward by liberalism's critics. The basis of critique, then, in neo-critical theory is the unacknowledged power of those who would make such claims, particularly when the claim of injury is made by a group or party that has seemingly captured the sympathetic engagement of the state. State power, combined with the powers of "commonsensical" understandings of social life, yield legal settlements that favor certain groups – notably women, gays and lesbians, and ethnic and racial minorities – at the expense of others, whose interests have not so congealed into claims of injury, state recognition, and power – poor people, working-class white men, non-American nonimmigrants (i.e., illegal immigrants). African American claims of injury have generated state recognition, through affirmative action plans and through claims of racial injury, women's claims of domestic violence and neglect of caretaking needs have generated state recognition through expanded protections of laws such as the VAWA that regulate sexual injury and the Family and Medical Leave Act (FMLA) that recognizes the needs of maternity, and gays and lesbians are in the process of garnering state recognition of dignitary and monetary injuries caused by their exclusions from various social regimes, from marriage to the military to private hospital rooms. These claims of injury, in neo-critical theory, rather than the rights that might cause harm, are the target, then, of neo-critical theory. "Left" legalism, rather than liberal legalism, is the new target for scorn.

This shift from "liberal legalism" to "left legalism" as the target of critique yields a different set of critical projects, and a different political valence, between neo-criticism and the critical legal studies movement, and particularly the moral brief that was at its heart. Both movements – critical legal studies and neo-critical legal studies – targeted various identity based political and legal movements. The similarity ends there, however, although here as well, the evolutionary story is complicated. The critics argued that liberal rights, including those that ostensibly protect various identity groups, protect, mask, legitimate, and insulate privately sustained harms – often the same privately sustained harms that the liberal right purportedly targets and the same victims the liberal right purportedly helps. Thus, the antidiscrimination norm in constitutional law provides a "right" against state sponsored discrimination but, precisely by so doing, constructs a wall of legitimacy around other patterns of race subordination that become all the more difficult to penetrate;[179] the "right to privacy" protects various reproductive decisions but, by so doing, constructs a wall of legitimacy around various private realms and the domestic or sexual violence that occurs within them;[180] the "right to contract" protects various contractual decisions and, by so doing, protects the exploitation of economic vulnerability that occurs within it;[181] and so on. To target what the right either advertently or inadvertently protects, critical scholars – *as well as* feminists and race scholars – argued that more is needed from the state than liberal rights of colorblindness, privacy, and neutrality: to address real racial subordination, the state would have to undertake a range of color-conscious remedial programs, including affirmative action plans; to address private domestic violence and sexual violence, the state will have to pierce rather than insulate the private and intimate realms; and to advance the interests of economically subordinated persons, the state will have to intervene in rather than remain neutral toward contractual or market allocations of wealth and privilege. Critical legal scholars then – *as well as* critical race scholars and feminists – targeted liberal settlements regarding race, gender, and class, and did so because those settlements protected rather than addressed the deepest, underlying causes of race, gender, and class difference and subordination. All of those arguments, in all three contexts, originated in an understanding of the harms done by racial, gendered, or class subordinations. Those subordinations work against the interests of the subordinated, render their needs invisible, and alienate them from their labor, true desires, and identities.

There was, to be sure, eventually a divergence between the goals of feminists and critical race scholars on one hand and critical legal scholars on the other. By the late 1980s, this divergence had developed into a deep fissure of purpose and organization between the various groups. CLS, feminist theorists, and critical race scholars all shared a distrust of liberal rights and remedies that addressed identitarian concerns: the "antidiscrimination" norm in liberal theory, as well as the "equal treatment"

---

[179] Bell, "Serving Two Masters"; Bell, "*Brown v. Board of Education* and the Interest-Convergence Dilemma"; Bell, *Faces at the Bottom of the Well.*

[180] MacKinnon, *Feminism Unmodified* 93–102; MacKinnon, "Reflections on Sex Equality under the Law," *Yale Law Journal* 100.5 (1991): 1281–1328.

[181] Hale, "Bargaining, Duress, and Economic Liberty."

strand of the Fourteenth Amendment was the subject of critique by all of these critical groups. However, the reasons for this animosity toward liberal rights of race and gender were different, and the differences eventually swamped the shared point of contact. Two sorts of differences emerged: the first, purely political, or pragmatic, and the second, theoretical. Feminist legal scholars and to a lesser extent race scholars, far more often than critical legal scholars, put forward affirmative arguments for particular legal interventions that might address the harms that liberal rights – the targets of both critical and feminist and critical race theory – had ostensibly either protected or simply ignored. In virtually every case, this came in the form of arguments for greater (not less) and affirmative (not negative) actions by the state into realms previously protected by liberal rights: affirmative action or other race-conscious policies, the VAWA, equal pay or comparable worth initiatives, living-wage initiatives, and so forth. Critical legal scholars had no stake in those purely legalistic arguments, or in the often quite ordinary politics that would produce them. One consequence was simply that feminists and race scholars were involved in ordinary law reform movements – to enact VAWA[182] or FMLA,[183] to defend affirmative action, to push for legislation against hate crimes,[184] and so forth – whereas critical scholars were not.

On the more theoretical side, both feminists and race scholars ultimately took quite seriously the existence of modes of private- and intimate-sphere subordination – patriarchy and white racism – that survive within capitalist societies, and their independence from class-based modes of subordination and particularly the class-based modes of subordination that the liberal state, at least arguably, exists to legitimate and to protect. If this is true, then it is not at all irrational or politically naïve to believe that the state can sensibly target those forms of subordination; they are, in fact, deeply illiberal. Domestic violence and sexual violence against women is, after all, violence, and the liberal state, generally committed to the project of preventing, deterring, or compensating for violence, might, then, if also convinced of the equal status of women, be convinced to use its weapons to combat it. The same is true of hate crimes against African Americans and gay and lesbian citizens.

---

[182] Violence against Women Act of 1994, Pub. L. No. 103-322, 108 Stat. 1902-55 (codified in scattered sections of 18 U.S.C., 28 U.S.C., and 42 U.S.C.). For discussion of VAWA, see Victoria Nourse, "Where Violence, Relationship, and Equality Meet: The Violence against Women Act's Civil Rights Remedy," *Wisconsin Women's Law Journal* 11.1 (1996): 1–36; Catharine MacKinnon, "Disputing Male Sovereignty: On *United States v. Morrison*," *Harvard Law Review* 114.1 (2000): 135–78; Reva B. Siegel, "Rule of Love: Wife Beating as Prerogative and Privacy," *Yale Law Journal* 105.8 (1996): 2117–208.

[183] 29 USC Sec. 2601, et seq. For discussion of FMLA, see Angie K. Young, "Assessing the Family and Medical Leave Act in Terms of Gender Equality, Work/Family Balance, and the Needs of Children," *Michigan Journal of Gender and the Law* 5.1 (1998): 113–62; Katharine Silbaugh, "Is the Work-Family Conflict Pathological or Normal under the FMLA? The Potential of the FMLA to Cover Ordinary Work-Family Conflicts," *Washington University Journal of Law and Policy* 15 (2004): 193–218; Michael Selmi, "Is Something Better Than Nothing? Critical Reflections on Ten Years of the FMLA," *Washington University Journal of Law and Policy* 15 (2004): 65–92.

[184] Matsuda, "Public Response to Racist Speech."

Thus, feminists and race scholars were attuned to the existence of modes of subordination that might be fully or partially addressable by the state that the critical scholars viewed as either peripheral or as conducive to a kind of false consciousness: concerns over racial slights or sexist treatment simply distract attention from more purely economic, and purportedly greater and more harmful, forms of subordination. Thus, there was an ideological divergence as well as a practical one. The two points of divergence, furthermore, were connected: if racism and patriarchy exist independent of the class subordination that is the primary interest of liberalism, and particularly of the liberal rights of property and liberty, then the tools of liberalism might well be put to use against racism and patriarchy: the violence at the heart of each, in other words, might be addressable through traditionally legalist means and for profoundly liberal reasons.

It was this possibility – that there exist modes of private subordination within liberal societies that are in some way profoundly *illiberal*, as well as subordinating, and therefore can be addressed through liberal legal law reform of a relatively traditional sort – that critical legal scholars never countenanced, and in my view, was at heart of the basis for the split between these movements. Nevertheless, the point I want to stress here, and that was later thoroughly obscured by the visible and public splits among critical race scholars, feminists, and critical legal scholarship, is that there was a shared logic in the initial critiques of liberal rights that formed the basis of each of these three legal movements. It was a critique, furthermore, that was initially penned by critical legal scholars, in their confrontation with liberalism: liberal rights, including liberal-sounding rights of nondiscrimination and privacy, mask and legitimate and, in some cases, aggressively protect in the name of liberty quite real harms and suffering. An understanding and appreciation of the harms suffered, and a respect for the claims of harm, was thus at the heart, not the periphery, of those critical claims.

The neo-critics have systematically turned these arguments on their head. The result is that there is a little noticed but important difference in both the target of critique among the critical legal scholarship, feminist scholarship, and critical race scholarship of the 1970s and 1980s *on one hand* and the target of critique of the neo-crits *on the other*. The former – CLS, Feminist Legal Theory, and Critical Race Theory– *all* argued, albeit in different ways and ultimately with divergent ends that the claims of neutrality and liberal equality norms mask, legitimate, and insulate private power. Critical feminists and race theorists further claimed, however, that at least some forms of that private power – forms that manifest themselves in domestic violence and hate crimes, for example – can be and should be targeted by the state, and by the state on its own liberal terms: that private violence is in fact as offensive to liberal and legalist norms as to feminist goals and purposes. To some degree, those efforts met with success: with limited state action targeting just those forms of power. Thus came about the passage of hate crimes legislation, VAWA, greater recognition of rape and hence rape reform movements, FMLA, and some protection of race-conscious remedies such as affirmative action.

The *claimant*, then, at the end of this process, is the person wielding the power: the claimant complaining of domestic violence, of hate crimes, enjoying the benefit of diversity initiatives and multiculturalism, and so forth. *That* power is then harnessed by the state – whether for liberal or radical ends – and at that point that power is congealed into "state power." At that point this power – "state" or "governance feminism," for example, as Halley calls it, becomes the newly found target of neo-critical focus.

Thus, from the neo-critical perspective, whether the result of this fusion of the power of the complainant with the power of the state furthers or alleviates the suffering of people is neither here nor there. The focus, following Foucault, is on the power that yields the claim of sufferance, the allegiance of the state, and then the constellation of state power and private interest. "Follow the power" (rather than "follow the money," which might be a better idea) is the rallying cry. Whether the newly congealed state power is being used for good or ill is not the point. The result of this transformation in neo-critical writing is a critique of claims of injury and the concept of harm that is libertarian in political orientation – although without traditional libertarianism's understanding of human nature or its commitment to individual autonomy. What it shares is libertarianism's distinctive and instinctive distrust of the state and of state power and, ultimately, its political commitments as well: against race conscious and state-approved affirmative action, against sexual harassment policies, against expansion of gay and lesbian rights (including marriage rights), against further regulation of rape and other crimes of sexual assault. All of these reforms, all of which had their genesis in some of the same ideas that motivated the original critical legal studies movement – wed the state to constellations of private interest that are expressed in the language of injury and harm. All are generated from interest and power and, once harnessed by the state, are complicit in the state's perpetuation of its own power, for its own ends.

Let me elaborate just a bit, taking them one by one, starting with race. Both critical theorists and critical race theorists in the 1980s argued that the antidiscrimination norm and the rights that are protected by it legitimate private-sphere discrimination and perpetuate unacknowledged and unreckoned harms to African American citizens by so doing.[185] The right to be free of state-sponsored discrimination legitimates the sufferance of the harms of private racial subordination, across a wide swath of private and social life, from residential discrimination to private patterns of employment, family formation, and civic life. Neo-critical theorists, prominently Richard Ford, shift the focus of the critic's attention from the harms suffered by racial minorities to the *claimed* harm propounded by multiculturalists; the "assertion" by multiculturalists, of racial difference.[186] The content of the latter claim of harm, in Ford's retelling, is the loss of diversity, of multiculturalism, and of the distinctive

[185] Bell, "*Brown v. Board of Education*"; Freeman, "Anti-Discrimination: A Critical Review"; Crenshaw, "Race, Reform, and Retrenchment."
[186] Ford, "Beyond 'Difference,'" *Left Legalism/Left Critique* 38–42.

and valued difference of racial or ethnic minority status.[187] This claim of harm, itself a product of interest and power, has been captured, in essence, by the state and has become the basis of state-generated race-conscious delineations. Diversity rationales for university affirmative action policies, for example, typically rely on the argument that students from different racial groups will enrich the university experience, that the racial composition of a university is therefore ideally diverse, and that pursuit of that diversity is therefore a legitimate academic and university function. The state, Ford argues, has basically accepted this argument, and the result is that the delineation of racial difference has become a state power.[188] That power is in turn pernicious – it gels racial difference, retards assimilation, and aligns the state with essentialist claims of racial categorization. There is a real difference in rhetoric here from the right-wing critique of race-conscious affirmative action as racial favoritism, which Ford is at pains to delineate.[189] However, there is no difference in the target of critique. For Ford, consistent with neo-critical theory generally, the claim of harm rather than the right that might protect the harm is the target of critique. The product of the neo-critique of the law of race, then, is a criticism of multicultural and diversity-based justifications of affirmative action plans, not, as it was for the earlier generation of critics, the liberal rights to color blindness that render that race consciousness problematic.

The difference between critical and feminist (collectively) writing on the one hand and neo-critical writing on the other, with respect to gender, sex, and sexual orientation issues, is even wider. What is suspect, from the neo-crit perspective, is *not* the violence in private life that was protected by liberal rights or legitimated by the gauze of individual consent; it is, rather, the claims of that sexual harm themselves.[190] The claim of sexual harassment is what causes harm, not the sexual harassment itself: the claim, which as often as not is founded on a sex panic or internalized homophobia, coupled with the state's need to regulate sexual life as well as economic transactions, does nothing but further entrench state power at the expense of private sexual freedom.[191] Coupled with a irrationalist and quasi-Nietzschean commitment to the value of sex of all forms, and a quasi-Freudian conviction that both sexual energy and sexual repression are constants of human life, what follows is a suspicion not of *liberalism*, or of liberal rights, or of liberal feminism, and certainly not of libertarianism, but, rather, of radical feminist critiques of sexuality in private life. What follows politically for the neo-crits is a deregulatory project with respect to sexual harms: a call to cut back or eliminate the civil rights cause of action for sexual harassment, and an insistence that all rape claimants, whether the claimed rape be in the context of war, domestic life, or by a stranger

---

[187] *Id.* at 41–44.
[188] *Id.* at 49–52.
[189] *Id.* at 65–68.
[190] Halley, *Split Decisions* 324, 345–47.
[191] Halley, "Sexuality Harassment," *Left Legalism/Left Critique* 94–102.

and at knife point, be treated with a very old-fashioned mix of distrust and contempt. Probably, the rape did not happen – she is lying. If it did, she likely enjoyed it, and cannot admit that. Even if she did not enjoy it, the harm is trivial in any event. The bottle here is new, the wine is old indeed.

Let me conclude this with a three-way comparison. In the 1980s, critical legal scholars and feminist and race scholars did indeed have a very public split on the relative importance of racism and patriarchy, compared with economic class–based oppression. Furthermore, for the former, some liberal commitments – notably, liberal commitments to squelching private violence and some related forms of private oppression – could be and should be addressed by law, within a liberal regime, and could be so addressed through relatively traditional liberal legalist tools: notably, the VAWA, hate crimes legislation, and race-conscious affirmative action plans. The logic of this is not hard to see: liberal legalism might well mask some harms suffered by women and ethnic and racial minorities, but it is also committed to domestic pacifism and fairness in the private sphere, and the latter commitment can be used to target racist and patriarchal violent and oppressive practices. Critical legal scholars were simply never convinced, as far as I could tell, of the relative importance of these legalist projects, and likely of the relative importance of the distinctive harms they addressed: patriarchal and racist hate or violence. They were accordingly never convinced of the relative value of using the traditional tools of liberal legalism – constitutional law, adjudicative decisions, interpretation, and law reform – as means of rooting it out.

Nevertheless, there was shared ground between critical legal scholarship and feminist and race scholarship that this conflict somewhat obscured. All three groups understood the dangers of liberal legalism as clustered in its legitimating and obfuscating powers, and in particular understood the dangers of liberal legalist reforms that addressed only the most innocuous forms of discrimination against these identity-based groups. Liberal antidiscrimination efforts that target only de jure state-sponsored discrimination carries the danger of legitimating, and mightily, deeper and more destructive forms of private discrimination, including race hatred, as well as legitimating other forms of market-based subordination thus rendered fair and just by antidiscrimination efforts. Both critical scholars and critical race scholars agreed on some form of this argument and put forward multiple critiques of traditional antidiscrimination law on the basis of it. The same is true of liberal antidiscrimination norms with respect to gender, as well as its legitimating effects on other forms of gender-based economic harms, from the failure to compensate comparably valuable jobs with comparable pay to the inequitable distribution of household and child-raising labor in the private home. Equal pay for equal jobs is a step forward, but arguably several steps back in legitimating more powerful forms of private economic disempowerment of women. Likewise, liberal privacy initiatives that ground reproductive and sexual rights run the risk of legitimating a sphere of domination and violence within which the subordinating forces of patriarchal control are insulated both from legal regulation and political critique. This argument, made forcefully by Catharine MacKinnon, was also echoed in early critical writing, including that of Mark Tushnet. All three arguments – that the antidiscrimination norm legitimates private racism, domestic maldistributions of labor, and private sexual violence – targeted liberal legal civil rights–era settlements. All three suggest that liberal legalist gains made ostensibly for these identity-based groups had the potential to backfire, and badly, against those groups. All three were made by both critical legal scholars and critical race and feminist scholars. Furthermore, all three were premised explicitly and directly on the sufferance of harm and injury by the subordinated groups purportedly protected by liberal norms of neutrality, privacy, and color- and sex-blind state treatment.

The neo-critical critique of identity scholarship and politics is entirely different. First, the neo-critique is simply not aimed at liberal legalism, the antidiscrimination norm, or the privacy doctrine that insulates and enshrouds sexual and reproductive life. Nor does it target the legitimating function of consent in sexual and private transactions; far from it. Rather, the target of neo-critical critique is almost entirely the attempts by critical race and feminist scholars and activists to employ law to address the deeper injuries that were purportedly protected by those liberal doctrines, particularly wherever those attempts have been successful: antiharassment actions, expansive rape laws, affirmative action programs. The result is a purportedly critical movement that in its political orientation is aligned, most often, with ultra-conservative causes (and often funded by ultra-conservative think tanks): along with right-wing women's groups and libertarians, neo-critics challenge various feminist efforts to address sexual violence in the home and in private life; along with right-wing anti–affirmative action activists and scholars, neo-critical theorists target race-conscious remedial actions taken to address private-sphere racial subordination. The arguments of the neo-critical scholars are different. Both libertarians and neo-critical scholars harbor a deep distrust of the state, but whereas the libertarian distrust stems from premises that are largely Hayekian, the neo-critics distrust is loosely Nietzschean: state power is to be distrusted because it invariably overrides private power, which should be unleashed not because it is private but simply because it is power. What is at the heart of this, in other words, is a love of power, not of the private sphere per se. Likewise, the blanket affirmation of sex-for-sex's-sake lies not so much in fear of the prying eyes of the state (or not only that) but rather in a view that sex is an expression of power (rather than of love or sentiment) and should be protected and celebrated for that reason. Its potential to express power trumps whatever harms it might (but probably does not) on occasion cause. Power is celebrated and harm denied.

Both the celebration of power and the denial of the coherence of the concept of harm distinguish neo-critical theory not only from contemporary identity-based scholarship and activism but also from the critical legal scholarship to which it nominally claims allegiance. The critical scholars were indeed committed to the unmasking of legal power, particularly where it went unnoticed, such as in judicial opinion writing. However, this by no means either implied or rested on the Foucauldian and trivializing claim that power is everywhere, nor on a love for it. They certainly had no love for private power in the economic, sexual, or racial private sphere. More important, and more clearly, critical scholarship, particularly as it pertained to racial and gender issues, was never premised on a denial of the coherence of the concept of harm, injury, suffering, or human need. Sympathy for the suffering, harms, and injuries of others is a likely prerequisite not only for moral life but for political alliances across groups, and the critical scholars were acutely aware of the human need for both. Recognition of the human suffering of others and of the urgency of the call for us to respond to that suffering is at the heart of progressive activism and must be at the heart of progressive legal scholarship, if the latter has anything at all to contribute to the former. Fault it in whatever way you wish, but the critical scholarship of Roberto Unger, Peter Gabel, Mark Tushnet, Michael Seidman, Robert Gordon, Joseph Singer, and scores of others was acutely aware of that fact.

CONCLUSION

The disappearance of the moral brief that once defined the critical legal studies movement is partly a response to particular countertraditions and trends in critical theory itself: primarily, the incoherence of that brief in light of the indeterminacy thesis, but also, the rise of Foucauldian and Nietzschean thinking, an "antinormativity" and "antipolitics" ideology that came to swamp moral and normative vision within critical theory more broadly construed, and tensions within and between critical legal studies on the one hand and critical race and feminist scholarship on the other. However, it was also a part of a much broader phenomenon in legal scholarship, and perhaps in legal education in toto, and that is a retreat across the board, and across the political spectrum, from the idea that legal scholarship should have any moral point or that the scholar should have a moral point of view. The law and economics movement, for example, was once routinely described as having both a "normative" and "descriptive" wing; the normative wing, largely identified with Richard Posner's writings in the 1970s and 1980s, has largely disappeared. Doctrinal scholarship, which is loosely normative virtually by definition, is increasingly squeezed by interdisciplinary and avowedly nonnormative or antinormative work. In part, this simply reflects the perpetual insecurity of the legal academy: its status is enhanced if it is hitched to the knowledge- and truth-seeking function of the university, and it is lessened if it is hitched to the justice-seeking function of the legal profession. University-generated and -constrained understandings of the ideal of knowledge, so to speak, has more cache than professionally generated and -constrained understandings of the ideal of justice. Furthermore, in part, it reflects an uneasiness about the meaning of moral ideals quite generally, and the meaning of justice in particular. The result across the board has been a demoralization of legal scholarship. Scholarship that is seemingly aimed at making the world better, rather than at better understanding, once the bread and butter of legal scholarship, is now quite routinely derided as "mere advocacy" at worst or embarrassingly normative at best: nonanalytically rigorous, slipshod, overly emotional, and sentimental.

Critical scholarship, however, has been particularly hard hit. The critics' late-twentieth-century moral brief was virtually by definition adversarial, explicitly normative, and highly sentimental. It was premised on a sympathetic regard for the suffering of people in the world – and a felt moral imperative to respond to it. Like all such appeals, it was impassioned, sloppy, sentimental, emotional, utterly nonanalytic, defied rigor, and unabashedly slipshod. It was, furthermore, about the effect of the law on people. It was emphatically and self-consciously not about the effect of law on texts about law, the effect of texts about law on law, or on other texts. It was not about the interplay of principles, interpretations, interpretive presuppositions, interpretive strategies, and so on. It was not about making our textual-legal premises and principles the best they can be, or about the interplay between competing textual interpretations. It was not, in short, about texts at all. It was about people, and their suffering, injuries, and the harms they sustained, and the ways in which law legitimates and masks them.

The *jurisprudential* projects of the critical legal studies movement, however, were very much about text: their indeterminacy, their contradictions, their genesis in power, their interpretation, the indeterminacy and contradictions of those interpretations, and their genesis likewise in power. As discussed earlier, there were very real tensions between the jurisprudential project of critical legal studies, which aimed for the elucidation of textual contradiction, and the moral project, which aimed to alleviate suffering. Minimally, the totalizing claims of the former – that all social life is a text, that all texts are contradictory, that all claims of suffering are texts that can be viewed accordingly, and so on – simply overwhelmed the latter: if the former are true, than the thing to be done with claims of suffering and harm is to deconstruct them, not sympathize with them, far less respond to them in a way aimed at the alleviation of the suffering that causes them. This leaves no room for a moral project. When the jurisprudential project is premised on Foucauldian premises, however, it obliterates it. There is no room for a sympathetic response to the suffering of others in a Foucauldian world. Both the articulation of the harm and the sympathetic responses are acts of power (as is everything else), and as such they must become the target of critique, not the motivator of critical scholarly work. Thus, the inversion: the articulation of harms caused by liberal rights that protect private spaces becomes itself the act of power criticized in neo-critical thought. When those harms become recognized and reckoned by the state through a legal victory – sexual harassment law is the clearest example, but race-conscious affirmative action is certainly another – those now state-recognized harms become the target of criticism: the private act of power has become state power. The neo-critical focus, then, is on state power, rather than the pockets of private power facilitated by state inaction or state recognition of private liberty. The claims at that point are either studiously descriptive – theory before politics and so on – or, to whatever degree there is a departure from studied antipolitics, they are starkly libertarian. Harms that prompt state intervention into private markets through sexual harassment policies or affirmative action policies that are race conscious are simply outweighed by state-generated wrongs: invasion of liberty, the demarcation of difference, the stifling of spontaneity, and so forth. The moral project morphed into yet another critique of the potential invasiveness of the state in private markets and the dangers that invasiveness poses to private power.

Critical legal studies, always on the defensive against charges of emotionalism, lack of rigor, and anti-intellectualism, could not sustain its moral project against both the internal challenge to it posed by the rise of Foucauldian theory and the external disdain of the legal academy. Something had to be dropped. What was retained was, first, the critique of identity politics, although this time, the target was radical feminism rather than liberal, and multiculturalist defenses of affirmative action, rather than the antidiscrimination norm. What was retained, secondly, was the disdain for left-wing lawyering. What was retained, finally, was the focus on text and the conceit that radicalism is a badge of honor worn by those with a detached attitude toward texts and whatever theories of justice they may express. All of this, I believe, is unfortunate. The real tragedy, however, lies in what was dropped, during the missing years when critical legal studies went into its coma, and neo-critical theory was in utero. What was dropped was the emotionalism, the sentimentalism, and the unabashed refusal to take one's eye off the prize, which was the alleviation of the suffering of the world's and the nation's and the community's poorest and most damaged peoples, whether that harm be occasioned by corporate or state power, individual acts in the home, or community acts against a people. What was dropped was the insistence that the scholar's purported neutrality in the politics of the day is unconscionable. What was dropped was the scholars' outrage at the nation's wars on dark-skinned people across the globe, and the use of napalm or drones against them, the wars on drugs or terrorism at home, the blind and blinding Lear-like refusal to turn swords into plough shares, and the state's frighteningly arrogant use of the rhetoric of law – international law, human rights law, Fourteenth Amendment law, the rhetoric of liberty and equality – in all of those deadly enterprises. What was dropped was the outrage against the corporate manipulation of belief and desire to effectuate profit at the expense of people. What was dropped was the acute awareness of the state's complicity through inaction in those harms, no less than its aggressive warmongering abroad. What was dropped was allegiance with the interests of those who have lives of almost unmitigated pain. What was dropped was the political, and, more simply, the passion. It is a terrible shame.

Conclusion

Reconstructing Normative Jurisprudence

I have tried to show in this book that over the past fifty years, three major movements in legal philosophy have all largely lost the normative dimensions that at one time defined them: contemporary natural lawyers only rarely discuss what justice requires of law; legal positivists have abandoned the censorial project of criticizing positive law on the basis of a moral measure independent of law itself, and critical scholars have basically renounced their once distinctive moral brief against liberal legalism. This did not, however, happen in a vacuum, nor are the three trends in positivism, natural law, and critical legal studies unrelated to each other. Rather, legal scholarship in general, over the past quarter century, has increasingly leaned against normative argument. Arguments such as the following are now often explicitly disparaged, particularly at the elite American law schools: "the law should be thus and so," "the law requires this but should not," "it should require that instead," "law forbids something that should be permitted or ignores a problem it should address," or simply "this law is unjust and should be changed" or "this social situation is unjust and therefore needs legal redress." These arguments, so the complaints go, are "moralistic," inappropriately political, "mere advocacy," "adversarial," or, worst of all, "brief-writing" rather than insightfully explanatory of some deep sociolegal phenomenon. The philosophical movement in the three jurisprudential traditions I have described away from normative interpretations is clearly reflected in this contemporary movement away from normativity in legal scholarship generally.

Nevertheless, analytic jurisprudence did not cause the larger shift in legal scholarship: jurisprudence is simply not that influential a subdiscipline within legal scholarship. It is much more likely, in fact, that the general movement in legal scholarship against normativity is part of the cause of the parallel trend in the subdiscipline of jurisprudence rather than the other way around. Whichever way the causal arrow points, however, the two phenomena are obviously interrelated. Therefore, by way of conclusion, I take up these broader questions: What is the origin of the current antinormativity movement in legal scholarship generally, and what are its costs?

I look quickly at the arc of this idea and its intersections with the same trend in jurisprudence, then its roots in the history of legal scholarship, and then its costs. At the end, I suggest that we should reverse it. Reversing the parallel movements in the major jurisprudential tradition discussed in the bulk of this book is only one way to start.

THE ARC OF ANTINORMATIVITY

The contemporary critique of normativity in legal scholarship is usefully reflected, and to some degree likely caused, by two influential and lively articles by Pierre Schlag, a major architect of the critical legal studies movement, which appeared in the early 1990s.[1] Schlag's target in those pieces was "normative legal scholarship," by which he meant broadly legal scholarship that criticizes, on moral grounds, existing law, legal doctrine, or large swaths of received legal opinion and does so toward the end of reform.[2] The worry expressed in these articles, repeated in a more pointed way fifteen years later by Schlag in a piece claiming the death of legal scholarship[3] is that normative legal scholarship – moral arguments in law reviews about the way that law should be – reflects, in an unthoughtful way, the givenness of legal structures and the immutability of political categories of analysis.[4] The moral categories on which normative legal scholarship rests are generally reflective of the givenness of the way things are and a web of beliefs in which the legal scholar is firmly embedded. For this reason as well as others, normative legal literature generally has no impact on actual law reform in any event and no impact on public understandings either. It is inconsequential. To whatever degree it does have an effect, however, that effect is unduly if unwittingly conservative. The claims made in normative legal scholarship for the desirability of shifts of legal doctrine at the margins simply serve to reinforce the rootedness of law in the main.

The second major contribution in the 1990s to the antinormativity "cottage industry" was a book by Professor Paul Kahn of Yale Law School titled *The Cultural Study of Law*.[5] In that book, Kahn makes the argument that the study of law will not mature or yield meaningful fruit until legal scholars abandon our unhealthy fixation on normative legal scholarship.[6] Legal scholarship generally, Kahn argued, should eschew its preoccupation with the way things ought to be, legally speaking, and focus instead on a better understanding of the way things *are*. The way things are, he

---

[1] Pierre Schlag, "Normative and Nowhere to Go," *Stanford Law Review* 43.1 (1990): 167–92; Schlag, "Normativity and the Politics of Form," *University of Pennsylvania Law Review* 139.4 (1991): 801–932.

[2] Schlag, "Normativity" 808.

[3] Pierre Schlag, "Spam Jurisprudence, Air Law, and the Rank Anxiety of Nothing Happening (A Report on the State of the Art)," *Georgetown Law Journal* 97.3 (2009): 803–36.

[4] Schlag, "Normativity" 905–9; Schlag, "Spam Jurisprudence" 829–30.

[5] Paul Kahn, *The Cultural Study of Law: Reconstructing Legal Scholarship* (Chicago: University of Chicago Press, 1999).

[6] *Id.* at 26–30.

suggested, is plenty mysterious and gives us plenty to occupy our time and energies. We have little understanding of it. We do not understand why the legal world is carved in precisely the way we see it, and we have no sense of how legal changes occur or why. We dimly sense that history, economics, and politics have something to do with all of that, but we have no real understanding of the machinations of legal change or even of law's origins.

One reason for our ignorance, Kahn argued, is that we lack a sustained, disciplined understanding of law's culture.[7] Legal scholarship, then, could usefully seek deep understandings of law's culture and law as a culture: its predispositions, its defining ways of thought, its "habitat," its ambitions, ideals, and practices. However, it cannot possibly achieve such an understanding if it persists in its current role of participant in the very legal culture it should seek to understand. Legal scholars do not, for the most part, participate in law as lawyers, but they do nevertheless participate: to commit oneself, as a scholar, to a normative legal project – to a claim about the way law should be – is to participate in the object of one's supposed study.[8] The ends of law, the normative scholar seemingly presupposes, might thereby be served, whether for good or ill, by that scholar's normative contribution. The ends of scholarship, however – an understanding of the way things are – will not be; if anything they will be further obscured. The legal scholar is participating, then, in the legal enterprise, not a scholarly one.

What I call the Schlag-Kahn thesis – that legal scholarship should not be normative, because normative legal scholarship is unduly conservative, or unenlightening, or, of course, both – has had a remarkably friendly reception despite the posture, or assumption, of both authors that they were bucking, and not simply reflecting, the status quo in American law schools; the presumption, shared by both scholars, that they were saying something radical. Both took as their starting point the givenness of normative legal scholarship, and both took as their task the work of making the purportedly counterintuitive and counterexperiential claim that legal scholarship should be avowedly antinormative or nonnormative at least plausible.[9] Both assumed that normativity was the status quo in the world of legal scholarship. This alone is odd. During those ten to twenty years since the Schlag-Kahn hypothesis first appeared, at least elite law schools have largely accepted the antinormativity critique. Normative scholarship is increasingly decried across the board, and not only by occasional iconoclasts such as Kahn or Schlag. It is decried precisely for being normative – not for lacking rigor, interest, or merit but simply for being normative, for being of the form, that is, that "law should be thus and so."

The same impulse is reflected in the elite law schools' most pronounced modern hiring trend – the sometimes obscene bidding wars that occupy the time of deans and appointments committees and drain the resources of such schools, for the junior law

---

7 *Id.* at 1.
8 *Id.* at 7, 19, 28–29.
9 Kahn, *The Cultural Study of Law* 7; Schlag, "Normativity" 932.

professor who enters the academy with no experience in the profession – increasingly not even a clerkship – but with a newly minted Ph.D. in a companion discipline (economics, history, sociology, and philosophy being the most marketable). A few law schools have quite self-consciously and explicitly refashioned themselves as housing the interdisciplinary study of law as their primary scholarly agenda: treating law as an object of study by scholars from other disciplines rather than itself being a "learned profession" within which study can proceed in a systematic and rigorous way. Thus, according to this emerging conception of the modern legal academy, the "law school" is a place where historians, philosophers, sociologists, and other credentialed scholars – whether or not they are also lawyers – gather to study law, and to study it in a disciplined way with the tools of an established academic discipline. One school – Northwestern – has now embarked on a plan to in effect split its faculty in two: to have the long-standing pedagogical mission of law schools – to train future lawyers – taught by lawyer-practitioners with no scholarly requirements for tenure and have the scholarly mission fulfilled by scholars who will all, by requirement, have a Ph.D. from another discipline (whether or not they also have a J.D.) and will have few, if any, teaching obligations.[10] Other top schools are trending toward the Northwestern model, even if not explicitly, by requiring less teaching of their most highly prized scholars and less scholarship of their best lawyer-teachers. The study of law is thus being, in effect, "deprofessionalized" – it is being turned over to scholars for whom the legal profession forms no part of their identity – and normativity is the first casualty of this transformation. The goal of the legal historian, the legal philosopher, or the legal economist is the articulation of some historical, philosophical, or economic truth about the subject of law. It is decidedly not to utter claims of what justice requires. The idea that law is itself a discipline within which to utter claims of *either* truth *or* justice is thus increasingly, and I believe unfortunately, marginalized.

Within this context, then, of law schools that are coming to define their scholarly mission in terms drawn from other disciplines, with law serving as the object of those disciplines, the ideal of nonnormative legal scholarship makes perfectly good sense – not radical in the slightest – and the view of normative legal scholarship as unworthy (or oxymoronic) follows quite naturally. It is hardly radical or edgy, and there is absolutely nothing political about it. Historical, philosophical, sociological, or economic scholarship (or teaching) that is influenced by the political or moral views of the scholar producing it is *rightly* faulted, pretty much universally, within the academy; as Stanley Fish has noted, the point of scholarship should be knowledge, and the point of education generally is to educate, not proselytize.[11] Historical scholarship about law should be no different: the point is to add to our fund of

---

10   Northwestern's website boasts, "Northwestern Law has the highest percentage (47%) of full-time research faculty with social science PhDs in the nation." "Faculty Research and Achievement," available at http://www.law.northwestern.edu/faculty, December 2, 2010.

11   Stanley Fish, *Save the World on Your Own Time* (New York: Oxford University Press, 2008).

knowledge about law and its history, not to lend the weight of history to a political or moral agenda. The same can be said of every other discipline: philosophical analysis of law should not be influenced by the philosopher's politics, and if it is, it is bad philosophy, bad sociological analysis, and so on.

This has been true and widely recognized for a long time. Lawyers are not academics or scholars, even if it is true, as it undeniably is, that legal arguments routinely and by necessity, rest on historical claims – and occasionally on philosophical or economic claims as well. This is a long-standing tension: legal arguments made by lawyers that incorporate historical or philosophical claims are routinely disparaged by the interdisciplinary scholar. The lawyer who makes a historical-sounding argument on behalf of a legal conclusion is engaged in "law office history," which whatever it is, is not history.[12] Obviously, the same is true of the legal scholar making a legal argument toward a normative conclusion: to the extent the scholar's legal argument rests on historical claims (and it is bound to rest on historical claims somewhat, because that is what legal arguments are), it is "law office history" regardless of whether it actually takes place in a law office. Thus, the reliance of traditional legal scholars on historical claims, including historical claims made by historians, toward the end of legal argumentation is a long-standing target of withering critique by historians themselves. From the perspective of the scholar, the subjection of law to the disciplines of the humanities or the social sciences, rather than the incorporation of insights drawn from other disciplines into legal thought or analysis, is what is meant by the interdisciplinary study of law. The end result of this is clearly further disparagement of "normative" legal scholarship. Normative scholarship is at cross-purposes with truly disciplined scholarship of any sort; indeed the phrase "normative scholarship," from the perspective of a core university discipline, has an oxymoronic sound to it.

It is not, however, only the influx of scholars drawn from other disciplines into the law schools that accounts for the contemporary appeal of the idea of antinormativity within legal scholarship. Rather, I argue in this conclusion that antinormativity today has broad appeal largely because the normativity that has dominated the legal academy over the past century is highly constrained; I call it, pejoratively, faux-normativity, and it is that faux-normativity that is the real target of the Kahn-Schlag thesis. Faux-normative claims are extremely circumscribed and even stylized normative claims about what the law should be, but they have two distinctive characteristics: first they are drawn from quasi-historical claims about what the "true" law really was; second, they are made within larger arguments about what the current law really *is*. The legal ought, in other words, is implied by the legal past, rightly understood, and is a part of an argument about what the current law actually

---

[12] *See, e.g.,* Jack M. Balkin, "Populism and Progressivism as Constitutional Categories," *Yale Law Journal* 104.7 (1995): 1935–90, 1955 ("[Cass] Sunstein's 'Madisonian' theory of the First Amendment is about as Madisonian as Madison, Wisconsin: It is a tribute to a great man and his achievements, but bears only limited connection to his actual views.").

is. I tendentiously call these constrained normative forms of argument "forms of faux-normativity" because although they are indeed normative claims about some state of affairs, they are made not toward the goal of some argument about what the law should be but, rather, within a larger argument about what the law is. The faux-normativity embraced at each of these three points of development, I claim, is a normativity that commits the scholar to the large project of articulating "truths of law," as Schlag has helpfully put the point, *rather than* truths about law – as called for, in different ways, by Kahn, Schlag, and the interdisciplinarian movements.

However, they also – and this is the point that has been lost in the current infatuation with the antinormativity thesis – moved legal scholarship away from making or even studying genuine claims of justice, or claims about what justice requires of law, or deeply critical claims about law's false promises or inauthenticity, or thoughtful claims about what the "common good" or common welfare, or even common happiness, is, toward which law should press, and hence, toward a more genuine normative stance. The dominance of faux-normativity, in other words, has moved legal scholarship, very generally, toward a self-understanding of the point of legal scholarship as being the articulation of truths *of* law rather than *either* descriptive truths about law *or* moral claims about the demands of justice, law's shortcomings, or law's promise. They moved legal scholarship away from both the pursuit of knowledge about law and the project of justice. Instead, faux-normativity has put the legal scholar in the business of making limited moral claims about the way the legal world ought to be, but toward the end of making limited claims about the way the world – at least the legal world – already is: toward the articulation of versions of claims that take the form "the law should be thus and so, and therefore it is thus and so." All three, in different ways, consequently gave normativity in legal scholarship a distinctively bad rap. The current antinormativity critique needs to be evaluated against that backdrop: what the critics are denouncing as "normativity" is, I believe, faux. True normativity – the study of justice and the good to which law should and might contribute – is not the culprit here; rather, normativity has been one of the casualties. My claim then is that before we dispense with normativity, we might first want to give it a try.

THE ROOTS OF FAUX-NORMATIVITY

Three distinct moments in the history of law schools, corresponding with three ongoing strands of legal thinking, contributed to the rise of faux-normativity in American law schools and, hence, to the favorable climate within which the modern antinormativity claim is now received: first, the establishment of law schools within the university rather than reliance on apprenticeship training in law offices in the last part of the nineteenth century, together with the formalist understanding of law and legal education that accompanied that shift; second, the rise of the legal realist movement in the 1920s, 1930s, and 1940s; and third, the return of various neo-formalist forms of legal writing and scholarship in the 1960s and 1970s. These three moments, and the forms of scholarship to which they gave rise – formalism, realism, and neo-formalism, respectively – constitute the "roots" of faux-normativity in legal scholarship and, hence, of our current dissatisfaction with normative legal scholarship. They also account for the contemporary popularity of the antinormativity critique and its otherwise paradoxical seeming claim to radicalism or marginality. I take them up in that order.

The first root was the most formative, and that was the extended "moment" in the latter part of the nineteenth century when the legal academy collectively identified law as a "learned profession" and the university, rather than the law office, as the place within which lawyers should be formed. If law is a learned profession properly housed in universities, then in some way the object of legal scholarship, as well as legal pedagogy, should be law, and the goal of such scholarship should be truth. University-housed legal scholars, then, should aim, in their scholarship, to say something true about the law that is their subject. What sorts of true statements can be said of law, within the profession, and independent of expertise lent by other university disciplines?

Christopher Langdell provided one sort of answer: the subject of legal scholarship is law, and the goal of it should be true statements "of law." Legal propositions themselves have truth value, and the goal of the legal scholar should be to utter true statements of law, particularly in areas in which the law is unclear.[13] Thus, a contract either does or does not require consideration to be binding, and a penny either can or cannot be consideration: these statements are true or false. Because the goal of the academy is truth and the object of study of the legal academy is law, the goal of the legal academic should be to state the legal truth of the matter. In common-law systems, as all first-year students quickly learn and as Langdell himself appreciated, this is not as straightforward as it sounds. The major premises of arguments that might yield legal truths with respect to particular questions can be hard to come by; rather than found in a code, they are themselves general propositions pulled from the evidence of past cases. In pulling those propositions, the legal scholar may have to engage in subtle forms of reasoning: he may have to discern a purpose behind more particularized statements about the enforceability of this or that promise to articulate a true and sufficiently general proposition of the meaning or content of the consideration doctrine. That reasoning may, furthermore, be strikingly normative: in deciding how to mash the cases to generate the general proposition, the scholar (like the judge) may be required to articulate some moral or political point to the holdings of those cases. Nevertheless, the cases themselves contain the seeds of the general proposition, and the scholar's work, no less than the judge's, is to unearth them. The goal of the scholarship is true statements of law, then, not claims of justice or of morality. The scholar should aim to state or restate the law accurately

---

[13]   Thomas Grey, "Langdell's Orthodoxy," *University of Pittsburgh Law Review* 45.1 (1983): 1–54.

and should focus on areas of legal unrest when doing so. The scholar's aim is not to criticize the law, to suggest what the law should be, or to suggest how to make the law more just. The scholar's aim is to restate the law accurately – the goal is truth, not justice, but true statements *of* law, from the internal perspective of the legal actor, so to speak, not true statements *about* law, from the perspective of the external scholar.

The pinnacle achievement of this understanding of the legal scholar's work, then, is not the law review article that makes the overtly normative argument that the law should be thus and so, that justice requires that the law be this rather than that, or that some swath of law is unjust and needs change. Nor is it the scholarly treatise that reveals the truth about law or legalism to be something other than it is understood by its actors. Rather, the pinnacle achievement of the legal scholar in this time is the law review article, legal hornbook, encyclopedia, or eventually the American Law Institute Restatements.[14] There is without question a form of normative argument embedded in this work, as the realists proved again and again and with considerable glee: in deciding that the consideration doctrine truly requires a genuine exchange of value, rather than a formal ritual, or that a promissory note can pass free of the fraud in the underlying transaction, and so on, the scholar, like the judge, may be making interpretive claims about case law that in turn require moral or political judgment. However, the normativity here is limited, or, as I called it earlier, faux: the goal of the entire argument is to unearth the true statement of law, not the better restatement of a political principle. The political morality that might form an explicit or implicit premise of the argument is the political morality embedded in the law, not a critical morality, or even the scholar's own moral sense. The scope of such reasoning is in any event limited: the gaps in the law might be real, but they are not overwhelming. Formal legal reasoning is just that: it is, for the most part, formal, not discretionary; it is, for the most, part legal, not moral; and it is, for the most part, reasoning, not arbitrary whim. It can, then, be sensibly placed in the university. The goal is truth, and the object is law. It is no different, then, from the physical sciences, in very general form, the goal of which is truth, and the object the natural world, or the social sciences, or even the humanities. The goal of all these fields is truth, although the object differs from field to field. The goal of the legal scholar likewise is the articulation of true statements of law.

The second such moment, somewhat paradoxically, was the legal realist revolt against Langdellian conceptions of law: following Holmes, realist legal scholars decried the false claims of law's autonomy, as well as its claims to closure. Legal questions cannot be answered solely by recourse to premises drawn from earlier cases.[15] Legal realism was, of course, a broad movement, touching on many aspects of both the legal academy and profession, and it famously gave rise to a profoundly

---

[14] Grey, "Langdell's Orthodoxy" 5, 38.
[15] Oliver Wendell Holmes, "The Path of the Law," *Harvard Law Review* 10 (1897): 457–78, 465, 467.

moral and political critique of the libertarian and regressive interpretation of the Constitution that a conservative Court had sought to impose upon federal New Deal reforms of the early part of the century. The part of legal realism of relevance here, however, is its jurisprudence, more narrowly defined. Its jurisprudential claims were remarkably conventional and had far more in common with the Langdellian paradigm than is widely acknowledged.

The realists rejected the Langdellian claims of law's autonomy and closure, as noted. They did not, however, for the most part, believe that either the judge or the scholar should or could have recourse to moral claims to resolve law's ambiguities. "I hate justice," Holmes famously opined, and he held nothing but scorn for the lawyer making recourse to claims of or about justice in the course of legal argument: it showed nothing but an ignorance of law.[16] The man of Blackstone, Holmes thought, was the man of the past.[17] It was the man of the slide rule – the economist – the man of social scientific fact, that would replace him, not the natural lawyer, not the moral philosopher, not the man of justice. Resolution of legal questions, where law itself fails to supply guidance, should come from the then-nascent social sciences and the facts they reveal about social needs, not from moral claims of justice. What was needed to render law modern, and useful for a changing society, were the tools of the social sciences. The realist was happy to concede law's open-endedness and happy to have the study of law reside in the universities. Nonetheless, the branch of learning to which law should turn, when the scholar or judge or lawyer hit law's limits, were social sciences, and particularly economics. These would be and should be the stuff of the informed and educated "public policy" that should inform legal analysis from the bench.

The realists, again following Holmes, then combined their ambitions for a judgment guided by the social sciences with a thoroughgoing Holmesian definition of law as the product of judicial decision making or a prediction of what the courts will do in fact.[18] The law, then, that becomes the object of scholarship, as well as of the attention of lawyers, is what courts do, rather than what legislatures do or what executives administer: it is the product of judicial deliberation. If we put the two claims together, then legal analysis consists of reasoning from judicial opinions toward future judicial opinions, guided, where precedent is insufficient to ground prediction, on whatever can be gleaned about decent public policy from the methods of the social sciences. This is indeed at odds with Langdellian or formalist conceptions of the judge's role, and hence of the lawyer's role, in ascertaining and interpreting and applying law. It directs the judge, and therefore the lawyer, toward what the law should be in the future, somewhat, rather than what the law has been

---

[16] Oliver Wendell Holmes, Letter to Doctor Wu, *The Mind and Faith of Justice Holmes: His Speeches, Essays, Letters, and Judicial Opinions* (New Brunswick: Transaction Publishers, 1989) 435.

[17] Holmes, "The Path of the Law" 469.

[18] *Id.* at 460–61 ("The prophecies of what the courts will do in fact, and nothing more pretentious, are what I mean by the law.").

in the past, exclusively. It exposes the role played by the judge's understanding of what sound public policy requires, in his pronouncements about the content of law. It directs lawyer and judge both toward a branch of social sciences – economics, and perhaps sociology as well – in ascertaining what sound public policy requires.

Yet look at what the legal realist revolt was not. For all their disagreements, Langdell and Holmes were as one on two fundamentals. First, they both eschewed the study of, and even the mention of, justice as a guiding ideal for law, albeit for different reasons: Langdellians had no need for it – law and law alone could resolve all legal questions – and Holmes and the realists had no taste for it – the social sciences, the slide rule, and the man of economics would rule the future, as the man of Blackstone had ruled the past. They were accordingly united in their disparagement of normative thought in law, if by normative one means discussion of what the law ought to be on grounds of justice. For Langdell, what the law ought to be should be determined by reference to what the law is; for Holmes, it was by reference to sound public policy. For neither, was it by reference to the demands of justice. Second, they were both equally court- or judge-centered in their jurisprudential understanding of the meaning of law. Langdell did not opine on definitions, but he disparaged legislation and codification and filled his "case-books" with judicial opinions: the stuff of law. Holmes famously opined that the opinions of judges were all he meant by law.[19] Combining these two, then, Holmes, like Langdell, disparaged justice, as did their respective realist and formalist followers, and Holmes, like Langdell, defined law, and hence legal studies, as the product of judicial decision making. Holmes, then, like Langdell, had no particular use for normative critiques of law based on claims of justice. If normative scholarship is about the criticism of law based on a moral account of what law ought to be or on an understanding of the demands of justice, Holmes, like Langdell, had no use for it, nor did the realists that he influenced.

What of "faux," or constrained, normativity – the incorporation of normative claims about the way law ought to be within claims about the way law is? Again, what is clear in retrospect is that the realists by and large did not represent a break from the Langdellian commitment to constrained or faux-normativity; it represented only a different course for it. Whereas for Langdellians, the lawyer and judge were perforce required to exercise some judgment in making interpretive claims about the meaning of preexisting law, Holmes, and many of the realists he influenced, were of the view that the judge might be required to exercise some judgment in making quasi-scientific claims about the content of sound public policy. The lawyer, then, might need, in a house-of-mirrors sort of way, to make some judgment about what the judge's judgment might be in making those quasi-scientific claims about the content of sound public policy, and the scholar likewise. The judge is making these claims about public policy toward the end of saying what the law will be, whereas

[19] *Id.*

the lawyer is making claims about public policy toward the predictive end of saying what the law is – predicting, that is, what the judge will say the law is. Neither actor, judge or lawyer, is making normative claims about what the law ought to be on the basis of a moral benchmark of what justice requires. The professional work of neither requires an investigation of or even a curiosity regarding the content of justice or its demands. The realist judge, like the formalist judge, embraced a faux-normativity that required limited judgment regarding competing claims of public policy, and the realist lawyer, like the formalist, would need to echo those understandings to produce a decent account of the law that is.

Where does this leave the legal scholar? The scholar who stays true to the realist jurisprudential revolution would hold the social sciences in high regard and doubt the formalist claim of law's completeness. The scholarly study of law, however, would not necessarily depart in any more fundamental way from Langdellian ambitions. The focus would remain on adjudicative law, the goal of such scholarship would be to say what the law is, and, most important for these purposes, claims of justice remain marginal, either as constitutive *of* law – again social science would guide law where gaps exist – or as a critical baseline against which to judge it. Law, for both the realist and formalist, remains a learned profession, and what is meant by that, is that some learning is required to render true statements of law: either learning in the law books or learning in the social sciences. What was not meant was that law would be the object of other learned disciplines; that would come later, with the interdisciplinary movement. What was also not meant, was that law would be the object of a learned profession, housed in the legal academy that would subject law to critical scrutiny, with moral baselines drawn from outside of law itself. Rather, the learned profession would and should continue to issue learned statements about law's content. The difference – and it was not negligible – was that the realist academic would make those statements through partial reliance on the forward-looking social sciences, toward the end of fitting law as a tool toward the end of sound social policy. What remained stable, although often overlooked, however, was more fundamental: the legal academic aimed to make true statements of law (not about law) and to do it without recourse to justice. Science and rationality were to rule, not morality, passion, or emotionalism. What remained outside the doors of the legal academy altogether likewise remained outside, in the transition from formalist to realist understanding of law's meaning: the normative criticism of the law that is, and on the basis of the demands of justice, or more simply, on the basis of what law ought to be.

The third such moment was the reemergence in the 1960s and 1970s of various neo-formalist approaches to judicial decision making and, with it, neo-formalist modes of legal scholarship. A range of liberal public law scholars – notably Dworkin – and private law as well, began to urge and model a form of legal reasoning that incorporated within it an appeal to a highly conscribed sort of moral principle: moral principles drawn from past case-law precedent that arguably fit within the controlling law that governed the resolution of particular legal questions.[20] As with older Langdellian formalisms, the neo-formalists were answering legal questions within legal frameworks, but unlike the old, they explicitly appealed to moral principles while doing so. Nevertheless, the moral principles were also, if the argument succeeded, legal principles, or law. They were, as Dworkin would say, the bridge between legal and moral norms or the connection between the law that is and the law that ought to be. They had the value of moral principle and the positive standing of positive law. They thereby closed the formalist circle. Neo-formalism then met the demand of legal formalism – that legal questions be resolved by reference to law – and the moral ambitions of a more liberal and capacious conception of law – that it be principled and in line with an evolving liberal morality that could itself embrace far more than the vaguely libertarian principles embedded in the common law.

As discussed in Chapter Two, as a regulatory ideal of adjudication, the Dworkinian turn to neo-formalism had plenty to commend it: it directed the interpretive energies of judges toward moral principles that are aligned with institutional facts – there is nothing wrong with urging judges to make law "the best it can be."[21] As scholarship, however, neo-formalism is clearly limited. The scholar's aim is true statements of law (not statements about law) – he or she is operating within law to generate claims of law. As such, if Dworkin was correct, they also aim to embrace a broad set of moral principles that have some measure of fit with preexisting legal institutions, including past precedent. This has the effect, however, of compromising both the descriptive and the normative dimension of the scholar's work. Descriptively, and as countless critics of Dworkinian formalism have pointed, out, the scholar's recapitulation of the law is saturated with his or her political "priors," or moral principles. The neo-formalist description of law is also morally compromised, however. These are not Kantian principles about what must be or utilitarian claims about what ought to be unadulterated by that which is. They are, quite self-consciously and avowedly, moral claims that are drenched in the institutional compromises from which they emerge. They are not even, potentially, the author's own moral beliefs; they are the best interpretations that can be rendered of the moral principles that emerge from the scholar's conscientious reading of prior cases. They become, then, at best, a way to nudge the law in a direction already foreshadowed by the law itself. They become at worst, and far more typically, yet another attempt to claim moral grounding for existing law – for discovering in the power of law the light of reason, or in the king's crown the rays of the sun. The liberal legal scholarship that emerged from the era developed into precisely the body of law decried by the nineteenth-century positivists: a body of scholarship claiming moral authority for legal commands.

---

[20]   Ronald Dworkin, *Law's Empire* (Cambridge, MA: Belknap Press, 1986) 176–274.
[21]   Ronald Dworkin, "Natural Law Revisited," *University of Florida Law Review* 34.2 (1982): 165–88.

Again, what was left out of the neo-formalist revival was twofold. First, the neo-formalist scholar, like the realist and the Langdellian, is engaged in the work of making true statements of law – not true statements about law. Legal commands are given a truth value, and then debated, as though they were claims about the natural world. Second, neo-formalism quite consciously forecloses recourse to any moral principles by which law could arguably be judged that are truly outside the scope of existing legal authority. The moral principles by which legal authority can be, at least arguably, developed, are internalized into law itself – and then claimed to exhaust the moral universe. Those moral principles are, then, the basis of neo-formalism's faux-normativity: the normative dimension of liberal legalism is defined by its limits, and those limits are set by existing positive law. Liberal legal formalism, then, not only fails to set itself the goal of generating genuine normative critiques of law. By its logic, it denies the possibility of doing so. The faux-normativity of liberal legalism thus exhausts the moral world.

Thus, my claim is that the faux-normativity of first the Langdellian formalists, then Holmesian realists, and then liberal legalists forms the backdrop, and eventually the target, of the contemporary critics of normative legal scholarship. When Schlag, Kahn, and others inveigh against "normative legal scholarship," they are attacking an existing practice that has gone on for well over a hundred years, not an abstract possibility. That existing practice is normative scholarship as it has existed in the legal academy for more than a hundred years. Normative scholarship, as it has been practiced, however, is faux-normative. It incorporates limited moral baselines into legal doctrine or discovers them there, but the moral baselines are both generated by past law, themselves become part of the law, and then serve to regulate its development. They are not independent of the law itself. They do not serve as external moral points of reference by which to judge existing law, whether the point of doing so is criticism or reform. They become rather a part of the law by which other parts of law are criticized, all toward the end of generating new and better descriptive accounts of the law that is. Normative scholarship – if by that is meant scholarship that develops a moral baseline by which existing law can be criticized or reformed – is not the intended product and certainly not the actual. Faux-normativity is the product.

Faux-normative legal scholarship is vulnerable to two critiques, which are roughly represented by the Schlag-Kahn thesis. First, faux-normative legal scholarship is not truly normative. The moral principles invoked are not independent of law, and they are not the basis on which law is truly criticized or reformed. Rather, they are drawn from law and then claimed to emanate from within it, then used to illuminate its true nature, and then mold its future development in a way that is aligned with its historical roots. It is a fundamentally conservative and legalist project: making law be true to itself. This has been at least a part of the Schlag critique of normativity from the outset. Second, faux-normative legal scholarship is not scholarship, and this is the heart of the Kahn critique. True legal scholarship should aim to say something true *about* law, not aim to make true claims *of* law. True claims *of* law are only true if some person in political authority says they are, and that is transparently a distortion, or perversion, of any sensible account of truth, even the most pragmatic accounts, that have or should have credence in an academic setting. It is a form of speaking powerfully and calling it truth, rather than speaking truth to power. Second, however, true claims of law are the province of the judiciary. The academy should be aiming for true claims about law, not true claims of law. There is simply no way such a study can get off the ground, if its potential practitioners are ensconced in the very professional practice that should be the object of their inquiry.

Kahn's solution to this is that legal scholarship should drop all claims of normativity. The legal scholar's job should not be to make any claims about what the law should be, or, for that matter, what the law is – particularly because the latter is more often than not merged with the former, in the ways discussed earlier. Rather, the legal scholar's job should be to make true claims about law, not true claims of law. Those claims might be made from any number of disciplined perspectives; the one that Kahn urges has been to date underutilized – and he is certainly right about this – is cultural studies. Thus, he calls for a "cultural study of law" and urges the cultural study of law as the proper province of the legal academy and of the legal academic. Another way, not Kahn's own, to put it is that what he is urging is the development of a field of "legal studies" – comparable to "American studies" or "women's studies" and so on – in which law is the object of study, and the goal is true statements about law (or about legal culture), rather than the traditional understanding of "legal scholarship," in which the legal scholar employs the same form of argument as the lawyer or the judge, and toward the same end: the utterance of true statements of law, with constrained normative claims as part of the legal argument.

THE COSTS OF ANTINORMATIVITY

Let me summarize. Schlag argues against normative legal scholarship on the grounds that the normative vision is cramped and in some way not genuine: the normative premises are themselves drawn from law and are deployed toward the end of claims of law. Legal scholars should drop all normative ambition. Kahn argues that normative legal scholarship is in a deep sense not scholarship at all: it does not aim to make true claims about law but, rather, aims to make claims of law and as such is necessarily normative, because legal argumentation itself is normative. Legal argument, as performed by lawyers and judges, always contains a normative dimension. Legal scholars, however, should eschew normativity, because they should eschew legal argumentation; the goal should be genuine scholarship about law and law's culture, not simply more legal arguments about law's content. What fills the gap for both is some form of study of law, taken from other disciplines: an amalgam of cultural studies, critical theory, and postmodern inquiry. One could clearly add, though, economics, history, and philosophy to the mix. The foundational shift is away from making arguments about what the law is or should be from within the discipline of law itself and toward arguments about the nature of law and legal culture, from a nonlegal but disciplined vantage. Both then urge an abandonment of "normativity" – Schlag because the forms of normativity the legal scholar inherits and mimics from the judge are tepid and Kahn because normativity is intrinsic to legal argument, and legal argument should not be the work of scholarship.

Both critiques, I believe, have merit: the normativity in legal scholarship is as constrained as the normativity in adjudication, as Schlag argues, and as a result is often unduly conservative or limited. The "scholarship" that is still undertaken by most legal academics is as Kahn describes it: legal argumentation, as done by lawyers or judges, that seeks to make the case for some statements of law, rather than statements about law, and to do so in a way that incorporates some limited set of normative principles. Nevertheless, both misfire, Schlag by overshooting his mark, and Kahn, oddly, by undershooting. Schlag targets "normative" legal scholarship, but the target of his attack – existing legal scholarship, as a practice – is only faux-normative at best. Standard doctrinal scholarship aims to state what the law is, and to do so, it incorporates constrained normative premises, themselves drawn from law, the point of which is to better illuminate law. Those premises must be embedded in a large swatch of legal opinion and consensus to be useable as legal, rather than just moral premises. They must appeal to the mainstream of legal opinion. They do not even aim for the disinterestedness, or objectivity, or nonfacticity of moral truth; they aim instead for acceptance. Kahn's target is likewise legal scholarship as it is practiced. He is right that legal scholarship as practiced employs forms of argument borrowed from the judiciary and the bar. Because it does so, it partakes in the forms of legal culture it ought, perhaps, to be studying. However, the culprit here is not normativity, the culprit is legal argumentation. Legal scholarship should be, on Kahn's analysis, about law rather than attempt to be law, if it is to make any headway in the project of coming toward an understanding of it. The target, then, of Kahn's attack should be the legal scholar's habit of assuming as his task the articulation of law – whether that articulation proceeds by way of constrained normative argument or something more purely legal.

I suggest friendly amendments, then, to both Schlag and Kahn's critiques, both of which leave plenty of room for a genuinely normative jurisprudence. Schlag's attack on normative legal scholarship, I think, ought to be directed at faux-normativity. Legal scholarship can and should be faulted, I believe, for embracing a faux-normativity, by which I mean a set of moral or political premises used to complete legal arguments when the law has gaps that are themselves drawn from older or simply other areas of law, and all toward the end of reconstructing law with slight modifications at the margins. Schlag is right that the sort of faux-normativity that comes from traditional legal scholarship will be tepid and inconsequential: when engaged in by judges, as it ought to be, it becomes an incremental step in the development of law; when engaged in by scholars, it disappears into cyberspace.

Kahn is right that legal scholarship should be about law rather than of law, and to achieve this, legal scholars need to stop participating in law's marginal creation or re-creation. Were they to do so, that would indeed, as Kahn suggests, leave room for a serious cultural analysis of law. It would leave room for much else besides: it would leave room for economic analysis, historical inquiry, literary analysis, and so on. It would also leave room, however, for normative analysis that is not faux.

What, then, are the costs of anti-normativity, whether of the explicit sort called for by Schlag and Kahn, or the implicit sort reflected in faux-normative practices? The costs are revealed by the jurisprudential gaps I have tried to expose in this book, both with respect to the particular branches of jurisprudence and as applied to areas of substantive law. They are threefold. First, we do not have from the academy a sustained accounting of how law achieves or fails to achieve justice. This is in part because we have neglected the development of a secular natural law tradition in the academy, but it is also because legal scholars across the board have eschewed the study or even the mention of justice. "I hate justice," Holmes opined, and we have followed suit, for more than a hundred years now. Perhaps because we both love and fear this graceful man, we have in effect been intimidated out of a sustained analysis of the concept of justice: wary of Holmesian scorn, of his eviscerating wit, of his contemptuous dismissal, we have followed the Holmesian "party line" that talk of justice is sentimental, emotional, or irrational. We have not, as a consequence, even investigated what we ourselves mean, or our students mean, or our opponents might mean when we claim that a legal practice is unjust, that a social practice is unjust and therefore calls out for legal redress, or that a university rule is unjust and cannot be abided. We do not know what it is we are impassioned about, when we make appeals to justice, in our own lives or the life of our nation. Justice is an imperative command, and, when we allow ourselves to, we experience and feel it as such: justice commands of us that we abide by certain ideals. However, we have not undertaken a study of justice, Rawlsian or otherwise, nor have legal scholars participated in the development of theories of justice that might guide a normative analysis or critique of law. We have developed neither theories of justice that might guide us nor even descriptive accounts of what appeals to justice seemingly entail. This is plainly odd: it is as though, in a way, medical schools were to eschew, across the board, all study of both the concept and content of human health. We cannot criticize existing law or social practices on the basis of appeals to justice if we have no conception of what justice requires or entails. Our continued avoidance of the concept of justice is a serious cost of our antinormative posture.

Second, we have no sustained inquiry into the nature of the good, beyond debates over the limits and meanings of cost-benefit analyses. Without it, we have no way to engage meaningfully or in a deep way in debates over public policy: what particular fields of law should be doing, what they might do better, what they might better not attempt to do at all. If law should lead to good lives, we have no way to describe what those lives must be or not be. If law should lead to good communities, we have no sense of what that means. Legal scholars have not taken up these questions, and it shows in our scholarship; in what we regard as legitimate questions of inquiry and what we do not. We can critique judge-made law on the basis of prior judge-made law. We have no sustained tradition, however, through which to argue for or against legislative initiatives, regulatory regimes, or statutory overhauls, on the basis of competing conceptions of the good. There are, of course, many reasons for this gap. In order of importance, perhaps: we have centered judicially made law rather than legislation as the subject of legal scholarship, and judicial law comes with its own baseline of criticism – older or other judicial law. Liberal legalists have too readily bought into a constrained conception of liberalism according to which varying accounts of the good life are not proper targets of criticism. Utilitarians and consequentialists have accepted a conflation of the concept of the good with the arithmetically calculable benefits, which has truncated the development of the idea of the good in both moral philosophy and political theory. To these powerful causes, however, can be added a fourth: the embrace of first faux- and then antinormativity in law schools.

Again, this is simply perverse. Why shouldn't law schools house sustained scholarly inquiry into the nature of the individual or social good that law ought to further? Other departments do. Political theorists and moral philosophers are engaged in active debates over the concept of the good, and public policy schools are engaged in equally lively and sustained inquiries into its application in various fields of law. The absence of either philosophical debate over the nature of the good, or its implications for the value of legislative initiatives or regulatory regimes governing various areas of social life, in law schools and in legal scholarship generally, is striking. Law schools study court decisions, largely on the basis of other court decisions, whereas other branches of the university study both legislative initiatives and competing conceptions of the good they ought to further. That is an odd division of labor. There is no reason other than inertia that law schools should not be central to debates over the value of proposed or existing legislation, as well as central to debates over the meaning and value of competing understandings of the good against which those proposals might be judged. Law scholars, presumably, would have much to contribute: lawyers and legal scholars know a thing or two about law, about what it does well, where it fails, and why. That knowledge of law and its value is oddly cabined, unengaged with debates over the possibilities of law's contribution toward the quality of public life.

The third cost of antinormativity is felt in our critical discourses, both narrowly and in a broader sense. First, as discussed in Chapter Three, the neo-critical legal theory movement has largely abandoned the normative project most squarely identified with the critical legal studies movement of the 1980s, the moral and political case against liberal legalism, and its three strands: the rights, legitimation, and alienation critiques of the liberal innovations most associated with the era. This development comes at an inopportune time: never have the features that were identified by the early critical scholars of liberal legalism been so exaggerated, and so harmful, as they are today. Let me look only at the rights critique. Critical scholars argued that rights shield private-sphere subordination by valorizing the private sphere as a realm of freedom, problematize governmental, public, democratic, and collective action that might address private subordination by constructing rights against it, legitimate regressive distributions of wealth by valorizing regimes of private property as domains of individual liberty, and falsely project alienated individuals engaging in transactions against and across walls of rights as the best forms of community of which humans are capable. None of this is any less true today than it was in the 1980s. The health reform bill faces a test of its constitutionality on the basis of the individual's right to opt out of insurance coverage, which, if granted, would valorize the private and vilify the public in precisely the way presaged by the rights critics; corporations have speech rights to influence political contests, which will further impede efforts at progressive redistribution, as again our rights critics fore-warned. First Amendment and privacy rights to pornography and sexual intimacy continue to legitimate sexual force and violence in intimate spheres, and reproduc-tive rights continue to legitimate the paucity of public assistance for poor parents in the private sphere of child care – pretty much just as was argued would occur, by those then newly crafted rights' critiques. The limitations and the regressive features of rights have if anything been borne out by the legal developments of the 1990s and aughts. That the rights critiques have largely disappeared from the literature cannot be explained as a natural consequence of the weakness of those claims.

If anything, the rights critiques did not go far enough. In what I believe to be a relatively new development, the rhetoric of rights is now used to shield citizens defensively from the consequences of a too minimal, shrunken government rendered incapable – because of budget cuts, ideological attacks, and political implosions – of doing basic governing tasks. The clearest example of this is surely the individual's right to bear arms, minted and declared by the Supreme Court after the articulation of the major rights critiques of the 1970s and 1980s. That "right" might have been originally conceived by an extremist militarist right wing as a right to forcibly insist on a minimalist government, or by hunters and hobbyists as protecting a private pastime, but by the time it was *litigated*, it had become, instead, a right to defend oneself against private violence. By the time it was litigated, it had become common constitutional knowledge that the state has no constitutional duty to protect individ-uals against private violence, or to protect against the elements, impoverishment, or any other privately sustained vulnerability. In a culture increasingly accustomed to identifying the breadth of moral obligation with constitutional obligation, if there is no constitutional duty borne by a state to do so, then there is no moral duty either. If there is no moral duty, there is simply no rhetorical resistance to the political mandate to cut taxes by cutting costs, and there is eventually no capacity to do what once might have been regarded as a central governmental function: the provision of a police force against private violence. Finally, if there is no capacity for the state to perform this central function, then individuals will have to perform this function, and if individuals have to perform what were once state functions, it stands to reason that they will have to have the right to do so.

Thus, the individual right to bear arms, in addition to the legitimating functions described by the critical scholars, serves an additional legitimating function in the 2000s that was unknown to the 1980s: it legitimates the incapacity of the state to continue to assume what was once this core state function. The right to homeschooling, now argued by a broad range of "family values" conservatives, the right to refuse health care, the right to die, and the right to abortion and birth control might soon come to have many of those same features. They all have, or will have if they are recognized, a legitimating function not even foreseen by the most far-ranging rights critics of thirty years ago: they legitimate the withdrawal of the state from functions once considered core. Individuals now have or might soon have rights to protect themselves with weapons that kill, a right not to buy insurance, a right to school their children at home, and a right to take their own life, as well as a right to abort a fetus. There may be good reason to grant individuals rights to do all or some of this, but there are also bad reasons to do so: individuals might have these rights to perform these functions precisely because states lack the capacity to provide the services that would render the right unnecessary. The result of that shift of responsibility – a shift of responsibility for protection against violence, for education, for provision of health services, for palliative care and child care – off the roster of state duties, and out of the realm of the public, to the shoulders of private individuals, will undoubtedly be a smaller state, a less credible, less competent, and less trustworthy government, and precisely because of that, a more unequal, and considerably more alienated, albeit freer, society of unequals.

The broader cost, however, of antinormativity to our critical discourse, is that if we embrace it, we will have lost the possibility of developing a distinctively critical legal voice. We have, oddly, not developed the legal perspective as a perspective from which meaningful criticism of law can be mounted. We have developed, rather, an entirely different normative project for the legally trained scholar: shadow brief or opinion writing. We have not, however, developed a critical legal perspective: a role for the critic of law, who criticizes law on the basis of values drawn from legal training or professionalism but not from law itself. This is, again, simply odd. Lawyers and legal scholars know a thing or two about law. They know something about its pitfalls, and they know something about the social chaos over which the rule of law might be an improvement. The point of university-housed scholarship should undoubtedly be to contribute to our store of knowledge, but the legal scholar is also a part of the legal profession, and a part of a larger society. The point of professionally based and societally based scholarship could be, as well, to contribute to our capacity and store of legal criticism: criticism of law, on the basis of legal expertise, and criticism of societal structures, hierarchies, or milieus, for law's lack.

CONCLUSION

Let me return briefly to the Schlag-Kahn hypothesis. Schlag and Kahn argue that legal scholarship should eschew normativity for two reasons: first, normative legal scholarship is unduly constrained, conventional, and inconsequential; second, normative legal scholarship, because it participates in the forms of legal discourse it should be studying, cannot possibly be enlightening: it cannot contribute to an understanding of law's culture, as it performs within it. They both then urge legal scholars to avoid normative argument. Find something to do other than make arguments of the form "the law should be thus and so," or "law is x and should be y" and so on. Legal scholars, Kahn argues, should be encouraged instead to study legal culture; they are in a peculiarly advantageous position to undertake the work of understanding why law is as it is. Schlag does not offer so precise a research agenda but urges analyses that will be more cutting, more radical, and more revealing than whatever might be uncovered willy-nilly through traditional forms of legal scholarship.

Normativity, however, is not the culprit. For Schlag, the culprit is faux-normativity, or the constrained normativity of the judiciary, transplanted for no good reason in the academy. Judges perhaps can and should develop lines of legal argument by reference to norms themselves drawn from other areas of law and toward the end of restating law. Yet there is no reason for the legal scholar's work on law to be so constrained. Normative legal scholarship need not, and should not, mimic the normativity of the bench. Legal scholars can and should criticize law on the basis of moral norms drawn from philosophical traditions, as I argued earlier: that law is unjust or fails to promote the common good, as natural lawyers have long argued, or that it fails to serve the happiness of the greatest number, or leads to more pain than pleasure, more suffering than welfare, or that its array of rights and liberties legitimates subordination, or ill serves the downtrodden, and so on. We have lost the greatest contributions of the natural law, legal positivist, and critical legal traditions if we strip them of their normative dimensions. However, there is no reason to so limit the reach of normative legal scholarship to the forms of argument preordained by established tradition. Legal scholars, if committed to truly normative rather than faux-normative projects, might likewise criticize law on the basis of cultural practices, utopian imaginings, cross-cultural borrowings, or historical pillaging.

And what of Kahn's claim? Legal scholars might well profitably study law's culture, as he urges. It is also no doubt true that legal scholars cannot do this if they are overwhelmingly committed to the shadow brief and opinion writing that I have characterized above as "faux-normativity." Furthermore, it is true that legal scholarship is situated within the academic community of universities. It does not follow, however, that the point of legal scholarship is solely to increase our store of knowledge regarding the culture of law. Legal scholarship is also situated within the profession, and within society broadly construed. As such, it can be normative, without being faux, and in ways that contribute distinctively to political and moral discourse, both within the profession and outside it.

Let me take up by way of conclusion a possible rejoinder to this thesis, one that neither Schlag nor Kahn would pursue or would be inclined to pursue but that nevertheless might be commonly felt: what is it, the conventional skeptic might respond, that *legal scholars*, of all people, can contribute, to the pursuit of legal solutions to contemporary problems? Why should legal scholars have any more to say on the demands that justice makes of law, the content of the common good toward which law should aim, or the nature of well-being that should be its goal than, say, Hollywood stars? Shouldn't legal scholars study the content of law, and perhaps its nature, but leave normative argument to the political process, or, in the interstices, the judicial? Why should we assume that legal scholars are experts on the demands of justice – whether legal, distributive, retributive, or social – rather than experts on the mechanisms and content of law? Shouldn't legal studies be descriptive and empirical? Again, what can legal scholars know?

First, it is worth noting the peculiarity of this objection. Surely justice should be the object of legal studies, no less than the nature, content, and demands of good health should be the object of medical studies. There is a good deal of hypocrisy, in fact, in denying this. We say that justice is the object of law, we carve into our walls the inscription that "law is but the means, while justice is the end" and we invoke it routinely in Law Day and Graduation Day and Commencement speeches, but we do not act on the assertion; we do not study, argue over, or teach the nature of justice in any systematic way. My point in this book is simply that we are right to say that justice is the goal of law and we are wrong in not pursuing the scholarly and pedagogical implications.

It is all the more peculiar, furthermore, at this point in the development of legal studies to assert that legal studies should focus solely on what law is, rather than what it ought to be. The last hundred and fifty years of legal education, adjudication, and professional advocacy have thoroughly dismantled the view that claims regarding the content of the law can be disentangled from the claimants' views of the legal ideal. Legal scholarship, no less than adjudication, as waves of legal realists and critical scholars have demonstrated repeatedly, is filled with stated and unstated normative premises, arguments, implications, and conclusions about the law we ought to have. What we do not have in the legal academy, and what the current trend toward antinormativity suggests we should not have, is any systematic study, or even discussion, of the content of our normative legal commitments. Not studying, or examining, or discussing those commitments is not a healthy insistence on empirical rigor or an admirable refusal to engage in empty or overtly political proselytizing. It is rather an acceptance of a form of argument that leaves normative premises that are very much there untouched and unexamined – it is a sort of capitulation to un-reason, and to superstition.

So, the hope, or plea, of this book is simply that legal scholars can and should contribute to the *criticism* of law, to its *reform*, and to its *formulation*, in ways that extend well beyond shadow brief writing, and well beyond the study of law's culture, economy, and history. The contemporary trends in jurisprudence that suggest otherwise – the intrapositivist movement toward the purely analytic or descriptive study of law, the absence of a secular and progressive natural law movement, and the neutering, in effect, of the critical legal academy – are missteps and unfortunate ones. Kahn and Schlag's scholarship are simply more explicit statements of the same underlying and, in my view, deeply mistaken position that underscores these trends: the position, that is, that the legal academy is the wrong place to look for criticism and suggested reform of law. We are not suffering from an excess of such scholarship. We are suffering from a lack of it.

Let me take these one by one – criticism, reform, and formulation – starting with criticism of law. It is apparent to all lay observers that law and the breach of as well as inadequacy of law's promises have been deeply implicated in virtually all of our current-day disasters. The oil that gushed for almost an entire summer into the Gulf of Mexico in 2010 and the financial meltdown of the late 2000s are both direct results of underregulation and underutilization of the tools of law that might regulate corporate greed. The illegal wars the United States has embarked on, the illegal use of unmanned drones in those wars, the imperialist thirsts and bogus claims of successive administrations, the perverse overincarceration of our cities' youth perversely coupled with the continuing carnage on city streets all represent a failing not only of American politics but also of American constitutionalism and American legalism – a failure *of law* – of the highest order. Yet somehow law and legalism emerge in the midst of these legal as well as technological and moral disasters fundamentally unscathed: *law itself,* or our understanding of it, or our articulation of its promise and ideals, we assure ourselves on Law Day celebrations and Constitution Day conventions, is not the problem. However, this is exemplary of the grossest sort of false consciousness the country could possibly ever witness. The legal regulation of deep-sea drilling for oil, of mining in Appalachia, and of the financial markets on Wall Street is labyrinthine in its complexity. The constitutional law governing abuse of power in the executive branch is miles deep and wide, as measured by Supreme Court opinions and law review articles. Our highest constitutional law and its practitioners are proud of our national and constitutional commitment to – insistence on – human dignity and the protection of the just claims to liberty of the lowliest criminal defendant charged with the most heinous crimes, as well as the guarantees to all of us, criminals and noncriminals, that individuals can articulate and live the good life by our own lights free of state or community intermeddling. Yet the oil gushes unabated, the miners die, the climate warms, the homeless sleep on cardboard on doorsteps one block from the nation's capitol stripped of dignity, corporations are handed the keys to our electoral kingdom in the name of liberty, and we incarcerate more of our citizens in worse conditions than any civilization on the planet or known to history. *Law* – the law we laud as protecting us from all of this – has somehow overseen all of this without seeing. We do not know why. Without a commitment to undertaking deep criticism of extant law, including a willingness to confront the extent to which law has used the tools of moral rhetoric, idealism, and ambition to cave to the ambitions of a few at the expense of the many, we have no prayer of understanding how our law can, and has, been so complicit in these disasters. We simply do not have that understanding.

Again, what might legal scholars contribute to a better understanding of how law – the idea of law – has gone so wrong? Why should legal scholars be the ones to study law's perverse calamities? Again, the question seems to answer itself: who else, precisely? Legal scholars know the processes and content and the history of the calamitous law that matters. If the calamities are rooted in something like a "fundamental contradiction," or perhaps a miswiring, rather than, say, simply an imperfection, a shortfall, or shortsightedness, in our basic legalist constructs, it will be legal scholars who have the knowledge close to the core of their expertise to root it out. Our Constitution may truly be inadequate to the resolution of the roots of today's inegalitarianism – corporate power, changing economic forces, internationalism – as it was to the resolution of the question of slavery in the nineteenth century. Yet with only a few exceptions – Sanford Levinson being the most prominent – the legal academy has not undertaken a critical examination of the adequacies of the Constitution in the face of contemporary inequalities (rather than the inadequacies of particular interpretations of the Constitution, or inadequacies of the particular make up of the Supreme Court at any particular time, and so on). Our tort law may be utterly incapable of dealing with the massive harms caused or threatened by environmental and pharmaceutical catastrophes, yet again, with only a few exceptions, the tort scholarly community has not taken up a broad-based critical review. The idea of law that drives adjudication – notions of horizontal equity between litigants for example – has not received much of a critical examination. Our criminal justice system is as broken as any system of law could conceivably be, yielding extraordinarily high incarceration rates for defendants only a precious handful of whom are accorded a trial, yet the deepest premises of our criminal law and law of criminal procedure for the most part get a pass. Our entire first branch of government – the legislative side of things – is seemingly paralyzed to take on the most pressing threats of our time, from global warming to crushing poverty. Yet legal scholars have yet to examine the legislative process seriously and critically, in anywhere near the detail so lovingly bestowed on the adjudicative. Legal scholars have neglected deep criticism of law and of constitutionalism, and in the past twenty years, since critical legal studies' self-induced coma, of liberal legalism as well.

Yet it is legal scholars, and only legal scholars, who have the knowledge base, the research tools, and the professional inclination to take on these questions. Legal scholars know tort law, the history of constitutionalism, the structures of government, the ideals of adjudicative legalism, the criminal law, and the law of criminal procedure. Others do not, either outside or inside the academy, except intermittently – hit and miss – as such knowledge has impacts on other disciplines or professions. If deep criticism of law and legalism and legal ideals is to come from anywhere, it will have to be from the legal academy. If it does not come from the legal academy, it will not be forthcoming. If it is not forthcoming, we will simply never know to what extent our current dilemmas are a function not only of unmet technological challenges, unharnessed political will, underdeveloped fellow feeling, or inadequate education of a voting public, but of the inadequacies of constitutionalism and legalism, their promises, their fundamental commitments, and their attendant pathologies.

What of legal reform? There is no good reason that legal scholars should not embrace the reform of law as the work of the academy. Law may have been complicit in our current dilemmas, but there is no question but that law in some form, whether conventional or not, will be essential to their resolution. Global warming will not be addressed without robust international law, and plenty of it. Law will be essential to the creation of a regime that provides incentives for manufacturers, commuters, polluters, and sovereign states that can trump the economic, and on a worldwide scale. The trafficking in arms, humans, drugs, and terror likewise cannot be addressed without law of both domestic and international reach; law will be essential to the creation of a regime that provides both mechanisms for policing against depravities and incentives to governments to respect individual liberties, worldwide. The macroeconomic forces contributing to the entrenchment of poverty both nationally and worldwide will not be addressed without the creation of a law that redistributes profit – and so on. There is also no doubt, however, that the legal changes requisite to the solutions to these problems – environmental, sociopathological, those related to global poverty – will not emerge from the evolutionary and domestic forms of legal change characteristic of common-law argumentation that have been the preoccupation of U.S. law schools for well over a century. It is increasingly clear that that preoccupation disserves our students, ourselves, and our world; nineteenth-century American common law and its principles is not the stuff from which the legal contribution to the resolutions of the world's and country's political, practical, moral, and environmental will come. They will come, if they come, from international as well as national legislative and regulatory initiatives and changes, yet those are precisely the forms of legalism we marginalize in both our study and pedagogy. International law is a boutique course and field. Expertise or even familiarity with legislative and administrative processes and accomplishments and challenges are required nowhere, and studied only intermittently. It is still the common law and its authors, the bench, that earn the respect and the meticulous study of the legal academy.

This is clearly perverse. The legal academy could and should participate in the formulation of those legislative and administrative initiatives. The formulation of sound "policy," and the formulation of law's contributions toward the making of sound policy, is work to which legal scholars, distinctively, can contribute. Legal scholars understand the forms, processes, and limitations of both legislation and regulation; have at their fingertips masterful histories of those fields of law; and have the tools to study the promises they hold out. Further, legal scholars have long understood, from the time of the legal realists to today, that "policy" has an impact on the decision making of judges and have long concluded that policy is therefore a part of law. What we have not acted on, at least within the academy, is the implied inverse: law is and must be a part of the formulation, in political and administrative branches, of sound public policy. There is no good reason that legal scholars should not pursue that work.

To do so in a systematic and responsible way would require a reorientation – not a revolution – of the academy's self-understanding and of its mission. Sound public policy requires a sound understanding of the nature of the good toward which law should aim, and for reasons explored in the first two chapters of this book, the legal academy has eschewed the philosophical study of that question, and its attendant features. Thus, we defer to other disciplines and other professions: to moral philosophy for insight into the nature of the good, to political theory for insights into the nature of politics, to history for an understanding of where law has been and not been. The legal scholar then examines ways in which judges "balance" competing policies or further one policy while abandoning another, and so on, while assiduously avoiding the evaluative: what policy is worth pursuing? What is "good" policy? This leaves profound gaps. It is the legal scholar who sees policy embedded in the forms of legalism that politics yields. It is the legal scholar who is familiar with the ways in which policies have been fruitfully furthered or not by law's processes. It is the legal scholar that is peculiarly suited to study whether a policy embedded in law is or is not furthering real human needs, capabilities, ambitions or whether it is pointlessly festering conflict. There is no other profession, and no other discipline, that lies at the nexus of moral philosophy, political theory, and political science peculiarly occupied, but then not acted on, by legal studies.

Lastly, legal scholars should be peculiarly capable of the moral and politically essential work of diagnosing the pathologies that follow from law's *absence*. The law we have might be in need of reform, but likewise the law we do not have, and should have, needs articulation. Liberty, or freedom from law's hand, can be exhilarating or nightmarish, and we cannot know which by the study of definitions or the espousal of ideals. Where there is no law, because of constitutional protections, an ideology of privacy, budget shortfalls, or otherwise, there may be, as a consequence, freer communities and more liberated individuals, or there may be crushing private hierarchies of power: harsh paternalism in family life; cronyism in politics, capital markets, or union life; economic oppression at work; bullying on the school grounds; and violence within intimate relations. There is no way to know whether private life, insulated against public law by constitutional or cultural protections, is Edenic or hellish, without a willingness to at least ask the question free of political dispositions one way or the other. There is also, however, no way to know whether the imposition or intrusion of law into those Edens or those hells on earth would be an improvement or a greater disaster, without knowing something about law itself – about its potential, its history, its shortfalls, its promise.

Law schools house such knowledge and legal scholarship in their repositories. The legal scholar, by virtue of expertise, is well situated to be a particular kind of social critic: attuned to social problems peculiarly caused, in part, by either the inadequacy or the overreach of a legal response. Legal scholars know something of the devastation too little law created in the lead up to the Great Depression and the clumsiness, but eventual effectiveness, of the federal government's response. Legal scholars know a bit about the risks of too little environmental regulation and of the inadequacies of the legal constraints on the war-making powers of the executive branch. Legal scholars know the human costs of too little legal protection accorded to slaves, to trafficked women, to abused wives, husbands, and children in homes some call "castles," or prostitutes fearing rape, or residents fearing drug lords or gang violence. Legal scholars know the pitfalls of too little or too toothless international law in the face of international catastrophe; the limits of unregulated market in the face of market failures; the theoretical limits of Coasean market-based responses to accidents in the face of offer-asking problems, false consciousness, or simply the lack of appreciation of long-term costs of sales or transactions impulsively wanted in the short term. Legal scholars know some of all of these and could know much more of all of them: of the ways in which too little law creates or perpetuates hellish states of nature, for which more law might be an effective, if unpopular, solution. Legal scholars know, likewise, the value of the legally untouched: the neighborhood that seeks self-governance; the sexual liaison that requires privacy; the commune that might benefit all of us if allowed to opt out; the sanctity of the prayer room, the synagogue, or the church; the pleasures of the private home; the private conscience and the private conversation free of state intrusion. The nature of these arenas of justified privacy – of freedom from law's inquiry as well as law's empire – is likewise within the professional knowledge of the legal scholar, as is the criteria by which we might distinguish the Edenic private recluse from the hellish.

Not to use the insights that the study of the history, content, and scope of law yields toward the generation of deep criticism of law seems like nothing so much as self-serving insularity. Surely the law is not too good to question. Only needing improvements at the margins? Our Constitution, to say nothing of our constitutional law, is not implicated *at all* with our current problems with self-governance, our lack of understanding of our obligations as citizens toward each other? Is it not even worth the bother of a suggestion that the Constitution itself – rather than its interpreters, any particular court, any configuration of theory that emerges from it – might be partly complicitous in the difficulties of contemporary democracy? Not to pose deeply critical questions of legal assumptions of law's value – including the value of constitutionalism itself – is worse than denial; it reeks of complicity in the generation of a massive intellectual fraud. To not use insights gleaned from our understanding of law's contributions to the creation of sound policies that have addressed this country's problems seems like nothing so much as a massive lost opportunity. Law, and laws, can create a better or worse world; law and laws do so whether or not the ways in which they do so are studied. Not to study how they do so, and how they might do so, is to commit to something that falls far short of a reasoned inquiry into the nature of the good. It is just not clear why legal scholars or the universities and the profession that supports them – and depends on them – would want that. Lastly, and most tragically, not to use the knowledge of the worlds untouched by law, either intentionally or willy-nilly, toward the improvement of those state-of-nature hells, or the protection of those private Edens, looks like nothing so much as either a reckless or indeed a willful professional blindness. Whatever else they know or do not know, legal scholars know something of the private chaos, subordination, or terror created by law's absence, and the arid rigidity, oppression, or stifling conformity that is risked by its overintrusive presence. There is no reason in the world not to expect – not to demand – of legal scholars that they give voice to those worries, when they feel them. Sensitivity to law's peril and promise is the content of their expertise. To willfully fail to act on the basis of that expertise – to fail to articulate in scholarship the basis of one's worries about law's overreach or of one's hopes for law's promise – is an unwarranted dereliction of duty. For a profession to do so, whether in the name of rigor, discipline, or a false humility, in the face of the demonstrated need for just that expertise, is shameful.

Index